Enfield Libraries

First edition
published in 2009 by

WOODFIELD PUBLISHING LTD
Bognor Regis ~ West Sussex ~ England ~ PO21 5EL
www.woodfieldpublishing.co.uk

ISBN 1-84683-083-4

A Pilot's Way

*Looking back on 55 years as a
military, commercial & private pilot*

M‍IKE H‍OLMES

Woodfield

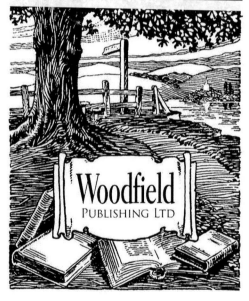

Woodfield Publishing Ltd

Woodfield House ~ Babsham Lane ~ Bognor Regis ~ West Sussex ~ PO21 5EL
telephone 01243 821234 ~ **e-mail** enquiries@woodfieldpublishing.co.uk

Interesting and informative books on a variety of subjects

For full details of all our published titles, visit our website at
www.woodfieldpublishing.co.uk

To my wife Gillian, who for years was marvellous in the way she put up with a husband who was either at home for periods which were inevitably too long or otherwise never at home when needed.

~ CONTENTS ~

The Author ii

Introduction iii

1. I'm Going to be a Pilot 1

2. Getting Started 18

3. Joining Up 40

4. Ode To The Tiger 52

5. Cold War Fighter Pilot 60

6. Harvards Over Kenya 77

7. Secondment to the USAF 93

8. Posted to Night Fighters 109

9. Varsity 131

10. An Apprenticeship 151

11. The Islands, the Link and the Oil 174

12. The BAC 1-11 and Ten Years of Routine 193

13. On Finals 218

The Author

Mike Holmes has written many magazine articles. The first of these, some years ago in *Autocar*, was about driving an ancient Hillman Minx around what was then Southern Rhodesia. He has also had a number of articles on aviation subjects published in magazines such as *FlyPast, Air Enthusiast* and *Today's Pilot*. He is also a keen naturalist and has written numerous articles on birds and bats, which have appeared in various society magazines and newsletters.

His first book, *Apprentice to the Red Ensign* (ISBN 1-903953-85-5), about his experiences as an apprentice in the Merchant Navy in the 1940s, was published by Woodfield in 2005. *Some Corners of a Birdwatcher's World* (ISBN 1-4120-93323-5) was published in 2007, followed by *Birds Bats and Travel* (ISBN,13 978-1-906146-38-2).

Introduction

To the south of me, on my right, rose the great chain of mountains that stretch along southern Spain from Almeria to Gibraltar. From where I was, Malaga and the Costa del Sol lay about thirty miles away on the far side of those jagged peaks, the western foothills of the Sierra Nevada. The city of Grenada was about fifty miles ahead, but I was only going for a short flight and would be landing on the little airstrip at Loja. It was easy to find, out on the plains, beside a main road just twenty miles east of Antequera, the ancient Moorish town that lay a couple of miles from the airstrip I had taken off from twenty minutes earlier.

Below me and stretching away to the distant northern horizon were rolling miles of green olive plantations, broken here and there by small, brown, rocky mountain ranges, which stuck up steeply from the Andalusian plain.

It was a day of incredible visibility. Rain the previous night had washed all the dusty haze out of the atmosphere, making those green and brown ground colours stand out in stark contrast to the clear blue, nearly cloudless Spanish sky above.

I kept climbing until I could see the Mediterranean through gaps between the mountains, with bright sunlight flashing silver across the waters, a sight I had not seen for over ten years. That had been before my retirement, after years of airline flying. In those days, I had seen it from the flightdeck of a BAC 1-11, not the cockpit the little microlight Thruster I was strapped to and flying now.

Suddenly, I found myself singing at the top of my voice. I can't sing, but alone in a little aircraft, high above Spain, that did not matter. Nobody had to listen to me. I was supremely happy. I was up in the air, flying, exactly where I loved to be and that love had lasted for a lifetime.

When I think of that occasion, and others when the same feeling has burst out, I'm reminded of that wonderful film,

Those Magnificent Men in their Flying Machines. I think of the airborne shots of all those marvellous old stick and string aircraft, up in the air after they have actually managed to take off and get away at the start of their race to Paris. I see the superb picture of the Italian Count, sitting up in his wide-open cockpit and singing at the top of his voice for the sheer joy of it. That's how I felt then and it is the way I have felt about flying throughout all my life.

This, then, is not an account by a famous experimental test pilot about his fascinating work and the daily hazards he encountered whilst developing some superb new prototype aircraft into an everyday working machine; an aircraft which would be of practical use in its role as a fighter, airliner or whatever else it might have been designed for. Neither does it recount the life and experiences of some high-ranking Royal Air Force officer who has commanded operations in wartime and probably had some effect on history.

Told here are reminiscences from the life of an ordinary working pilot, one who knew when still very young that when he grew up he would follow a career in flying, and then loved it when he did so. One who would not have been really happy doing anything else.

I am that pilot and have written of my career, together with my awareness of aviation matters during my childhood and the aircraft I saw around me then in the 1930s, together with happenings in the world of flying during those days, happenings which are now part of our history.

Apart from home and family, flying was the one great thing in my life. Though I was sidetracked between the ages of seventeen and nineteen, because at the end of World War Two, no pilot training that I knew of was available to me, I was a professional pilot throughout my whole working life until retirement at sixty. After that, I started flying again – gliding to begin with, but then in the microlight world.

I can't say that I enjoyed every minute of it. At times there were difficulties that had to be overcome and learnt from, but they were but a minute percentage of the whole and were soon set in their right perspective.

This then, is the story of a pilot's life, which started with an awareness of aircraft at an early age in the 1930s and was followed by a lifetime of professional flying, via a first solo with a flying club in 1948.

The flying ended 55 years later, when arthritis made it impossible for me to bend enough to get into the Thruster microlight I had shares in. It was then that I finally and reluctantly had to hang up my helmet and goggles.

1.   I'm Going to be a Pilot...

After leaving the RAF in 1966, I worked for a few years as a flying instructor at a flying school, owned and operated by BOAC and BEA in unison, some time before their amalgamation into British Airways. It went by the grand name of the College of Air Training and was situated at Hamble on Southampton Water, where there had been a well-known flying school since the 1920s. We trained *ab-initio* pilots, who were sponsored by the two airlines and, having qualified for their commercial licence, could make their careers with either one of them.

A university degree was one of the qualifications required for trainee pilots, so the students I taught were generally pretty intelligent people. Inevitably we would discuss the reasons why they had decided to make flying their career. It was a normal topic of conversation between pupil pilots and their instructors and I was always interested to learn just what it was that motivated my students. It often helped me to iron out any difficulties that might pop up.

At Hamble I found reasons that were often quite different from those that my fellow cadets and I had all seemed to have when we had started our RAF wings course many years before. Again, when I became an instructor in the RAF, I had generally found amongst my own students, the same motivations that I had had when I first started. Basically, we all just wanted to be pilots and to fly, though as might be expected, wanting to join the RAF for its own sake was also very important to some people. Personally, I had just wanted to become a professional pilot and really had no other thoughts about it. Joining the RAF had seemed the obvious way to start down that road. Everything else took second place to just flying, but naturally it would be great to be in the RAF, I thought, and that was exactly what I found.

At The College of Air Training, it was different. I found that some students did not want to become pilots in order to fly. Flying was just secondary and they wanted to become airline pilots with BOAC or BEA because it was a job from which they would have plenty of time off. This would enable them to do all the things that they thought that they would really like to do, things that other careers would not allow them sufficient time to become involved with. Then, with others, it was just a job where you were paid a good salary, which would enable you to keep yourself in the manner to which you thought you should be kept, without having to work too hard.

Some of my students actually said this to me quite openly, and although I did not say so to them at the time, I was horrified. It seemed to me that they would probably soon have 'another think coming,' and I wondered how they had managed to fool the selection board. It amounted to sacrilege as far as I was concerned. People with an outlook like that should never come into aviation.

I was quite different. I was one of those small boys who had 'always wanted to be a pilot.' As far back as I can remember, there had never really seriously been anything else. Though I had been side tracked by circumstances a couple of times whilst on the way there, I had managed at the age of nineteen, to get into the flying world and then remained as part of it in one way and another, until I reached seventy five.

From a very early age, I was aware of anything to do with flying that happened to be going on around me. This was during the 1930s, when aviation was new and thriving, being accepted as a permanent part of the everyday scene. It was the fashion to be part of the crowd at an air show such as those that were held at Brooklands. Sport flying was something that almost everyone became excited about and air races like the Kings Cup always made headlines. The RAF shows at Hendon, where Bristol Bulldogs, and later Gloster Gauntlets, performed formation aerobatics whilst roped together, were the World's finest air displays. Paris was only as far off as Croydon airport and a seat in luxury on an Imperial Airways airliner. In those days it was the height of fashion to make the journey in the stately great Handley Page HP 42 biplanes. Aviation was the latest exciting thing and in one way or another, was always in the news. I lapped up as much of that news as I possibly could.

This was less than twenty years after the end of World War One, which was still spoken of as the Great War. My father and my friends' fathers had all been involved in some way or another and talk of the exploits of the Royal Flying Corps were the most exciting things that I could ever listen to. Spitfires and Hurricanes, Lancasters and Halifaxes are the stars of the stories about World War Two today, but then, the tales were all of BE2c's, Sopwith Camels, SE 5a's and Handley Page 0-400's, plus many more. The enemy were Fokkers and Albatross,' not Messerschmitts, Dorniers and Heinkels. Our heroes were aces such as Albert Ball and Mick Mannock.

We avidly read the books and magazine stories by Captain W.E. Johns, about the adventures of Biggles, who was our great fictional flying hero. We discussed them in detail at school. Somebody would always say that their father thought that his exploits were impossible and such a saying would at once provoke the most heated of arguments. Biggles could do no wrong, both in my eyes and those of many of my friends. Looking back now though, perhaps those fathers were right in some ways. But I still enjoy Biggles.

Aero model clubs were part of my elder brothers' schools. Skybirds were the 1/72nd scale models of those days and were made of wood and wire, not plastic. The first plastic models came in the latter half of the thirties. They were Frog Penguins, which were followed years later by Airfix. There were Hawker Furies, Gloster Gauntlets and Gladiators, a beautiful, blue DH 86 in Imperial Airways colours and at the top of the fleet, a wonderful Shorts S23 Empire Flying Boat.

I remember being absolutely fascinated when one of my elder brothers showed me the model room in his prep school, where a large table had been rigged out as a flying field. All the Great War types were lined up in front of the canvas hangers and crashed German machines were placed in the fields round the edges. In the middle of the airfield was the wreck of a poor old BE2c. At the side was a more modern display of Moths and Imperial Airways aircraft. Other exciting types flew overhead, hung on strings, which were fixed to the ceiling.

For a part of World War One, my father had soldiered in India, fighting on the Northwest Frontier. Tribesmen had been stirred up by German agents working from Afghanistan and this was another very real part of the Great War, though one that does not appear in any histories. There always had been fighting there, and there still is, though it is no longer comes under the heading of 'Empire.' My father told me all about the BE2c's, which were the first British military aircraft to be operated in that part of the world. Such was their hot and high performance, that they were unable to take off after ten o'clock in the morning and were only used to carry out early morning reconnaissance flights, up through the passes if they were not too steep, in the hills at dawn.

There was another thing, which thrilled me at my brother's school. It was not far from Farnborough and was situated right under the circuit. Farnborough was then, and remained so for many years, the legendary testing centre where all new aircraft that were destined for the RAF, had to undergo a part of their trials. Whilst watching a football match with my father, when my brother was a member of the team, I would have a grandstand view of lots of exciting aircraft flying round overhead. They were much more exciting than my brother's football. Here it was that one November afternoon, I saw the prototype of a single engined low winged monoplane. Painted silver and gleaming in the afternoon sunshine, it went round and round the circuit for quite some time. It was quite a new one to me and I had no idea what type it might have been, but it was possibly the Fairy Battle. Nobody seemed to know what it was and I heard the grownups discussing it. The existence of new military aircraft was kept very secret in those days, with none of the modern publicity. We were looking at the shape of things to come, which was far removed from the biplanes that were still the mainstay of the RAF and were the usual, everyday sight in the skies.

Woodley, just on the east side of Reading, was our nearest aerodrome. The Miles aircraft company, which was based there, was then at its heyday and built many sorts of light aircraft. We lived where the land rose up towards the Berkshire Downs, between the Thames and Kennet valleys. This was obviously a favourite area for flying club members and owners of light aircraft, who would fly out to at weekends and during the long summer evenings. Whenever the weather was fine, there would be a continual stream, consisting of many types, passing overhead. Even at the age of five, I would stand and watch, bubbling over with envy and wondering just who those lucky people flying such machines, might be.

I did my best to identify all the types that flew over. I expect that I actually made many mistakes, though I would loudly tell anybody who might be listening, just what type of aeroplane any of them might happen to be. De Haviland Moths were of course very numerous and easy to recognise. They were mainly DH60's, the predecessor to the Tiger Moth, but there were also high winged Puss Moths amongst them. The shape of the Puss Moth's wing was very distinctive and easy to recognise from below.

Being so close to where they were made, Miles Hawk Majors were also common. This was the type that was developed into the Magister, one of the basic trainers that the RAF used during the War. Like Tiger Moths, when peace came some Magisters were made available for clubs and private ownership, and in 1948 at Thruxton with the Wiltshire School of Flying, I learnt spin recovery on one

I flew about ten hours on it altogether and always thought that after the Tiger Moths, which I had flown previously, it landed in rather a strange manner. You would think that you were all set up for a perfect three pointer, which I must admit, was seldom the actual situation for me, when suddenly the tail wheel would touch first. The main wheels then came down with a thump, which again always surprised me. However, I liked it because you flew it solo from the front cockpit, which I always thought was where an aircraft should be flown from, not from the back like most of the other tandem two seaters at that time.

Any boy who was interested in aeroplanes knew the Miles Hawk Major because a beautiful balsa wood, flying scale model kit of it was marketed by the Frog Company. I was a very poor model maker and their construction was beyond me at that age, but I was very lucky; I had an elder brother who enjoyed making them for me. He did so when, at the age of about eight, my parents gave me one for Christmas. Sometimes it could be induced to fly beautifully; at others it just crashed directly after it was launched. That was probably because I threw it into the air rather clumsily when I should have let it fly smoothly off; a hazard that any model of mine had to face. They could often be found sitting about the house in a damaged condition, usually in a state that was quite beyond my ability to repair.

It was possible to get them to take off from the ground in realistic manner if you could find a smooth enough, flat surface. A tennis court provided the required surface, but to climb out over the surrounding net was beyond most models' capabilities.

The simplest and cheapest model that flew was the Frog Imp. This was made of just two thin sheets of balsa wood, one for wings and one for the fuselage. A small elastic band powered it and it only cost about a shilling. There were masses of them at my school, and they were very unpopular with the staff, as they often seemed to fly down passages and collided with masters, who were carrying piles of books. At other times they might be released from the back of a class and so disrupt some dreary math's lesson. Most Imps went through periods of being grounded, due to their habit of being confiscated and locked in the staff room cupboard. This could sometimes last right through for the rest of a term, so making it an essential for parents to send a replacement. In my case, when the reason for such a request was found out, the answer was inevitably 'No.' Airspace became restricted when a school rule was eventually introduced, which forbade the flying of Imps anywhere except in the gym, and then only during half holidays.

Not all models came as kits. The commonest, other than those such as the Imp, was the Frog Fighter, which had strong, reinforced cardboard wings and an aluminium fuselage. The wings, which were cambered in a proper aerodynamic shape, just became detached in the event of a crash and did not break. In fact, mine had to survive many crashes, usually at the end of each flight when they hit the ground, a tree or the side of a barn. Very seldom though, was there the lasting damage that often occurred to delicate balsa wood models. The Frog Fighter cost five shillings, which amounts to just twenty five pence now, but was a small fortune for a boy in those days.

There was another exciting innovation in their propulsion system as the drive to their propeller from the elastic motor was geared. Extra revolutions were thus obtained, which considerably enhanced the aircraft's performance, making it seem very powerful when compared with other models that only had straight through transmission.

The vast cost of the Frog Fighter necessitated sending messages to Father Christmas, asking for it especially, as my number one choice. The only other chance of ever getting one came in the form of a birthday present, but birthday presents were usually rated at lower cost.

There were though, two other larger and more beautiful models which Frog produced. These were the Puss Moth and the Hawker Hart, but I was always told that they were well beyond the economics of my family, or words to that effect. All that I was able to do, was to look at them longingly when they were displayed in toy shops

All these were also elastic powered, the rubber band being wound up by turning the propeller by means of fittings, which were part of the box in which they came. It allowed a small handle to be attached to a geared cog, which was connected to the propeller. This could be turned and so the wind up was performed in a much faster manner than just twiddling the propeller in the usual way with ones fingers. The rubber band had to be soaked in some sort of oil, which had a marvellous and quite unforgettable smell, and made it more supple, so less easy to break. Tiny internal combustion engines had not arrived on the scene by then.

Surely the Hawker Fury was the most beautiful of all the single seat biplane fighters of those days; anyway I thought so then and still do. I had three plastic Frog Penguin models of the machine and they were my favourites.

A real one put on a show that will always be indelibly etched in my memory. On two occasions, a single Fury carried out a sequence of low level aerobatics beside a line of trees, which bordered our land, near to our house. Whether he was putting on a display for either his girl friend or his family, I don't know. Perhaps he just found this a convenient open space to practice over, somewhere where he thought that he would not get caught low flying, but for me it was the most marvellous air show to watch. Both performances took place during the early evenings on clear sunlit, summer days. At the time, I thought that the shining, silver aircraft with its bright scarlet and white No.1 Squadron markings, painted right across the top surface of the upper wing and only visible when it was upside down, was just about the most beautiful thing that I have ever seen. It all made a scene that I could never possibly forget.

I knew that it was No.1 Squadron as those were the markings on my Frog Penguin Hawker Furies. The three that I had made up a flight, which was always lined up in formation outside my model hanger.

No.1 Squadron was based at Tangmere, its home for many years, and Tangmere was about fifty miles in a straight line to the south from where we lived. I always wonder, therefore, just what it was that drew that 1930s fighter pilot to our part of the world, who he was and what happened to him. The War started about three or four years later and I sincerely hope that he survived it. I really would have liked to thank him for those two wonderful aerobatic shows, and always hoped by some extraordinary chance, to meet him one day and to tell him how he had helped to seal my fate. I just *had* to be a pilot like that when I grew up, although Furies were very much a thing of the past when it did come to be my turn.

The bombers we saw flying over then, were such types as Fairey Hendons and Handley Page Heyfords, the latter being huge great lumbering machines, but they looked very potent and businesslike in the air, as things went in those days. A few years later they gave way to Witleys, Wellingtons and Fairey Battles. One day, during the 1948 Munich crisis, my father pointed to one as it flew over, heading towards the northeast.

'There they go,' he said. 'The bombers have been flying over like that all day. They're going to their war stations on the East Coast.'

I don't suppose that that was actually the case at all. It was probably only part of an exercise, but at my age, I did not realise just how serious the situation really was when Hitler's armies marched into Czechoslovakia.

On an afternoon of alternate showers and sunshine, some time before the war, I looked up as usual when I heard an aircraft overhead and recognised a Lockheed Vega skirting round the edge of a nearby thunderstorm, flying at about two thousand feet. It had been raining heavily, but the air was now washed clean and clear, with a bright sun silhouetting the edge of the clouds and shining on the silver machine. I had never seen a Vega before, but I knew it and recognised it from a book that I had about American aircraft. I have never been able to find a reference to a Vega on the British register for that time and often wonder now if, perhaps, this was one of the American round the world record attempts. It must have been in about 1936 or 1937, I think, which was some years after Wiley Post, but I am not sure who else's route came in our direction.

There was one thing lacking in my sightings of aircraft. We lived a long way from any airport where civil airliners operated and as there were no air routes which passed over our part of the world, I was never lucky enough to see the classic airliner types of the thirties. However, during the early months of the war, when Imperial Airways were moved out of Croydon, to their temporary base at Keynsham near Bristol, we used to see the wonderful great HP 42s passing over. Another unforgettable sight.

It was no wonder that my greatest ambition during my boyhood years was to go up in an aeroplane. It never happened. Just as the possibility arose, somebody would always interfere and say 'no' and I would be stuck on the ground. There were two occasions when I nearly made it, but I was thwarted on both of them.

The first was when Sir Alan Cobham came to Woodley with his flying circus and I must have been about six years old.

This was something I just *had* to see. I had always longed to do so and I badgered my father to take us there for a day out. Much to my surprise he agreed and, together with our nanny and the maid, we all piled into the Morris Isis. Oh yes, in those days nannies and maids were not uncommon additions to country families and I soon realised they were almost as excited as I was. In fact, I was bubbling over with excitement. This, I thought, was the greatest thing that had ever happened to me.

I had the most fantastic time watching all that went on; stunt flying and crazy acts performed by Moths and ancient Avro 504s but, as ever, my greatest ambition was to actually go up. In that I had a huge disappointment.

There were flights in what was billed as 'The Airliner.' I'm not absolutely sure what type this was, but I remember a great big old twin-engined biplane, most likely a Handley Page W8, which seemed to carry about ten passengers. If it was a Handley Page W8 (and Sir Alan Cobham's company did have one at the time) it must, in the past, have been part of the Imperial Airways fleet. Alternatively, Alan Cobham's Airspeed Ferries were available. All were busy giving joy rides and when I asked for a flight, I was sure that my father could not really say 'No.' Everyone else there seemed to be waiting in line, in order to take their turn, so why couldn't we go up. He had happily paid for Nanny and the maid to have a flight. They had been enthusiastic when they got back and were sure that they had seen our house in the distance. Now it must be my turn

My father refused and the day was nearly spoilt for me. On one occasion, whilst we watched the passengers from the airliner disembarking, a small boy about my age rushed out and stood under the tailplane being violently sick.

'There,' said my father. 'That would have been you. How lucky you didn't go up.'

I was furious. Of course I would not have been sick in the way that that sissy had been! I knew that I would have been perfectly all right and my father was quite wrong. Oh well... but I've never forgiven him.

The second occasion when my ambition was thwarted occurred in North Devon where, each year, my mother took my younger brother and I for our summer holidays. We stayed in a house which belonged to her mother and was always packed with her sisters and cousins, together with their children. Fathers were generally frowned upon and were seldom there. Anyway, they probably had to remain at work.

Not far away was a small airfield, locally known as Braunton Aerodrome. Its official name was quite different but I don't think it was ever used and I don't even remember what it was now. It disappeared when RAF Chivenor swallowed up that part of the land. There was the usual flying club based there, together with a small company that operated air services round the Bristol Channel. All the flying that went on fascinated me as usual and on more than one occasion my mother, who was also secretly interested, took us there to watch it.

There were the usual Moths, which anyway were the commonest aircraft to be seen in Britain during the thirties. There was a Short Scion and also a Monospar, which operated the daily service to Lundy Island. From our house, high on the cliffs of Baggy Point, overlooking Barnstaple Bay, I could sometimes see it in the distance, out at sea flying quite low over the water as it returned from Lundy.

I think that my mother must have been almost as keen as I was, because one morning she told me that, as a treat the next day, we were going to fly out to Lundy for the round trip. She announced it again at teatime and everyone at the table heard her plans. This was a ghastly mistake, as one of her younger sisters had been allowed to bring a prospective husband to stay with the family and so to meet his prospective in-laws. He now needed to demonstrate his importance and told my mother loudly, in the hearing of all the rest of the family, including Grandma, who ruled the roost, that such a venture was extremely dangerous and must not be allowed.

'The pilots who work for small companies like that are generally very poor and dangerous,' he pompously announced.

My unfortunate mother had no option but to cancel her plans, so my second opportunity to go up came to nothing, and I know that she was just as disappointed as I was. The prospective husband joined my list of hates and I noticed that my mother was not very happy either. What a pity it was that she had told them all about it before it happened. It would have been a super surprise to have related our adventures to them at teatime the following day, when the trip had been successfully completed.

Harwell was then the nearest RAF station to where we lived, but for many years now it has been the atomic energy research station and its RAF background is quite forgotten. However, if you drive past and know what to look for, you can still recognise the unmistakable pre-war RAF buildings, which were exactly the same on almost all the RAF stations of that era in Britain. In some cases, I later noticed, you could see exactly the same sort of buildings on overseas stations as well. Most were a result of the expansion period of the 1930s.

Each year in the early autumn, the RAF holds open days and flying displays. For years they were known as Battle of Britain Displays, but prior to World War Two they were called Empire Air Days. Harwell always put on just such a show and in 1938 my parents suddenly told me that we would go and that I might bring a couple of my school friends along with me.

That was marvellous and I was sure it was going to be just about the most exciting thing that had ever happened to me. It also meant a day out from boarding school, but naturally when the day came, it poured with rain. The cloud base must have been no more than about five hundred feet at the very most, with dismal visibility in continuous rain. It went on without a break all afternoon, which obviously meant that there could be very little flying. The static display had to be the main attraction as it was inside, in the hangers.

There was one thing that we had to keep going back to. In fact, it is just one of two things, apart from the rain, that I remember with any clarity at the show. This was a Bristol Bulldog, which was set up so that boys like me could sit in the cockpit. It was something that nobody was going to drag me away from for long. My memory of that cockpit layout may be very hazy now, but it is no more a hazy memory than some types of aircraft on which I later flew many hours. However, I can still remember standing in front of it and I have a vivid picture in my mind of the big Bristol Jupiter radial engine with the beautifully smooth, dark brown, wooden propeller

The flight sergeant, who was there to look after the machine and lean over the cockpit whilst explaining things to small boys, must have been a very patient man. I do remember him saying to my father that this was just a very old aeroplane, long since superseded by much more modern types. It was only used as the station hack, which was why it had been put at the mercy of small boys. Well, to me it was just the greatest. This was the first cockpit I had ever sat in.

Now, it really is something to look back and think, 'I have actually sat in the cockpit of a Bristol Bulldog.'

Harwell was then a base for Fairy Battles and the second thing I remember from that Empire Air Day is a flight of them getting airborne in the rain and putting on a low-level bombing display. As usual, a canvas contraption made to resemble a building had been erected on the far side of the airfield and this was the target to be 'bombed'. Three times the Battles appeared out of the murk and flew over the contraption. Each time the usual explosive charges, which had been laid in the ground, were detonated in order to represent bombs. This was still the practice many years later when I was in the RAF. I expect it still is. They made as much flash and bang as possible and on the last fly over the whole contraption was caused to collapse in a heap.

The Battles flew low and slow and even then, at the age of ten, I thought that they must suffer from ground fire. I had learnt a few things from my Biggles books. I also thought the aircraft did not really look quite right and must be under powered. Later I realised that they must have been among the aircraft that, only a year later, were sent across the Channel as the bomber arm of the RAF Advanced Striking Force, to fly low and slow during the Battle of France and be massacred during the German blitzkrieg in the summer of 1940.

The pilots, who flew low over the canvas contraption on that wet Berkshire afternoon, must have been some of those who had to fly their under-powered, poorly armed machines against a vastly superior enemy. Very few of them came back and it's possible that all the aircraft I saw there at Harwell on that wet English September day could have fallen to German guns less than two years later.

There were many other types, totally obsolete but still flying at the beginning of the war. One grey morning of low cloud and drizzle during a dreary Latin lesson at school, a Blackburn Shark flew down the valley just two or three hundred yards away from the classroom windows, low in front of our school. I shouted, 'Look, look!' and the whole class rushed to the window. The observer was leaning out of the rear cockpit and waving. There and then, another memory for life was printed in my mind, but I spent much of the next half holiday in detention writing lines, as the Latin master considered that I had undermined the class. Perhaps he was right, but the view was worth it.

Latin was much more important than aeroplanes there. In fact one ancient, long-retired Indian Army colonel, who eked out his minute pension by teaching at my prep school, told us all one day that aeroplanes were terrible things as they had 'completely spoilt warfare'. Those were his very words … and this was just before the start of World War Two.

Whenever I recall the aircrew that I came in contact with, however remotely, during those 1930 days, I wonder if they survived and just what happened to them in the war. Only a small percentage were still alive when VJ Day came around. What about the pilot and observer of that Blackburn Shark, who had waved out of their cockpit at the schoolboys leaning out of their classroom window? I hope they made it.

As the preparations for war built up, a searchlight with a listening station was set up in the next field just below our property. The crew with a sergeant in charge, lived in the usual basic Nissen huts that were erected nearby.

My parents would invite them all to tea in the garden and on one occasion, very early in the war, on a clear day during the late summer, we saw four aircraft flying very high in formation above the Berkshire countryside. Somebody rushed indoors to get the binoculars.

They flew in close box formation, tiny specs together against the blue sky. The binoculars showed the long thin shape of their fuselages and the light blue colour of their undersurfaces.

The sergeant looked grim faced.

'They're Dorniers,' he said. 'Flying Pencils.'

My father looked equally grim. How could these enemy aircraft have flown unhindered, deep into the English countryside so far from the coast, without being intercepted by our fighters. In fact, we learnt after the war that they had been doing this for some time and had mapped much of Britain using aerial photography. However, they were the first enemy aircraft that I had ever seen, and as a boy, I was just excited at the sight of them.

Our part of the world was not somewhere where German bombers often came in the daytime. Very distant contrails might have been all that I saw of the Battle of Britain (as it would later be known) but with the rest of the family I listened, glued to the BBC six o'clock news on the wireless every evening. We avidly took in all that the announcer said about the battle and the tally of the enemy shot down for the day. Often there would be air battles going on over Kent, not all that far to the southeast of us, even whilst the announcer was reading the communiqué.

One day, however, on a fine but partly overcast evening, my father and I were standing in the garden when a Ju 88 descended into the clear below cloud just above us and flew west towards Hampstead Norris, our nearest RAF station. We heard the sound of machine guns, the crump of bombs and then the Bofors replying. Later we learnt that the enemy aircraft had been shot down by the airfield defences. Somehow, a few days later, via a friend, I managed to obtain a very small piece of its fabric; a magnificent trophy at that time, and one which any boy like me itched to get hold of.

Later, when the bombers came at night, the unsynchronised thrump-thrump of the German engines became a not uncommon sound. Though officially we were told that it was not possible to tell the aircraft apart by the sound of their engines, any boy my age could do so with no difficulty. One night, when by chance I happened to be looking up into the sky, streams of tracer suddenly flashed out high in the darkness and the sound of machine guns accompanied the thrump of enemy engines as a night fighter engaged the Hun. Unfortunately on that occasion there was no plummet of fire towards the ground.

The glow in the sky from the London Blitz, seventy miles away was also something we could see on a clear night and sometimes bombs would be jettisoned over the open countryside, occasionally falling not far from our home. You heard the scream as they fell, followed by the explosion when they arrived.

An old man, who lived in a cottage in woods nearby, told me one morning after a raid that he had heard the whistle of a bomb falling quite close, the last in a stick that had fallen in woodland. There had been no explosion, it was a dud, and he showed me the hole, about a foot in diameter, where it had hit. The bomb, with perhaps five hundred pounds or more of high explosive, must still be there, but brambles have long since grown over the hole.

Later in the war, we would see huge groups of American Fortresses and Liberators climbing in wide circles as they gained height and picked up formation before heading out to attack targets in Nazi-occupied France.

'St Nazaire or Lorient again today,' my father would say.

Then, during the build up to the Normandy invasion and for some time after the landings, RAF Bomber Command was used on daylight raids as part of the air support for the ground campaign. The Lancasters would pass over in great gaggles on their way to their targets in France. They might not fly in an orderly formation like the American Eighth Airforce, but they tucked in tight together in order to give one another mutual cover against any attacking German fighters.

A first cousin of mine, a squadron leader in the RAAF, who flew Lancasters and was on his second tour, described these attacks and said how they were a 'piece of cake' compared to the night raids deep into the heart of Germany. There,

Bomber Command met the full force of the German defences. Unfortunately, during a raid on Hamburg one night, when nearly at the end of his last tour, he met those defences once too often. He was expecting his posting home to Australia any day and was looking forward to the flying that he would do when he got back there. He had applied to go onto Liberators. He told us how he hoped to leave the air force as soon as the Pacific War was over and join some airline flying in the Outback; but it was not to be.

I had envied him in his work as a pilot. He was a teenager's hero. The fact that few pilots flying operationally in Bomber Command survived to reach the end of the war never really crossed my mind. I longed to be old enough to begin flying training, but it was another four years or so before I actually managed to have my first lesson.

2.   Getting Started

It was just a week since I had walked down the gangway of a ship in Avonmouth docks after my sixth trip to sea as an apprentice in the Merchant Navy. I came ashore with the certain intention of never going back. The seagoing period in my life had come to an end and I had no intention of ever doing another trip. I had lost interest in sitting for my second mate's ticket, which I would be qualified to do after having amassed just a few more months' sea time. I was determined that somehow or other I would start flying as soon as I could find a way.

Now, just a few days later, I was in the rear cockpit of a Tiger Moth belonging to the West London Aero Club, which was based at White Waltham, just outside Maidenhead in Berkshire. I was having my first flying lesson.

This was also the first time in my life that I had ever been up in an aeroplane and I cringed down as low as I could in what seemed to me to be a tiny little, totally unprotected cockpit. There seemed to be nothing but some very thin canvas between me and eternity with a vast distance to the ground below. I just did my very best to avoid looking out at it in any way. I had the usual thoughts that I am quite sure many other pupil pilots aloft for the first time must have had in the past and still do, though very few would admit it just then. 'What on earth am I doing here?'

However, even after such a short period in the air and in spite of my nervous state, I was already certain in my own mind that I had found out exactly where I wanted to work for the rest of life. The cockpit of an aeroplane was the place where I belonged. The nervousness would vanish; well at least I hoped that it would

I was nineteen years old. Many young people, who want to fly, start just as soon as they can when they reach seventeen, seventeen being the age when you may first hold a pilot's licence or when the RAF would then take you for pilot training. I had been side tracked into spending those few years at sea, but now I had to make up for it.

I was totally in awe of the person in the front cockpit, the back of whose head I could see through my little windscreen and whose voice I could hear through the Gosport tubes. The voice was calling me 'Mister Holmes,' which I thought did not sound at all right. I wished that she would address me just as Mike, with none of this 'mister' business. In any case at the time, I was far too nervous to take in much of what she was saying and though she must have been trying to teach me the first of all pilot training exercises, *Effects of Controls*, I could not have been responding to her instructions at all satisfactorily. I do remember though, that the first time she told me to take the controls, to actually touch the stick and rudder pedals of a real aeroplane, up in the air, I was totally thrilled, but I don't think that it made me feel any the less nervous.

I can easily imagine her thoughts. In later years, mine could be similar sometimes. 'Oh here's another incompetent young idiot, and that means a lot of hard work will be needed to get any sense into him.' Or something like that anyway.

My instructor was Joan Hughes, who was already well known for her ATA service, but whose name was later to become a household word in British aviation. I always consider it a great honour to have had my first flying lesson with her, but unfortunately it was to be the only one. She was in the process of leaving White Waltham and moving to Wycombe Air Park, where she was to work as a flying instructor for many years, also taking part as a pilot in a number of films, such as 'Those Magnificent Men in their Flying Machines' and the 'Blue Max.'

Bill Hampton, also ex-ATA, was the instructor who had to put up with me after that one lesson with Joan. He looked after me all the way through, until I had obtained my 'A' Licence. The 'A' Licence, which had been in existence since flying licences were first thought of, is now of course the PPL, whilst to fly commercially then, you had to have the 'B' Licence.

My parents did get a bit of a shock when I told them of my intentions. They were pleased that I had decided to give up the sea, but considered that I should now settle down, go to Reading University, and slip back into a farming life. No such thing, I had decided to make the move at once, whilst the urge was still strong and there was no time to get side tracked again. Two days after I got home, I caught a bus and went to the nearest flying school that I knew anything about, the West London Flying Club at White Waltham.

I had been pointed in that direction by one, David Mason, who was the doctor aboard my last ship, the *City of London*. He had an 'A' Licence and wherever we docked, Durban, Beira, Mombasa, he would rush ashore, find the local flying club and talk them into letting him fly with them. It was he who had stirred up all those interests in flying, which had been lying dormant inside me during the seagoing years

I met Doctor Mason again years later in Portsmouth, at the now long deceased airport where he was a flying club member and part time instructor. It was great to see him after all that time and to thank him for helping me to finally make my mind up to leave the sea and start a flying career.

Another thing that motivated me had been the sight of the great BOAC flying boats, landing and taking off alongside us, when we were made fast to the quay at Basra on the Shat el Arab River in Iraq. This had been one of their stopping places ever since flying boats were first used on the Empire routes and I was seeing it all only a few years before the day when those wonderful old aircraft came to an end.

To the displeasure of the Second Mate, whose cargo watch I was on, instead of looking down the holds and making sure that all was going on correctly, I used to lean over the side of the ship, fascinated by the flying boats as they took off and touched down not far away from us. I would go up to the bridge, and borrow the ship's binoculars, peering through them at the crews as they came and went on the smart support launches. I could pick out the captain with all his gold braid, and thought him to be a very grand person. I was sure that one day I must be one of those people. That was the world for me, not this one where I was firmly stuck on a ship in a totally different life.

Now, in a Tiger Moth, I was just starting off in the flying world, but as ever, there were the usual difficulties. The journey that I had to make in order to get to White Waltham, entailed a bit of an effort, but I was pretty powerfully motivated and made it as often as I could. It first entailed a walk of about a mile, which was followed by a bus journey of about eight miles in order to get to Reading. Then I had to catch another bus along the old A4, Bath Road, to a cross roads near Maidenhead and walk a further mile or two from there to the aerodrome.

Looking back, it does seem to have been a big effort, but it never struck me as such at the time. It was all well worth it, and exactly what I had decided to do. After a few weeks, I managed to come by an ancient Morris Minor, ancient even in 1948, but it served me well and things became much easier after that.

So, on the 16th September 1948, bubbling over with excitement and not a little apprehensive, I had walked up the road beside White Waltham aerodrome, towards the flying club entrance for the first time. There I could see the usual row of aircraft parked out on the grass, beside the fence near some old wartime buildings. These were the kind of buildings that were designed to be temporary, but had been there ever since they were first put up in a hurry when the war was still just a threat. Some are still standing to this day. There were numerous other similar sites to be seen on many of the small airfields round Britain at that time, but that was all quite new to me just then.

Of the aircraft, I was easily able to recognise two Tiger Moths, but the rest were not types with which I was at all familiar. Every boy of my age knew what a Tiger Moth was. Anyway for a number of years during the War, they had been a common sight in the sky above my home as they operated from an RAF flying school of some kind at Theale, which was not very far away.

All of these aircraft at White Waltham were clean and most of them were painted in a very smart colour scheme with blue fuselages and silver wings. I learnt later that the other types were Hornet Moths, which made up the bulk of the club fleet, a Fairchild Argus, a Proctor, a Miles Messenger and a Gemini. The Messenger was painted green and the Gemini was yellow. Though my aircraft recognition had been superb in the days when I was a schoolboy, I had rather neglected it whilst at sea. I remembered some of the names, but was unsure of the faces.

In spite of their temporary war time status, the wooden buildings, which I walked up to, looked nearly as clean and smart as the aircraft. They were newly painted and did not have the rather derelict, neglected appearance, which many such buildings seemed to adopt when they served as flying club accommodation on other airfields round the country.

It was three years since World War Two had ended and by then, many flying clubs in Britain had got settled down and were working reasonably well, though on rather a thin shoe string. I think that many of them were possibly on the way to going broke rather rapidly, but surprisingly as the years went on, quite a few did manage somehow to survive. Just as they do now, they had to keep increasing their prices all the time. Some aspects don't change. But the actual cost of flying certainly has.

At the West London Flying Club, I paid two pounds ten shillings per hour for dual on the Tiger Moths. Solo cost just two pounds. The other types were a little more expensive. The Hornet Moths cost another ten shillings per hour and for the Proctor you had to pay six pounds.

In most flying clubs at that time, the instructors were almost all ex-wartime Royal Air Force or Fleet Air Arm pilots. There were some who had been professional flying instructors in clubs before the war and a number of them had even been instructing at Elementary Flying Training Schools in the RAF throughout most of the war. Also there were some of course who had done operational tours. When the war ended, a number of these instructors had just taken up their old jobs, where they had left off in 1939, and got on with it. They were different people inside though. They now had their hard earned, wartime flying hours with the associated memories and experiences, none of which could ever really be forgotten. Many had been demobbed for only a short while, so I walked straight into an atmosphere and way of thinking that was still akin to the RAF.

At White Waltham however, the basics were all a little bit different. It was not the RAF that held sway there, but the Air Transport Auxiliary, well remembered as the ATA, the organisation that ferried the aircraft from the factories and engineering works to their assigned RAF units. Almost all the staff, the instructors, those in the office and the engineers at the West London Flying Club, had been in the ATA, and many of them had been stationed here at White Waltham which was one of the main ATA bases. Now the club occupied the buildings that the ATA had used for those wartime years. As part of the business of forming the club, money had been spent on them and they had been put into good repair. My first impression of fresh paint and general tidiness was born out when I walked through the bright blue door.

I found a room with somebody sitting at a desk and somewhat hesitantly introduced myself, saying that I wanted to learn to fly. The person behind the desk was Mac. I never did learn his last name, but he was Mac to all and sundry. He seemed to be the one who ran the show and did some commercial air taxi work in the club's Proctor as well. Now he gave me a very friendly greeting and told me that I had come to the right place and would be very welcome.

He asked me what type of aircraft I would like to learn to fly on and the answer was obviously the Tiger Moth. It was the only one of the aircraft which I had seen parked on the grass outside, which I knew anything about. Also it was the type that all my cousins, who had been in the RAF and RAAF during the war, had learnt to fly on. To follow in their footsteps, did seem to me to be the natural thing to do. Mac said that it was the best trainer ever to have been built and also, of the types that the club owned, it was the cheapest to fly. That was obviously the deciding factor.

Mac also said that he was sorry, but it was a Monday and all the instructors had the day off. This was the usual thing because, as might be expected, the weekends were their busiest time. I made the first booking that was available.

Doing your basic training on Tiger Moths was quite the normal thing in those days, but looking back, I think that I was very lucky to have done so, both as a start in the civil flying world and then in the RAF. Compared with modern training aircraft, which in comparison often seem highly sophisticated to me, the Tiger was totally basic. But learning to handle her really properly, as was certainly required during the RAF training, taught you a very great many tricks that you needed to know when you flew far more advanced types later on.

Mac told me the cost of flying, which was a little less than what David Mason had warned me to expect. I was living at home and so with a little care I could afford it, but I had to add on the cost of the journey from home to the airfield, which I would have to make nearly every day.

That flying cost seems staggering when you think of today's prices. As I visited other clubs later on, I found that West London was generally a pound or ten shillings cheaper than most, but even so, in those days flying costs were something that could be afforded much more easily. They didn't put many people off as they must do now; just as soon as they are first mentioned. Ex-military aircraft were cheap and easy to come by. Spares were plentiful and again very cheap, so overheads were a good deal less than they are now.

However, balancing that, flying instructors' salaries were minute and mainly dependent on the amount of hours flown, as in many cases they were actually only paid by the flying hour. A lot of students were needed to keep them going. Because of that, there was at times, an unfortunate tendency amongst some instructors not to send their students off solo when they really were ready for it, but to wait until that momentous event could obviously not be put off any longer. More dual meant more pay.

Clubs were expecting to get masses of work, partly hiring out aircraft to ex-wartime RAF and Fleet Air Arm pilots, who were now demobbed and working in everyday jobs, but who wanted to keep up their flying. Also there were expected to be hundreds of other people, who would be bound to want to learn to fly in their spare time now that peace had come. Flying was then a popular idea and those in the trade thought that it was going to be something that would attract scores of people. There were memories of the 1930s golden era of sport flying. By keeping their costs so low, the clubs hoped to entice in all these hordes of would be aviators. In fact, it did not quite happen like that and most had a hard time, with quite a number of them failing to make ends meet.

West London had two tiger Moths, G-AIRJ and G-AIRK. I had that first flight with Joan Hughes in G-AIRK. Doing my training on either one of them, I later flew my first solo in G-AIRJ. In 1998, during the annual PFA show at Cranfield, I was wandering around the visiting aircraft park and came upon 'RK.' I had never thought that she could still be alive and I stood looking at her in amazement. To me just then, she appeared absolutely beautiful. She was still in the blue and silver club colour scheme, which even fifty years later, I remembered so well.

I was fascinated and thought it the greatest thing, fifty years on, to find the actual aircraft in which I had made my first ever flight. I peered into the rear cockpit, and vivid memories of sitting there huddled up on that first occasion, together with the later training when I had overcome my fears and was taking a real interest, came flashing back. What good that crouching down might have done, I have no idea, but I well remember doing so. Unfortunately, 'RJ,' in which I had flown my first solo, was written off in a crash during the early nineteen fifties.

I duly turned up at White Waltham again, a day or two later. Mac had told me that I would be taught by an ex-ATA instructor, as he was himself, but I had not met any of the others during that first visit. He told me all about the ATA and the ferry work that they did, explaining how they had had their own training set up and that many of their pilots were women. Even so I was surprised when I met Joan and found that I was to have a woman as my instructor. I had not realised that such people actually existed and at that time, apart from what Mac had just told me, I had not really understood the very vital part that women pilots had played in the ATA.

However, by the end of that day, and over the next few weeks, I met more of them. They still hung around White Waltham and this was their club with their culture, just as it had been when they worked there through all the war years. When I listened to their stories and learned more about them I was just amazed, and soon developed tremendous respect for all of them. Now, looking back, I think that it was another great privilege for me to have met all those people and to have been a member of that same club, even though I was a very junior member indeed, just a very basic sprog pilot starting out on his career, one who they did not lower themselves to talk to.

In the usual way, Joan took me out to the aircraft, explaining a bit about what we were going to do and what was generally going on. I don't think that I really remembered the least little bit of what she said and certainly cannot recall anything now. I was probably trying to hide my nervousness, which must have just about overwhelmed me. She strapped me in, and somebody swung the propeller to start us up. After the mandatory four minute warm up period, which is the law for a Gipsy engine, we taxied out and got airborne. I had not the least idea what was going on, and it could not have been until we had levelled off at about two thousand feet that I began to take any notice of things at all. I can just remember the view over the side at that point, but have no real recollection of anything that happened before then.

Afterwards I went home in a complete daze, but made sure that I had a series of bookings for the days ahead, often at least two per day.

I first met Bill Hampton when I came in for my second lesson. It was a surprise, as nobody had told me that there was to be a change of instructor. I did all my dual with him after that and he was also the examiner for the tests that were necessary for my 'A' Licence. For years I wondered why Joan had given me up so quickly and thought that I must have annoyed her at some time during that first flight. I would see her about the club sometimes, but was much to much in awe of her to ask why it was that I was no longer flying with her. It was a long time before I heard that she had been in the process of moving on and was doing no more flying at White Waltham. I wish that I had met her again in later years. I think that we could have laughed about it.

The qualifications required, and the A Licence test that I had to pass, were very different from the present day PPL requirements. I had completed less than twenty hours total flying when Bill told me that he thought that I was ready to take it. There was no navigation training and cross country flying was not part of the syllabus. Navigation had never been mentioned except in bar talk, when jokes were told about following the wrong road or railway and having to come down low in order to read the names on the pub signs. The last resort was to land in a field in order to ask the way; a not all that uncommon happening, I learnt.

The test itself, was flown solo. First I did a dual run over the procedure with Bill and then he sent me off to carry it out whilst he stood outside the clubhouse, watching. As a start, I needed to climb to two thousand feet, where a number of figure of eight turns had to be flown with some degree of accuracy. A barograph was carried in the small baggage compartment behind the cockpit, which gave a record of my height keeping. This had to be within two hundred feet either way. I'm not entirely sure now what other exercises were required to be witnessed, but I do remember that a straight forward, power off stall and recovery came into it. Then, from two thousand feet overhead the airfield, a glide approach had to be made, down to the designated touchdown point on the patch of grass, which formed the landing area.

As today, the 'Landing T,' positioned beside the touchdown point showed you the direction of takeoff and landing, and where you must touchdown. As on any grass field, there was no runway as such. You took off to the left of a line of marker boards and landed to the right of them. Obviously there are still one or two airfields like that now, but today the majority of grass fields have definite marked out runways laid down across them.

Except for a short oral exam which Bill also gave me, that was all there was to the test. I was then eligible, not only for the British 'A' Licence, but for the International Aviators' Certificate. I have to say it was easy, though I'm sure that I didn't think so at the time, and modern trainee pilots can only be envious of my generation. Qualifying for even a basic PPL nowadays is a major operation compared with anything that I had to do in 1948.

This then was the moment when more adventure was beckoning me on. I wanted to take the Tiger away from the local area where I had done all my training and to go exploring the sky all around over Berkshire, and just like many new pilots, the first thing that I had in mind, was to fly over my home. This was about fifteen miles away in a straight line, on the other side of Reading.

I had always been an avid listener to those stories in the bar about getting lost over the countryside, told by experienced club members and instructors, together with the other ex-ATA pilots who were always around. There were many such tales, and they told of how wrong railway lines had been followed because the direction of the line had not been checked against the aircraft's compass, or how the compass had been set up incorrectly to begin with. Then, just as a mistake could be made on the ground, an incorrect road could easily be taken at an intersection.

There were stories about the searches for familiar pubs when you were not quite sure where you were. But the great regret was that railway stations no longer had their names painted on the roof, as some had had in the 1930s.

Everybody seemed to have been lost in one way or another on more than one occasion, and pilots vied with one another to tell the best story about it. The stories fascinated me, but I did my best to learn from what I heard, and I think that some tales were told with just that intention in the mind of the experienced and seasoned old pilots who were out to teach, as well as to impress the sprog.

As well as all those stories, it was always firmly drummed into me that if the weather ever became bad ahead of me on my route, I must turn back and land, either at my departure point, or at some convenient airfield. Never try to push through until I had a lot more experience and knew just what I was doing. Crashes were cited, giving examples of those who had tried to push on unwisely.

So I had a fair idea of what I should try to do when one fine afternoon, I booked out for a local flight, but followed the roads away to the west where my home lay. I could not miss the great sprawl of Reading with the river and railway running through it. I knew the way that the Thames fitted in with the Kennet. Between the two valleys, I was able to recognise how the land rose to the Downs, clear and open to the west and beyond. Those landmarks pointed me without difficulty to the part of the country where I had grown up. I knew every farm, wood, lane and rabbit hole there. Afterwards, by following the main GWR railway line towards Maidenhead, I even found the way back to White Waltham after my escapade. I was surprised how easy it had actually turned out to be.

This was really flying; I was on top of the world. After that I just extended my 'local' flights a little further away each time, as far away as I felt safe and from where I would have no trouble in finding the way back. I leant to recognise and remember the major landmarks and lie of the land across the countryside down into Wiltshire and Hampshire. I made sure that I would always have a very good idea of just whereabouts I might happen to be and how to find my way back to White Waltham. I kept my bump of locality working hard and on top line.

Club flying was a great sport then. Controlled airspace had not yet really become part of the scene, so there was far more freedom, and only very few of the present day restrictions had come into force. If you wanted to go somewhere, you just pointed the aircraft in that direction and flew, following the railways, rivers and roads that would take you there.

The West London Flying Club was a marvellous place for someone like me. I hung around there as much as I could, and spent as much money on flying as I was able to, much more than I could afford. Bill had a fund of stories about flying in the thirties and then about the ATA during the War. I wish that I could remember them all now as such stories are very much part of our aviation history, much of which has disappeared for ever.

Before the war he had, amongst other thing, worked as a company executive pilot for some time, flying an Airspeed Courier, which carried four or five passengers and was powered by a single Armstrong Siddley radial engine. The Courier was also one of the first British civilian aircraft to be fitted with a retractable undercarriage and was built by Airspeed at Portsmouth Airport, which was then a thriving little airfield. As you drive past the site now, no trace of its aviation history is visible; even the old terminal building has been knocked down to make way for development; another loss for British aviation. The Courier led to the Envoy and then the Oxford, which became a workhorse for multi-engined RAF training right through the war and into the early nineteen fifties. The type also did useful work as squadron and station hacks. The Airspeed Consul was its civil version, which followed when the war was over.

There were many characters around the Club in those days. It was well run with a good bar and restaurant in cheerful, newly painted rooms. I think that the Van Dam family had a strong interest in the business set up. Sheila Van Dam had been an ATA pilot and I often saw her there. She flew a General Aircraft Cygnet, which was usually parked on the line with the Tigers and Hornet Moths. The Cygnet was designed towards the end of the war and was an attempt by the British aircraft industry to produce a popular light aircraft. With competition from much cheaper and easily obtainable ex-military aircraft, it sold in only very limited numbers. It was however, a very interesting design, being one of the first light aircraft to have a tricycle undercarriage at a time when tail wheels were totally the norm.

The Van Dam family owned and operated the Windmill Theatre, which was tucked away behind Piccadilly Circus, just off Shaftsbury Avenue. Its motto was, *We Never Closed*. It never had. It stayed open right through the Blitz, even when bombs were falling all round, very close to it. The Windmill was always a great attraction to servicemen and it certainly was now to a nineteen year old, just home after nearly three years away at sea. What greater attraction could there be, than the Windmill Girls, who danced or posed in the nude on the stage. That may be nothing special in this day and age, but then, 'Wow.' Such a thing was almost unheard of.

The Windmill girls were encouraged to learn to fly and were given cheap rates, so there were always a few of them about, which meant plenty of social life in those days at the West London Aero Club.

There were also many other flying characters about the place, most of whom, from my youthful view point, seemed to be very ancient. Some had backgrounds in aviation that reached back a long way before the war and I remember one particular old gentleman, who had been both a pre-war club member and then an ATA pilot. He had his own chair, reserved specially for him in a corner of the club house and it was where he had always sat when it had been the ATA pilots' crew room. Now his own private Hornet Moth was parked outside. When he felt so inclined, he would put down his copy of the *Times* and go out to fly for a little while. During the war he had left his chair in the same way when he was rostered to go out for a ferry flight. About twenty years later I was driving past White Waltham and decided to drop in for a quick visit. There, in the same chair, was that same old gentleman, but now very ancient indeed. The Hornet Moth had given way to a Cherokee, which sat outside the clubhouse in the same place as its predecessor. Every now and again as before, he would get up and go out to fly it.

In the late nineteen forties, White Waltham was a very busy aerodrome. The RAF still occupied a large site on the south side of the field, which was home to the London University Air Squadron and an RAFVR flying school. Both of these were equipped with Tiger Moths.

There were also Harvards based there and I got close up views of these great radial engined beasts as they waited for takeoff, running up their engines beside me at the holding point. Bill told me lurid tales about the way that they tended to swing on landing, to say nothing of various other difficulties, which were to be encountered when flying them. As they towered above me there, whilst I was waiting for a green light to take off in my little Tiger Moth, I was in total awe of the monsters. The thought that I would probably have to fly them during my training in the RAF, did make the way ahead seem perhaps a bit daunting.

On the north side, were the hangers and works of the Fairey Aviation Company. A lot of flying went on from there, mainly the production testing of new Fireflys. These were to become the standard carrier based attack aircraft for the Royal Navy and in two years time would form the Navy's bomber arm right through the Korean war.

Faireys were also testing the prototype of what they hoped would be the successor to the Firefly. This was a huge radial engined aircraft, which I think was called the Spearfish. It was not chosen for production, the Westland Wyvern eventually filling that hoped for slot. There was also an old Swordfish, which I sometimes saw and I suppose was used as the company hack. Together with much of the rest of the British aircraft industry, Faireys have totally disappeared now, having been destroyed by the clumsy intervention of a succession of governments.

Being the proud possessor of an 'A' Licence and having more than twenty hours on Tiger Moths in my logbook, I wanted to fly the club's Hornet Moths. There were four or five of them in the West London fleet. Bill checked me out in one, and that made me feel as if I had really climbed up a full rung of the ladder as with their enclosed cabins and my inexperience, they gave me the feeling that I had a much larger aeroplane in my hands.

G-ADNE was the one that I flew most often and it has since featured in a magazine article about its restoration. I found it a the 1998 Cranfield PFA show at the same time as my first Tiger Moth, and met the proud owner, who was standing beside it. The aircraft was immaculate, but was no longer in the club's blue and silver colours like the Tiger Moth that I had found. That I thought, was a pity, but it was great to see her and note how beautifully she had been looked after and to hear what her owner had to say about her. I also flew G-AEKY, G-ADNB and G-ANBL, but I have no idea where they are now.

Unfortunately, the cost of flying either the Fairchild Argus or the Proctor was more than I thought that I could afford, though I really did want to get my hands on both of them. To me, they seemed to be a definite step up the flying ladder, being four-seaters with much more power. However, when I balanced it against the amount of flying that I could get on the Tigers for the same price, I decided not to. The cost was then up to seven or eight pounds per hour I think, but I do regret now that I never had a go on either of the types.

Denham Flying Club operated Piper J3 Cubs, and they were definitely a type that I wanted to get my hands on. I had heard a lot about them and how they were the aircraft that had been the most popular pre-war light aircraft in America, besides being one of the types used for communication work by the American Army. Everyone had good words to say for Piper Cubs. I suppose that I was already a type hunter and so I visited Denham one Sunday. However I found very little going on and the people there, that day in 1948, did not seem at all friendly. I was not given anything like the welcome that I had had when I first went to White Waltham. However, they saw that I wanted to spend some money and so gave me a check out in the Cub, after which I did a few solo circuits; enough to just get the feel of the aircraft, which was great. Ever since then, all forms of Cub have ranked amongst my favourite aircraft.

A small charter company called Sunair rented a blister hanger and office in the club area at White Waltham. They had a Proctor and an Airspeed Consul, their one pilot being Mike Seeley, who had recently left the RAF and still sported a massive moustache. I got on well with Mike and one morning when I came in, he told me that he had got me a job. I was to fly a Fairchild Argus for Denham Studios, the film makers. They would contact me in about a week's time but he would first let me know just what was required.

That took me aback. With only an 'A' Licence, I had not really thought about trying to get a job, and by then I was definitely orientated towards the RAF. However, it seemed a pretty good idea so I thanked him profusely and hoped that something might come of it. But nothing did. A week later he told me that they had decided to look for somebody with a 'B' Licence, which was what I expected anyway. However, I have always been able to say that my first flying job was working for a film company with a Fairchild Argus. I have to add that I only held the job for an unconfirmed week, and then just vaguely. Also that I never actually flew and was never paid; well, hardly a job.

My elderly parents took exception to the life that I was leading and as there would be at least three months before the RAF actually absorbed me, it was decided that I should go back to the land and work for my keep on a farm belonging to one of my brothers. This was in Wiltshire, which was much too far from White Waltham for my liking, but there was no option. My visits to the club there would no longer be possible, as apart from the distance, I would not have enough free time to do so anyway. Besides, I was running out of money. It meant that I had to say goodbye to the West London, to its Tigers and Hornet Moths, plus the friends that I had made, and all that I had enjoyed there.

However Thruxton was not very far away from my new home and I did occasionally find enough spare time to visit the place. The club which occupied that aerodrome was the Wiltshire School of Flying, as it still is today. As soon as I could, I went along, introduced myself and joined them, but with the inevitable shortage of money and long hours of farm work, I had to cut down the amount of flying that I could do quite considerably. Well, that's an on going story for all those who fly in their spare time.

The Wiltshire School also ran a B Licence course which I thought hard about, but it cost far too much. They had recently moved to Thruxton from their pre-war airfield at Highpost, which was beside the road between Salisbury and Amesbury. Unfortunately it was also just off the end of Boscombe Down's main runway, which meant that operating a flying club from there was not at all feasible. The club accommodation at the new airfield, was in the old RAF control tower, which seemed fine to me, though rather shabby compared with the smartly painted buildings at West London.

There was even a bunk room upstairs where overseas students lived whilst they were doing their 'B' Licence course.

Nevertheless there was an unhappy atmosphere, the instructors did not like Thruxton and were generally not pleased about the move. The airfield though, was much larger than Highpost and the tarmac runway that the RAF had put down there was still in good condition; so generally, I was never quite sure just what it was that they thought was wrong with the place.

I found that the atmosphere at the Wiltshire School of Flying was quite different from anything that I had known before and I missed the familiar ATA surrounds. Three of the four instructors were ex-RAF and I was first allocated to one who had been a Lancaster pilot. The person who owned and managed the club was still known by his RAF rank and always addressed as 'Sir' by the other instructors. There was much more supervision of members and that meant that I was very much a student once again, which might have been a bit of a bore, but it did me no harm. As ever, I had a lot to learn.

At Highpost, the club had operated Tiger Moths, but much to the annoyance of my instructor they had all been replaced at the same time as the move to Thruxton. I now had to learn to fly Austers. Two species of Auster were used, one being the Autocrat, which was then brand new and considered to be the cream of the fleet. It was some time before I was allowed to touch one, but I was checked out on the two seaters. Four of these were owned by the club. They were not really Austers at all, but Taylorcraft Model D's, which had been built under licence in this country by the newly created Auster company and had formed the basis of the firm's initial production. They were ex-military, as both the Army and the RAF had used them during the war for communications work and spotting. My instructor grumbled about them, but I enjoyed flying them and they were a new experience for me, much warmer and more comfortable in the winter than a Tiger Moth. There was no danger of my map suddenly blowing up round my face and then disappearing away into space, as had happened in the Tiger.

At White Waltham, I had not been taught how to enter or recover from a spin and my new instructor did not think much of that at all. Quite rightly I suppose. They considered it was very remiss of West London to allow me to fly a Tiger Moth solo without any spin recovery training and the gap in my knowledge would have to be remedied straight away.

Miles Magisters were used for aerobatics and spinning, which meant again that there was another new type for me to be checked out on. That pleased me and made my total up to five.

One afternoon in a Magister I had an hour and a quarter of stalls, spins, basic aerobatics and circuits. I must have coped, as I was then sent off solo, which was exciting, I thought. Now I was flying a low winged monoplane, which to my sprog pilot mind, was just like a fighter. Sitting on top of the wing and looking down at it produced quite a different sensation from anything that I had felt when I was either in a cabin hung underneath a high wing, or sitting in between two of them in a biplane. Also, you could actually fly a Maggi solo from the front seat, which made it even more exciting. Except for the nose of the aircraft, there was nothing to block your view out ahead of the small windscreen in front of you, no struts, upper wing nor bits of a cabin. I felt that the sky was all wide open and that I had really become part of it. It was great and another thing for me to enjoy, another step forward.

With the lesson on spins and aerobatics, the Maggi taught me a little bit more about flying, which would help a great deal when later on I started my RAF training and had to take it all far more seriously.

One dual cross-country, which I had to do, in order to satisfy the new club, could have ended in a mess. When I look back at it now I can see a funny side, though there was little that was funny about it at the time. We went from Thruxton to White Waltham for the first leg, which was easy. As an extended local trip, I had done it on more than one occasion, unofficially without telling anybody. From White Waltham, we set off for Broxbourne, where there was a club, which was said to have lots of girl members.

A high pressure system dominated the country, and a light south easterly drift filled the sky north of London with a thick industrial haze and smoke from coal fires. The further we went, the worse the visibility became. There was no horizon and I became hopelessly lost without realising or understanding it. I learnt a lot that day about flying in reduced visibility. We should have turned round and found the way back, but the instructor, who was not my usual one and with whom I had not flown before, remained firmly silent. It took me a little while to realise that his silence was caused by his being lost just as I was, and not having a clue where we were.

I pressed on until suddenly we flew low into the circuit at Hendon, which was then the RAF Transport Command airport for London. It seemed to be busy and a number of aircraft were lined up at the holding point, waiting for takeoff. A ball on the signal staff above the tower indicated that instrument approaches were the order of the day. We flashed across the airport and from what he said and the way that he said it, I gathered that this instructor was not at all happy.

After a little while, he decided that we would have to stop and ask the way. Suddenly the jokes in the bar at White Waltham were real, not just bar talk as far as I was concerned. Now it was the real thing. He took over and we landed in a field. It was rather a small field and had a line of oaks at one end. I gathered from what he said, and the way that he said it, that it would be touch and go as to whether we could make it out in one piece. There was every chance that we would crash into those trees when it came to trying to climb out over the top of them when taking off.

The inevitable youth on a bike arrived. He might have been me, only a few years earlier. We asked him where we where and that obviously shook him. He had not realised that aeroplanes got lost sometimes. We were near Potters Bar, so to this day I can never hear the place mentioned without laughing. But however often I have looked for it since then, when flying over that part of the world, I have never been able to recognise the small field with the row of oaks at the end. It was probably turned into a housing estate anyway, as the years went by.

Well, all that taught me quite a bit.

We went on to Broxbourne and found no girls there; big disappointment. After that we flew back to Thruxton in silence. There was a rather tense atmosphere in the cockpit of that Auster.

Also at Thruxton, I had my first effort at night flying. It was quite unofficial. I had a friend who flew from Fairoaks, so one day I set off in an Auster in order to go and see him. We sat and talked in the club there as the afternoon went on. Time went by. This is a classic story of stupidity and how a very inexperienced young pilot did not think ahead and plan properly. You've heard it before and you can guess what happened.

It was a late winter's afternoon and by the time that I took off for the return flight, an early dusk was starting to set in and would soon turn to darkness. I had found my way from Thruxton to Fairoaks by following the main Southern Railway line that runs from London to the West. Steam trains were easy to see from the air at night, as the fire in the cab was very obvious when the door was open to stoke the boiler. Also the trains themselves were well lit and there seemed to be plenty of them on the lines in those days.

The obvious way to find my way back home, was to follow the railway again in the reverse direction, as it was not difficult to stick to the line past Basingstoke, and on as far as Andover. After that I had to work out the pattern of the roads and follow the headlights of cars to where I thought Thruxton must be. Luckily I got it right, and luckily, I landed successfully in the rapidly darkening winter afternoon, even though there was no airfield lighting in any way.

I could see the lights of the clubhouse and taxied up towards them. The one instructor, who was not ex-RAF, and who was considered by the others to be just a mere civilian with the minimum of flying experience and thus of a much lower order, saw me from the windows of the caravan where he lived, and came out spitting blood. I think that he was a friend of the management, as he always seemed to hold a lot of sway, even though he lacked experience, and was not popular.

I was rather surprised that I had not crashed, that I had managed to find Thruxton and then had actually landed successfully in near darkness. I knew that I had done a stupid thing and I was rightly expecting to be torn off a strip, but did not like it coming from this particular person. What was happening to me at that moment was not at all a surprise. However, the surprise came when my own instructor emerged from the clubhouse and broke in. He loudly congratulated me on the way that I had found the airfield and landed without crashing in the dark. Thereupon, the two instructors started arguing heatedly with each other, so I sneaked away, put the aircraft back in the hanger and slipped off home.

Taking all these incidents into consideration I think it's quite surprising that, having received my orders from the RAF to report a few days later, I was able to walk through the gates of RAF Cardington in one piece. However, they were all incidents that still happen to many inexperienced pilots. You see the write ups about them when they appear in magazine columns, which are entitled, 'I Learnt About Flying From That.' My trouble is that I am often prone to forget what I have learnt.

One thing that do I remember very well, is the happy time that I had in the air, flying those club aeroplanes during the winter of 1948/49. Just starting my lifetime career in aviation in such a way, made me feel as if there was great freedom in the sky. There it was, full of wonderful opportunities stretching out ahead of me, as far as I could see into the distance. That feeling never left me, but there was a lot of hard work to go with it.

3.   Joining Up

The more time that I managed to spend at flying clubs, the more flying that I managed to do, and the more time that I spent with flying people, just continued to convince me that my way ahead lay in aviation. It was obvious to me that the best thing for me was to join the RAF as soon as possible, which anyway was what I intended when I walked down the gangway of my last ship.

After the halt when the war ended, the Service had started recruiting people for pilot training once more, and I had every intention of becoming one of the lucky ones. So, one morning in November 1948 whilst staying in London, but going down to White Waltham as often as possible, I went to Kingsway and walked into the recruiting office; very cocky and sure of myself. I had been flying for over a month by then, and got my A licence.

There was a long thin corporal standing behind the desk. He had a rather dreary expression on his long thin, pale face.

'I want to join the RAF,' I announced cheerfully.

The answer was a noncommittal grunt.

The grunt was followed by, 'Oh yes then lad, what trade do you want to train for.'

'I want to be a pilot,' I said

The answer to that was just another grunt, but much more contemptuous this time, accompanied as well with a look of utter disdain. Here was another stupid young lad who had quite ridiculous ideas about himself.

'Fill in this form and put down a trade,' he said.

Having duly written in 'pilot' and handed it in without any other second choice, I was told to return at eleven o'clock the next morning, in order to take some tests and answer some questions.

When I duly reported back next day, I found that I was one of a group of about half a dozen. The same corporal took us across the street to another office where there was a row of desks. We sat down and were given more papers with more questions that had to be answered. The questions were simple; so much so in fact, that I wondered what on earth it was all about and thought that there must be a catch in it somewhere. After that we were simply sent home again and told to wait. We would be contacted.

A week or two later a letter with more forms to fill in and a demand for references arrived from some department or other in the Air Ministry. Then after a few more weeks, I was ordered to report to the RAF station at Hornchurch in Essex, where I would go through the aircrew selection procedures. Well, that was great, I was on top of the world. In spite of the contemptuous grunts from the lugubrious corporal, I had managed to make the first step in the right direction.

Selection at Hornchurch lasted for one week and consisted of masses of practical and academic tests, medicals and interviews, tests that were certainly not simple like the ones that I first had to answer in the Kingsway office. I was one of sixty would be aircrew members who made up the week's batch and at the end of it, about a tenth us were called in for a further interview. I was one of those lucky ones and was told that I had been selected for pilot training.

'Go home now,' they said. 'You will receive a letter, telling you when to report to Cardington, which is where you will actually join the RAF and get kitted out.'

Naturally, that news put me right on top of the world again. I had really managed to get into the Royal Air Force. I had never had any doubts about it until the week at Hornchurch where it had been made obvious to me that some things were not always at all easy to achieve. They sometimes required quite a lot of hard work, and this was just such a thing. I found that I felt a bit humble, but it did not stop me hanging around London for a day or two and celebrating.

For a number of years, almost all new recruits, of whatever trade or status, had had to start their careers at Cardington when joining the RAF. It was where I was ordered to report and a railway warrant came through the post. It would pay the train fare from London, but by then I had long left the Big

City and was living in Wiltshire, working on my brother's farm. That made no difference, London was where I had first walked through the entrance doors of a recruiting office and that was what counted. It was where my railway warrant would run from.

The vast airship hangers, which stood out, high across the Cardington skyline, could be seen from miles away and dominated the surrounding Bedfordshire countryside. They had been built during the twenties and still stood firm, having lasted much longer than the great flying machines which they were supposed to house. These had soon failed and been scrapped, long before they could become the envisaged lifeline of the Empire.

Now the RAF used the hangers just as storage sheds. Rows of so called temporary, wooden huts were laid out in long dreary lines beside them and used to accommodate all that was needed for the new recruits, their living space, cook houses, administration offices and such like. As ever, there was a parade ground, or square as it was known, right in the centre of things. It all seemed to me to be a very dreary place and an almost overwhelming sense of depression swamped me as soon as I first walked in through the gates.

Nearly sixty of us were brought together there, on that cold, windy March afternoon in 1949. There was bright sunlight in between heavy showers and I had been soaked with rain at some point on the journey. It was all very strange and rather daunting. I felt homesick in a way that I had never done when I had joined the Merchant Navy and had made my way to my first ship in the Mersey docks. That was a great adventure, but somehow I could feel no sense of adventure in these surroundings. The sight of the rows of wooden huts, which made up the camp, brought on that fit of depression immediately and it lasted through a lot of the time that I had to spend there.

The attitude of the corporal who was waiting for us at the guardroom, did nothing to dispel the feeling. He rounded up the small bunch of us who had come off the train from London together, and greeted us in a manner, which was hardly cheerful and welcoming. The sight of the austere barrack hut accommodation to which he took us, only added to my gloom.

We spent less than a week at Cardington, during which time we signed on and got issued with our basic uniform and kit. We also started to get to know one another. Two months previously I had met four of the others at Hornchurch, but the remainder were complete strangers and came from every walk of life, and part of Britain. It was good to see those other four again, and thus not be just on my own amongst a mass of total strangers. Even if they were little more than familiar faces, we had at least shared an experience together in the recent past.

Though quite a number were destined to drop out along the way as our training progressed, the bunch of us who came together on that March day, would stay together as an entity for nearly two years. Those who did survive all the way, would only split up after we had got our 'Wings' and were then posted to continue our training, flying different types of aircraft and working in one or other of the various roles that were part of military flying.

The few days at Cardington consisted of such dreary things as having our first drill sessions and being shouted at. We were given lectures about the Service by various officers who, as might be expected in having to do such a job, were totally uninterested. We were fitted into uncomfortable uniforms that having been kept in store for many years, smelt strongly of ancient decay and cheap mothballs. But first we had to sign on. That entailed swearing allegiance to King and Country.

To go through the signing on routine, we were taken in groups of about twenty each, into a classroom where bibles were handed out to us. We were supposed to hold these in our left hands whilst we quoted the oath of allegiance. One of the disinterested officers recited the words, whilst we repeated them back to him.

I had never believed in taking oaths on the bible. I had always considered that if I said I would do something, then I would jolly well do it as best I could. Besides, if at sometime in the future, I should decide to do something contrary to the oath, I would not want to have the breaking of it on my conscience. I stood at the back of the class, where I would not be noticed and put the bible down on a chair behind me. I kept quiet and did not repeat the words at all. I was not the only one to act like that. One other of my course mates, who stood beside me, had the same idea. We looked across at one another and grinned whilst it was all going on, and some sort of flash of understanding passed between us. However, we later had to sign a form, which I suppose made me obligated to the system in a manner that I had to accept.

The inside of the cavernous hangers was an extraordinary sight and I was quite unable to imagine what it must have been like in the days of the airships. Now they were stacked almost to the roof with rack upon rack of uniforms, and items of kit that had to be issued to new recruits. It seemed to me that an airforce, far larger than the RAF might ever become, could have been kitted out at Cardington. The designers of those great airships must have turned in their graves when they got word of what had happened to the hangers where their dreams were to be housed.

On one of the dreary afternoons, I was standing in the queue which was part of the way of life in the hangers, and dragging heavily on a cigarette. I was waiting my turn to be issued with a hat, a greatcoat, or a sewing kit or something, and was as usual, very bored and rather miserable. In order to get the last possible puff out of it, I held the end of the butt between my finger and thumb, when suddenly, the same chap who had stood beside me at the oath taking ceremony and who had also refrained from saying anything, came rushing up.

"I can see by the way that you smoke that fag, that you've been on the dole like me mate", he said.

The sun shone, suddenly there was light and colour; I roared with laughter. I had never been on the dole, but I had been in the Merchant Navy and knew all about the dole. I had worked on farms for my keep and I knew what he meant. From then on, I was able to grin and bear it. The guy's name was Fred and I still remember him with great affection. He saved my sanity on that dreary afternoon in the cavernous great airship hanger.

After that our way led to the aircrew holding unit at Kirton in Lindsay in Lincolnshire. There we joined up with others who were ex ground-crew, and already tradesmen in the RAF, but had only then been selected for pilot training. These new members who had first been through apprentice training at Halton, made our compliment up to sixty, which was the number that the RAF appeared to require for a course. Now we were drilled into some semblance of military personnel and became a single entity.

This was one of those years when the winter decided to hang around well into March, and what better place to do so than the Lincolnshire Wolds. Inevitably, we were accommodated in temporary wooden huts, but in each one there was a pot-bellied stove, which could be filled with coke and soon made to glow bright red. This could probably have become a very real fire hazard, but there were thousands of such stoves in wooden huts, throughout the British military world and I never heard of one causing a fire. There might be a freezing north wind outside, but we were always warm inside, and our wet clothes could be hung round it to dry over night. Our huts needed to be warm; there was nowhere else for us to go to. Those of our group had been in the services before, warned us about the horrors of NAAFI beer, so keeping us well away from that institution. The nearest pubs were a long cold walk away and in any case, we had no money.

We spent the days being drilled by an RAF Regiment sergeant, being taught how to lay out our kit by a corporal with a noticeably low IQ, and being given lectures about the Service by another very bored and disinterested officer. But, one day he suddenly told us that we would be on the next draft to No 4 Flying Training School, Royal Air Force Heany, near Bulawayo in Southern Rhodesia, now Zimbabwe. There we were to go through our wings course, and so become service pilots.

That was the best news that I had had since that day at Hornchurch, when I had been told that I had actually been accepted for pilot training by the Royal Air Force. Now, after a number of trips sailing round Africa whilst in the Merchant

Navy, and visiting numerous ports on the coast of the continent, I was going to fulfil another of my ambitions and see some of the great lands that lay up country, far from the ocean.

However, the prospect of going overseas, did mean one thing that was not too pleasant; we all had to have numerous vaccinations and inoculations. Just as now, it was always routine at that time in the Services to fill everybody up with masses of substances. These would supposedly immunise us against any conceivable disease that might exist in the corner of the world to which they were bound. Rhodesia, we were told, was full of many ghastly illnesses, to which we would inevitably be exposed. I found later that the Rhodesians themselves did not really agree with that, and would shake their heads in amazement when told about it.

To receive all these jabs we were divided into groups of ten, each group being formed into a circle. We simply walked round in our circles and each time we passed the particular medic who was dealing with our lot, we would have something or other pumped into us. Much had been said about fainting on such occasions, perhaps half-jokingly, but enough to have got the thought of such a thing working firmly on our subconscious minds. Whether we admitted it or not, we were all a bit scared of the possibility, though hoping that it would happen to others, not ourselves. As we circulated, people began to fall out and collapse on the floor. The medics expected this; they had seen it often enough before. There were a number standing nearby, and it was their job to simply pick up the fallen, sit them down on chairs and wait for them to come round. As soon as they could walk once more, they were returned to the circle. At length, we all received our jabs.

When the procedure was complete, we were all herded back into the changing room, where we were to put our shirts on once more. I was happily congratulating myself on having remained upright when our sergeant looked hard at me and growled, 'What's the matter with you lad?'

I suddenly realised that I was lying on my back at his feet and looking straight up into his face.

'Perfectly all right, nothing wrong with me thank you Sergeant,' I replied, and stood smartly up to attention once more.

Luckily, everybody laughed.

One day in April 1948, we were taken in trucks to Lincoln station and by dint of changing trains many times, arrived that night at another crop of wooden huts that grew out of the ground at Hednesford on Cannock Chase in Staffordshire. Here there were more uniform stores, but this time they were filled with khaki drill, tropical kit. As at Cardington, all this uniform had been there for many years, and smelt similar. The shape and length of the shorts, with which we were issued, indicated the era from which the kit originated. They were the sort known universally throughout the RAF and the Army as Bombay bloomers, voluminous great wide baggy affairs that came right down to the knees and looked ridiculous. British servicemen had warn this pattern before the War in such places as India and Mesopotamia, during many past years of Empire. There had been no change to a more modern style

Those who had been in before and served overseas, knew all about it. As soon as you got the opportunity, you had a cheap local tailor make reasonably shaped ones, specially for you. There was just that sort of person somewhere in a corner of every RAF station overseas, and he made his living creating reasonably shaped shorts and shirts at low prices.

From Hednesford, we were taken to London and accommodated for one night in a block of flats near Regents Park, which was used as a holding camp for overseas drafts. It had been used as such throughout the war, and had the reputation of providing many people's last ever bed in Britain. The boat train took us to Southampton the next morning.

Just what the normal civilian passengers on the Edinburgh Castle on their way to South Africa thought that afternoon, when they realised that they would have to share their journey with a large bunch of rather rowdy and unruly, RAF cadets, I have no idea. We were formed up into threes on the quay side by the NCO's who had escorted us from London. It was something that we knew well how to do by now, and automatically jumped to it when we heard the shout, 'Get Fell In.'

When all the other passengers were safely on board, we were marched up the gangway with our kit bags over our shoulders.

I was on my way to Africa and, apart from the prospect of the flying training to come, which was the reason for it all, it was all a very exciting, great new adventure for me.

We did have to put up with some sort of discipline aboard ship, as there was an unfortunate young pilot officer, who was supposed to be in charge of us. He travelled first class, as officers do, whilst we were far away down in the stern, right at the bottom end of the pecking order. We never saw him. There were also two NCO pilots, who travelled with us. They were on their way to Heany as well, and were to become instructors there. In fact, both were friendly and one in particular had great stories about flying Thunderbolts in the Dutch East Indies, stories which I could not get enough of.

We lived nearly as normal civilian passengers whilst at sea, except for having to wear uniform in the evenings. Nobody shouted at us, made us fall in, in threes, or marched us about. The two NCO pilots, who travelled with us, were not really bothered with discipline, but we had hardly any money, so could do little more than spend the hot days lounging around the swimming pool. Well, there's not much wrong with that really.

Reality hit us, and gave us rather a shock; on docking in Cape Town, it all changed suddenly. We were herded down the gangway in a line and there on the quay, were real live sergeants and corporals, waiting to shout at us. They were South African Army NCO's, and they knew just how to shout. They formed us up on parade on the quayside, and marched us off to some waiting busses, which we clambered aboard. These took us through the town to the ancient British Army barracks in Cape Town Castle, where we were to wait for the train which left that night. The train in its turn, would carry us for three days on the rest of our journey, a long way up country through Bechuanaland, now Botswana, to Bulawayo in Southern Rhodesia.

These barracks were another part of British colonial history. They were built of great solid blocks of stone, which looked as if they could resist even the largest cannon ball, and were seemingly meant to last for at least a thousand years or more, just as was the British Empire. I thought that the building must have been old when Queen Victoria came to the throne. Then it had housed the British regiments that had been based there to guard the route to India, many years before the Suez Canal was even envisaged. After that came the thousands more British soldiers, who had disembarked from ships as we had done that day, and were on their way to fight the Boer, many never to return. After that there were all our predecessors, the aircrew who were trained in South Africa and Rhodesia during World War Two.

In 1949 it was still a number of years before the 'Wind of Change' speech, which heralded the end of British rule in Africa, and at that time, the possibility of the British Empire coming to an end, was not really seriously part of the picture.

The view that I had of Cape Town that day, was very different from any that I had had on my previous visits as a Merchant Navy Apprentice, so it was all something new and exciting.

Later, that evening we once more formed up in threes on the parade ground outside the castle, and were marched to the usual waiting busses which this time took us to the railway station.

Nobody could have described the train journey that followed as being in any way comfortable, but I was fascinated just watching Africa, whilst we travelled up through the Karroo, past Kimberly and Mafeking; then into Bechuanaland, now Botswana, and so to enter Southern Rhodesia at Plumtree. I had got away from the coast, and was seeing the interior at last.

So, early one morning, about three days after coming ashore from the Edinburgh Castle, the sixty of us tumbled sleepily, and untidily out of the train onto the platform at Bulawayo. Once again, we were formed up in threes and shouted at by NCO's, but these were our own RAF NCO's from Heany, three corporals and a sergeant, who we would get to know well over the next eighteen months. They would drill us and be in charge of our discipline throughout the course. Somehow, in spite of giving us the usual spiel about our being a shower and the lowest form of life in the RAF, they were almost welcoming. Once again we were loaded onto rickety old busses, and these took us the last twenty miles out of Bulawayo to our new home at Heany in the central African bush.

My first impression of Heany was silver and grey on brown. The rains had not yet arrived and the bush all about was brown, with the earth showing brown through the sparse covering of withered dry season grass. The brown was broken by rows and rows of hastily erected, grey wartime huts with corrugated iron roofs, on which the sun beat down hard and hot. The corrugated iron accounted for the silver appearance, as here it was quite different from the usual dark colour that corrugated iron takes on in Britain. The silver memory has persisted, as later when I flew over it day after day, its rows and rows of silver and grey rectangles against a brown background, were firmly imprinted in my mind.

Three of these huts, each containing twenty beds, were allotted as accommodation for our course and we were dumped off in front of them. Once again the NCO's welcomed us in their time honoured manner: "Now you lot, get fell in and listen to what you're told".

It seemed that we were Number 11 Course, which meant that we were the eleventh group, each of sixty cadet pilots, to enter No 4 Flying Training School, RAF Heany, since it had reopened and flying training had started there once more, following the post-war shut down.

First we would have six months of ground school to live through but then, if we passed all the exams, we would start flying, first on Tiger Moths, and after that on Harvards.

I would fly the great monsters that I had been so in awe of when they parked beside me and ran up their engines at the holding point on the grass, whilst I was waiting for take off in my little club aircraft at White Waltham.

Now they roared overhead as they took off or joined the circuit here at Heany. At last, we had arrived at an RAF station where there were aircraft, and in time we would be flying them. We had got somewhere. The sixty of us were bubbling over with excitement.

4. Ode To The Tiger

It had been quite a surprise to me, when I learnt that basic training at Heany was still done on Tiger Moths and they were therefore to be the first RAF aircraft that I would fly. Here was I, a pupil pilot in an airforce that operated Meteors and Vampires, which at that time were still the most advanced operational jets in the world, about to climb into an ancient wood and fabric biplane.

The Tiger Moth had been an outstanding aircraft in its time, but now I thought, it should be giving way to the far more modern types that had taken over its roll at the Flying Training Schools back in the UK. I might have started my flying career by getting my first civil licence on Tigers, but had never expected to see them much more after those club flying days. To my youthful and quite incorrect way of thinking, the type was little more than an antique, and at that age I was certainly not interested in antique aeroplanes; just the fastest and most modern jets that there were then.

How wrong I was. The Tiger's successor, the Prentice was a totally unsatisfactory and characterless flying machine, with none of the ability which the Tiger possessed, of being able to instil into its pupil pilots the finer details of aircraft handling. It could never give the really firm grounding that the Tiger did to anyone who made their basic start on it in the flying world.

Right from the time that I first started learning to fly at White Waltham, I had been told, 'Anybody can fly a Tiger Moth, but if you learn to fly it properly, you will be able to cope with any aircraft that you may have to fly in the future, whatever its size or performance may be.'

Now in the RAF, I was hearing exactly the same thing from my new instructor, one Master Pilot Paddy Mulrooney. Sadly the RAF no longer has NCO pilots such as he, but in those days they were indispensable to the whole operation and were often the working backbone of a squadron. Paddy

Mulrooney, who had flown Lancasters during the War, had a vast amount of knowledge and flying skill, which he would try to pass on to me. I hope that some of his teaching sank in.

So, having managed to survive the six months of Initial Training Wing, which consisted of a rather dreary half year with nothing but solid, unending ground school, it was time to start the Basic phase of the flying course, and learn to fly the Tiger properly. It was the machine on which I was to enter the world of military flying and it was Paddy Mulrooney's job to teach me how it should be flown. It could not have been an easy job for him as I had masses of faults left over from my club days.

There was a lot that I had to learn. The club training that I had been through definitely harked back to pre-war ways and thinking. Some of things that I had been taught were frankly, a load of rubbish. Paddy Mulrooney had to wash all that out of me and instil the up to date methods, as laid down by the RAF Central Flying School

Though it did take a year or two to actually do so, I did come to realise that it had been a tremendous privilege to have started my RAF flying on the Tiger Moth and I have every reason to be grateful for the chance that I was given to get such a good basic grounding. The Tiger Moth was one of the stars that shone amongst the many stars from De Haviland.

This period at the beginning of the flying training programme suddenly became a time of great stress for almost all of us pupil pilots. There was a huge hurdle to overcome. We had to go solo, and doing so was the first big step in learning to fly. The stress was noticeable in the barrack hut where twenty of us, a third of our course, lived. The main topic of conversation seemed to be about reaching that moment at last, when we would be all alone in an aircraft. Those who had not yet done so were obviously a bit worried.

We would surely get scrubbed and be on the next boat back home if, after one of those traumatic sessions of circuits and bumps, we had failed to reach the moment of truth when our instructor was able to say as we taxied in at the end of it. 'Right, I'm getting out now and I'll make the harness secure in the front cockpit. Off you go; do just one circuit on your own and don't break the aeroplane. You'll find that it'll climb faster without my weight in the front cockpit.' It was a standard bit of instructor talk, always used when they sent someone off for the first time.

In fact, the threat of being scrubbed hung over our heads for the whole remaining year of the wings course. It happened to nearly half of us, but in this case I had a tremendous advantage. Only once ever in a life time can you fly your first solo, and I had done that nearly a year before at White Waltham, so together with a few others, who also had had some previous training, I did not have to fight that particular battle. There would be plenty more hurdles to overcome and battles to be fought before our training was over, but in this case after three dual flights, Paddy Mulrooney handed me over to the flight commander for a check and I was sent off on my first RAF solo by him.

In fact this was not my first solo over Africa. When we had first got settled at Heany, still with the prospect of six dreary months of ground school ahead of us, a friend and I had joined the local flying club at Bulawayo's Kumalo airport. We had got our British licences endorsed to cover Southern Rhodesia and had managed to get checked out on the club's Cessna 120's. However, after only a couple of flights, the RAF authorities had got wind of this and much to my annoyance, had stopped it. The word had come down from the station commander at Heany; cadets were not to fly club aircraft. Well, it had been fun and I had got another type in my log-book, but typically, it was something that went against authority's way of thinking.

The club flying had been just local circuits round Bulawayo, so the Tiger introduced me to flying out over the Africa bush. This was always wonderful, and gave me a thrill that never faded. There below and all round me was this wide brown land, which stretched to a hazy horizon, a seemingly never ending distance away. Depending just where you where, there could be mountains of all shapes, sizes and colours rising out of the vast plains. MBA, Miles of Bloody Africa. I loved it.

The basic part of our flying training at Heany, was divided into two halves. We flew about thirty five hours on Tigers, hours which were intended give us a good grounding as just very junior, young pilots, but after that we converted to the Harvard for the remainder of the journey to our 'Wings.' It was always the thought of gaining those much coveted wings, which kept us going through the many months of flying training, however hard the course might seem to us at the time.

Throughout the War, the Harvard had been, and in many cases still was the backbone of pilot training in numerous airforces. It was a well known aircraft and it only took me one close up look and a short time sitting in the cockpit, to endorse the healthy respect that I already had for the great monster. Add that to the sense of awe that I had had ever since those days at White Waltham when it's great radial engine had towered above me at the holding point, belching blue and grey smoke whilst making its deep growling roar, and you can get an idea of how I felt about the type that I was to fly for the rest of the course at Heany. Apart from that noise when just ticking over on the ground, the distinctive noise that a Harvard makes when airborne, was another factor. No other aircraft makes anything like it.

That feeling of awe had remained with me ever since I had first heard it, but up until this moment at Heany, the thought of actually having to master the beast had been no more than something which might have to happen to me in the far off future. It was something that did not need to be worried about at that particular moment. 'That Moment,' had become 'Now,' and had to be faced.

The Harvard's cockpit was also daunting, and after the Tiger's simplicity with a lack of anything at all complicated, I had no idea how I would ever find my way about and learn just what it all meant. Also, these Harvards at Heany were in fact, basically US Navy SNJ's and lacked the standard RAF instrument panel, which all Canadian built RAF Harvards were fitted with. That was another thing to add to the complication.

But the Tiger had given us all the good grounding that it was renowned for, and as far as I can remember, converting to the Harvard did not in fact turn out to be much of an event, in spite of all the terrible stories that the type carried in its wake. Had there been a problem, I would certainly have remembered all about it. What I do remember though after the Tiger Moth, is the sense of power that I got when I sat behind the Harvard's seemingly huge Pratt and Whitney radial engine and knew that it was firmly under my control. I had mastered it, and felt that I now would always be able to master any new, and initially daunting types that I might come to fly in the future.

More rumours and stories about the aircraft kept popping up all the time, and were boosted by those on the course, who had started their training in the RAF during the war, or had previously been in the Fleet Air Arm. They had had their first session of flying training abruptly cut short when World War Two ended and they had been demobbed. Now they were starting all over again, and had many stories to tell those of us who were right at the beginning of it all.

The Harvard would not easily recover from a spin. It often swung on landing when you least expected it, and then the swing would develop into a ground loop. That meant that you were definitely in trouble. It flicked off the top of a loop. All sorts of ominous and off-putting stories about it circulated, and were discussed in the barrack room. However, when I got to know the aeroplane a bit, it seemed to me that most of them were rubbish.

Well, if you let it, it could and would do many of the evil things that were spoken of, but it also taught you how to avoid them and deal with them if they ever started to happen to you. When the aircraft did bite you, it was usually your fault. With the basic grounding provided by the Tiger, the Harvard could soon be mastered without much difficulty, which was something that surprised me straight away. The feeling of awe soon vanished, just as it always does after a few hours on a new and more advanced type.

Years later, when I flew the aircraft operationally in the ground attack role after being on jets, it was easy stuff, but I will never forget the feeling which came over me when I first saw it close to, near the takeoff point at White Waltham and then had to first master it at Heany. Also, though it might have become easy stuff, I never lost my respect for it. It was another superb aircraft.

I consider myself very lucky to have had that start on Tigers and for years have known it to be a great privilege. Very few of my future colleagues had the luck to be given the chance of such a grounding for their pilot careers, and secretly I have sometimes felt a little sorry for them, though I have never let them know it. Even Chipmunks could never completely fill the gap that the Tiger left, though they certainly came close to it. Many other types have tried and failed, but apart from the Chipmunk, the only aircraft, which I flew and found to come anywhere near to instilling the basic feel that the Tiger managed to do, was the very odd Pegasus AX3 microlight, but that's quite another story.

Together with an Oxford, we had a Tiger for use as a hack at Biggin Hill when I was stationed there on 41 Squadron. That was great and I always grabbed the opportunity to go off and fly it whenever I could persuade my flight commander to give me an hour away from what he thought I should really be doing. I was there to fly Meteors and get on with all the exercises which that entailed. I wasn't there to go off jollying around in the Tiger. A fighter squadron was not a flying club I was told; together with various other things like that.

Also the Oxford was another new type for me, so I volunteered to fly it whenever a job for which it was needed came up. That even took me as far as RAF bases in Germany, which was good experience.

However there was an occasion when I actually got the chance to fly the station Tiger as a mail plane. One Wednesday afternoon our station commander gave me the job of carrying what he told me was a very urgent letter for the station commander at Northweald, near Epping in Essex on the other side of London.

This package had to be delivered by hand personally by me, and must indeed have been extremely important from the way that he talked about it. However its contents remained a mystery as far as I was concerned, and I was never told what it actually was.

Wednesday afternoon was utterly sacrosanct as far as the RAF was concerned in those days. It was an organised sports afternoon for everybody, so unless it had to do with some sort of organised and approved sport, everything closed down completely on all RAF stations. I always felt that some secret gentleman's agreement must have been signed with the Soviets, and they had been made to understand that we just did not fight wars on Wednesday afternoons. They were never to attack us at that particular time. This Wednesday sports tradition had existed as long as the RAF, and nothing was to change it.

Francis Drake had set the precedent with his game of bowls on Plymouth Hoe, those many long years ago. Then the Spaniards had to wait to be defeated, but now if the Soviets came on a Wednesday afternoon, they too would have to wait. Sports took priority, and even though the Spanish Armada had sailed up the Channel hundreds of years before the RAF came into existence, the pattern was still followed. No flying on sports afternoons; an enemy would have to wait until the games of rugger, cricket, soccer, golf or whatever it might happen to be were over, and everybody had had time for a shower and a change followed by a drink in the bar. After that, we would all come to readiness and join battle as required.

However this Wednesday sports routine was discontinued shortly before I left the Service. A simple little bit of mental arithmetic will show that the one extra afternoon must have increased the work output of the RAF by about ten percent.

I had a happy time that afternoon; I played no sports. Sitting in my biplane with its open cockpit, I cruised along at about fifteen hundred feet over northwest Kent, keeping just to the south of London until I came to the Thames near Tilbury. There, there were factories that spewed out thick green smog and on the run in to land back at Biggin in our Meteors, we would pass over them at about four thousand feet, doing about three fifty knots. Even then, in an enclosed cockpit and breathing oxygen, we would smell the filthy sulphur stench. Now, at fifteen hundred feet and eighty miles per hour, the pollution was horrible, but after a little while, I was through it and heading up across the Essex countryside.

I made for the northeast corner of Epping Forest, and there, ahead and out to my right, I saw North Weald. As expected, it was sports afternoon there also, and nothing was working as usual. The signals square had a big yellow cross on it, so I picked a nice looking patch of grass, landed and taxied in towards the control tower.

I was amazed, the organisation was working. The orderly officer was there to meet me and as I stopped the engine, the station commander drove up in his staff car. Success; I was able to hand over the packet directly to him.

I was really happy. I had done a job of work, actually flying on a Wednesday afternoon and used the squadron Tiger Moth to do so. To me the Tiger has always been one of the greatest.

5.   Cold War Fighter Pilot

Every fighter pilot must surely consider his squadron to be the best, not only in the airforce in which he happens to serve, but in the whole world. It is one of the things that goes with the essential high morale on a fighter squadron. May fighter pilots always have such an outlook, it's a necessary part of their make-up and helps to attain the very high operational standard that is required.

In June 1951, just six years after the end of World War Two and a little less than three since I had walked into the recruiting office on Kingsway, I joined my first squadron. It was No 41 at Biggin Hill, in Kent just south of London, and I have never had any reason to doubt my first impressions. This definitely was quite the finest fighter squadron in the world. I'm sure of it, though I expect that some other past or present fighter pilots, who have not had the privilege of serving on 41, may have different ideas. However, I know that I am right; 41 was the best and I'm quite certain that it still must have been so, right up until it became a reserve unit in 2006. Now it must be the best reserve squadron, though it deserves better.

Earlier that summer, I had completed the course at the day fighter operational conversion unit flying Meteor 4's and, though I still had a lot to learn, the long period of official pilot training was over. I had finally split away from the last of the friends with whom I had spent the previous two years and three months, the period that had started on one Lincolnshire evening in March 1948, when the sixty of us had all been brought together in the snow at Kirton in Lindsey. There we had been made up into the group of cadet pilots, which had become Number 11 Course at RAF Heany. Some had dropped out along the way and later, I had lost contact with those who had been posted onto bombers or other forms of RAF flying. Now I had said goodbye to the last of them, who like me had gone through the Meteor training, but were to join different squadrons. At last, I was quite on my own with none of those old friends around me.

I had survived. Of that sixty of us, who had set off together on the adventure into Africa, only about half had managed to stay with the system and get their 'Wings.' The others had been scrubbed at some stage and I was lucky not have been one of them. But now I was about to join my first operational squadron and ahead of me was the life of a day fighter pilot, as part of the defence of Britain itself.

During our time on the course at Stradishall with Number 226 OCU, we had all wondered just where we would be sent to when it was over, and what station we would call home for the following two years. It was one of our main topics of conversation in the crew room, the mess bar, or the pub. We awaited our postings with some trepidation. There were about twenty regular squadrons equipped with Meteors in Fighter Command at that time and we could be posted to any one of them. They were on stations scattered all up and down the country from Leuchars in Fife on the east coast of Scotland, to Tangmere on the south coast near Chichester in Sussex.

I was lucky, but just why I was lucky I don't know. By going to 41, I got what I definitely considered then, and still do, to be by far the best of the postings that were dished out to us. I considered myself doubly lucky as I would catch up with two particular friends, who I had first met when on advanced training at Middleton St George in County Durham. They had already completed their training ahead of me and were now operational members of 41. I was looking forward to seeing them again soon.

Biggin Hill was in 11 Group and being on the southern outskirts of London, was one of the fighter stations that made up the defence of the Capital. Dating back to the days of World War One, it was steeped in the history of the RAF and particularly in the Battle of Britain. What more could a brand new pilot officer dream about for his first squadron; it was without doubt just the best in every way.

Unfortunately the day that I joined was a very bad one for both the station and the squadron. As I drove along the road beside the airfield, bubbling over with excitement at seeing this historic place for the first time and knowing that it was to be my new home, a Meteor overshot its landing roll and skidded off the end of the runway, crossed the road in front of me and exploded as it crashed into the front of a house. I could just see the 41 Squadron markings on the fuselage, before they were obscured by the smoke and flames.

Then a flight from one of the other squadrons on the station came in overhead to break formation for landing. The number two did not keep his eye on his leader and must have looked down at the wreckage just as he broke. There was a collision in which the tale of the leader's aircraft was knocked off and they both crashed in the valley below the airfield. It was too low for either pilot to bale out successfully, as the Meteor 4 had no ejection seat.

It was not really a very good way to be introduced to one's first squadron, but unfortunately it was all part of the way things were then and part of the high attrition rate, which went with life on that early generation of jets. However, there was only one more fatal accident during the whole of my two and a half years on 41, which was more than could be said for most other squadrons in Fighter Command during that period.

Whilst I was doing my flying training in Rhodesia, there had been a visit by a bunch of senior RAF and USAF officers, who were on a tour round British overseas bases from the Flying College at Manby. Speeches had been made to us cadets and one American had told us how we were the young pilots who would be the future guardians of the free world and would fight the next Battle of Britain. It was probable that this would take place very soon. Such words meant very little to me at the time and I did tend to think that we had to listen to lot of hot air from senior officers anyway. However, when I was posted to an actual fighter squadron at Biggin Hill, in what would be the front line, I began to understand what he had been getting at. Almost all our flying was in preparation for just that possibility.

Fighter Command squadrons had a strength of either 16 or 22 aircraft, No. 41 being equipped with 16 Meteor 8's. These had only just arrived as a replacement to the Mark 4's, which in their turn had recently replaced the Hornets which the squadron had been flying for some years. I was disappointed to have just missed that super derivative of the Mosquito, but at the time, I looked upon even the finest piston engined aircraft as relics from the past and no longer my thing. I had been trained as a jet pilot and that was that, as far as I was concerned.

The Meteor 8 was new to me, and a great improvement over the Mark 4 which I had got to know during my training at Middleton St George and then Stradishall. To begin with, it had a Martin Baker ejection seat, which was good for morale, and though I'm glad to say that I never had to use it, it certainly saved the lives of some of my friends. The cockpit seemed roomier and more comfortable. The controls were laid out in a much better way and the traditional British spade grip stick had at last given way to a pistol grip. I considered that a great improvement, one which I had become used to on the version of the Harvard that I had flown at Heany. The critical Mach Number was 0.82, which was another improvement over the Mark 4's 0.79, and that was important.

At the time, this all appeared to be quite a leap forward, but with its straight, unswept wings, the Meteor was already becoming dated. Its performance was not really up to that of the fighters which were entering service in other airforces, such as the American F86 Sabre and the Russian Mig 15. The latter was the one that was often in our thoughts, and a frequent topic of bar and crew room conversation. It would be the one that we would have to meet in battle, should we have to go to war. That war suddenly did not seem very far away and we were certainly being honed for it.

Three squadrons made up the Biggin Hill Wing. The other two were No's 600 and 615, both Royal Auxiliary Air Force and still equipped with Meteor 4's. They did most of their work at weekends, the members having ordinary civilian jobs throughout the week, but becoming fighter pilots on a part time basis, mainly at weekends. To make the Wing viable, we also worked through the weekends and had our time off on Tuesdays and Wednesday morning.

At the period that I joined however, the political situation was critical due to an escalation in the Korean War and the attitude of the Russians over Berlin once again. Because of this, the Royal Auxiliary Air Force had been temporarily called up for full time service. It was thought that World War 3 was imminent and the full strength of Fighter Command would therefore be needed at very short notice. We had to be absolutely ready and trained to tip top capability in order to meet the Soviet threat.

Being regulars, we made it plain to the Auxiliaries that we were very superior people and could out-fly them in every way. There was a great deal of friendly rivalry and competitive spirit, which all helped to generate a high standard of flying and morale on the station; just the situation that should exist between the different squadrons on a fighter station.

Fighter Command, the organisation responsible for the defence of the UK against air attack, divided the country into a number of sectors. We were part of Met Sector, the Metropolitan Sector, whose task it was to defend London and the Southeast. Given a task like that, we were totally sure that there wasn't anybody, who could even remotely approach our high standard. We knew that we were the tops.

North Weald was another fighter station in Met Sector. It lay in Essex, just to the Northeast of London, but the squadrons there were far inferior in our estimation as they were only equipped with Vampires. We always spoke of Vampires, as 'Kiddy Cars,' and considered that we could outperform them in almost every way. In a dogfight, they could turn more tightly than us, but that was all. However, about a year later North Weald did re-equip with Meteors, as did Odiham near Basingstoke, another neighbouring fighter station in Met Sector, which was also equipped with Vampires.

Some way to the South of us in Sussex, lay Tangmere, another famous, old time fighter station, which just like Biggin Hill, had been heavily engaged in the Battle of Britain. Number 1 Squadron was based there, and had been since before the war. There was always a very strong and healthy rivalry between the two squadrons, 1 and 41, which was probably another thing that helped us both achieve extremely high standards in the way that we operated, in our gunnery scores and the amount of flying that we managed each month.

Having gone through the usual procedures that one had to when joining a new station, it was time for me to meet my Squadron CO, start training with the squadron and be introduced to the Meteor 8. The CO at that time was Sammy Osborne, but he was posted away after I had been on the squadron for only a few weeks and his place was taken by Dusty Miller.

There was no initial dual check with my Flight Commander or a Qualified Flying Instructor. I just sat in the cockpit of a Meteor 8 whilst another pilot leant over and showed me the various controls, pointing out the differences between it and the earlier types of Meteor. Under his guidance, I started the engines and then taxied out.

Apart from it being in this case my introduction to the new version of the Meteor, a pilot's first flight from a new and strange station was always known as a sector recce. One flew round the local area and got to know it, learning the landmarks and carrying out an instrument approach.

I remember that I was suitably impressed, enjoying the more comfortable cockpit, the pistol grip stick and the improved, nearly all round visibility. The latter though, had one very bad point. The rear of the canopy was not transparent perspex, but made of an aluminium sheet. Thus the pilot had a blind spot right in his rear and could not see an enemy right on his tail. In Korea, this naturally proved to be a killer, but was not rectified until the Australian pilots on 77 Squadron RAAF, who flew the Meteor against the Mig 15, complained very strongly. They quite rightly said that it was unacceptable.

Having had my introduction to the aircraft and the sector in which we had to operate, it was then time for me to work up to an operational standard. I first had to learn to fly as the number two of a pair in battle formation. This would be the number two or four position in a flight of four aircraft. The pair was the basic unit in combat and the two aircraft worked together, totally as a team. Good teamwork was an essential for all fighter operations. As soon as a formation became involved in a dog fight, it broke down into its pairs. The number two covered his leader and acted as the eyes in the back of his head. Thus the leader could concentrate on his attack, knowing that his tail was guarded, and that no enemy was able to attack him without warning.

It was the most heinous crime for a number two, or wing man as he was sometimes called, to lose his leader. As a wing man, you just had to stick to your number one through all the manoeuvres that he made whatever they might be. This was quite a problem in itself, but you also had to make sure that your own tail was clear and that no enemy could come unseen, into a position that enabled him to attack either you or your leader. You had to have eyes in the back of your own head and look after yourself as well. I found all of this to be incredibly exciting, but it took a lot of practice and hard work before I achieved anything like a satisfactory standard.

On one occasion during the debrief after a squadron battle formation exercise, the CO bluntly told me that unless I learnt how to keep up and fly in the right position, I would be shot down on my first operational sortie. I would be dead. That sunk in, and I made sure that I very quickly got it right on all future flights.

Then there was cine gun work, and as there was no enemy at that time all the practice combat was against friendly aircraft. Instead of firing live ammunition, we took film, which was later assessed in order to determine if we would have scored any hits. I soon learnt that to be successful you had to get in as close as you could behind the target, fly steadily and aim correctly; then fire in short bursts. All that was fine in theory, but it took a lot of practice, and would be very different with someone shooting back at me.

Our CO kept drumming just that into us. 'The only way to be sure of a kill is to get in as close as you can, line astern behind the target, and shoot straight. Don't just hose the sky.'

Every morning, the first thing after Met Briefing, which was when our day started, he would go over the cine gun film that had been taken on exercises the previous day and make sure that we understood exactly where we had gone wrong. He did not mince matters, but bluntly told us off when we did not come up to the required standard.

To bring it home to us, we were shown actual gunnery film from some of the fighting early on in the Battle of Britain. There were pictures of formations of German Heinkels spread right across the frame, indicating that the attacking pilot had indeed just hosed the sky, whilst well out of range of the bombers. He had used up all his ammunition without doing the slightest damage to the enemy aircraft. It was explained how the pre-war tactics and gunnery training in the RAF had left a lot to be desired. Lessons that had been well learned by the RFC pilots in World War One when dog fighting, first when flying DH 2's, then Sopwith Camels and SE 5's, had to be learned again the hard way, in the heat of new battles during 1940, first over France, and then over Britain.

'Get in close behind and shoot straight in short bursts,' was the word

To further drum this in, we were also shown gunnery film of Migs being shot down during the Korean war, which was at its height just then. It was obvious, 'Get in close behind.'

Our main task in Fighter Command was to destroy bombers, and the proscribed method of attacking them was known as the high quarter attack. We positioned ourselves out to the side of the enemy formation and a little way ahead of and above our particular target; then rolled in towards him, closing fast and tracking him in our gun sight. This was known as a curve of pursuit and you opened fire when you had him in range and were holding the sight steadily on him. It was no good trying to shoot unless you were tracking steadily; you would simply just hose all your ammunition away round the empty sky, as in the films we had been shown.

This manoeuvre caused you to end up in line astern to the bomber, which was of course, exactly where you needed to be in order to cause him the most damage, as long as you were close in. Also it was of course, exactly where the bomber's tail gunner wanted you. You would then be a sitting target for him. From his angle there would be no curving flight, so just like you, he would not need to lay off any deflection for his shot. It would be difficult for him to miss. You just had to make sure that you put him out of action first, before he did just that to you.

Having flown in as close as you dared, you broke away hard at the last moment, underneath the bomber before you crashed into his tail. Stick fully forward and hard over into either front corner of the cockpit, trying to get out of range of his belly gunners at a moment when you were most vulnerable and could not shoot back at them. It was far from the smooth use of controls as taught by generations of flying instructors. On fighters, you soon learnt that the only way to stay alive, was to be as ham fisted as possible and fly with crossed controls except when actually lining up and aiming your guns. Then all flying had to be perfectly balanced.

To practice the basic method of carrying out these attacks, two Meteors would work together as a pair. Having climbed to thirty or thirty five thousand feet, they then split up to take turns, one aircraft stooging along as the target and the other making practice attacks. The attacker would of course, take cine gun film, which was assessed for its accuracy and shown as usual after met briefing the following morning. At thirty thousand feet, the Meteor handled well and you could make really good attacks, but at thirty five the aircraft was labouring; you were flying right on your limiting Mach Number and could easily run into compressibility problems. When you did so, the aircraft could certainly not be controlled smoothly and you were no longer anything like a stable gun platform. Also in your turn, as you tracked the target at that height, you could easily get into a high speed stall situation. The need to get in close and straight behind the bomber was obvious, even though at that point you knew that you were a sitting duck for the rear gunner.

It took a great deal of practice, before we were able to make attacks that were anything like satisfactory and would have been damaging to an enemy bomber. Luckily in the Cold War, we had time to really work at these exercises and did learn to handle the Meteor in a way that would have made life very difficult for any enemy force that might have attacked Britain in the early nineteen fifties.

In order to make what we had learnt when practising these high quarter attacks on one another more realistic, the next exercise was bomber affiliation. The bombers called this fighter affiliation and of course, their gunners needed the practice against fighters such as us, who were simulating attacks against them. We both gained experience. Our targets were Lincolns and Washingtons from Bomber Command or B50's from the USAF.

The Lincolns flew at about twenty thousand feet, often in groups of at least ten or dozen. They were never in close formation, like the Americans, but bunched together in a tight gaggle, and when attacked, they would carry out evasive corkscrews, just as the Lancasters had done when attacked by German fighters in World War Two. A lot of skill was needed, but it was a lot of fun trying to follow these and keep your sights on the target. You had to slow right down, lower a small amount of flap sometimes, and try to turn very tightly inside the bomber in order to keep your gunsight just where it had to be.

The Washingtons, as the RAF called their Boeing B29 Superfortresses, flew between twenty five and thirty thousand feet, which made them easy to attack with high quarters. The Meteor handled really well at that altitude and you had a superb weapon platform under your control. In order to make yourself a difficult target for their gunners, you tried to attack whilst diving as steeply as you could, with as much angle off as possible, though your shooting could then never be as accurate as a straight run in from behind.

I really enjoyed myself when exercising with Washingtons as I developed a system of attacking them, which really thrilled me. I would fly almost right over the top of them and then start a kind of descending barrel roll, which would put me in position to come down in a really steep, diving curve of pursuit. This then became a perfect high quarter, which made it very difficult for the gunners to track me with any degree of accuracy. At least, that was what I hoped it would do.

After one session of attacks against a Washington, the pilot passed a message on the radio via our radar interception controller, saying that these were the best attacks by fighters that he had ever seen. My wing man and I flew back to Biggin doing aerobatics all the way, and it really did make me think that perhaps I had actually managed to achieve something in the game of learning how to be a fighter pilot flying interceptors. Nevertheless, I was always conscious of the fact that I could never really be sure of that until I had defeated a gunner who was shooting back at me for real. Luckily I never had to do that, though naturally at the time I was stupidly itching to get a chance

The American B50's of Strategic Air Command, usually flew rather higher, and in close formation; in the way that the old B17 Fortresses had over Germany during the World War Two. I never found them easy to attack. There ahead of me would be a block of bombers filling half the sky and rapidly getting very close in a frightening manner. All their tail guns would be pointing straight at me and sometimes, if I had closed right in, I could see what looked like the gunners in their rear turrets. These guns were radar aimed and I knew, could not miss. Then by the time that we had closed in so tightly that we had a chance of doing the bombers some real damage with our guns, we were at the point where we had to break off. Suddenly there seemed to be no spare bit of sky left to fly through, and the break had to be really hard in order to avoid them all, getting away clear underneath, and then zooming up in order to position for another attack.

I had always had a profound respect and sympathy for the crews of the American Fortresses and Liberators that had had to fight their way in daylight across Germany against the masses of German fighters. Now the memory of those formations of B50's which we had to attack, if only in practice, also causes me to have a lot of respect and sympathy for the Luftwaffe fighter pilots. I felt that it would have been interesting to meet some of them and talk to them about it as they could certainly have given all of us many useful tips. I suggested this in the mess bar one evening, but the senior officers present were horrified and I felt that I had nearly been labelled as a traitor. I had better keep quiet!

The Red Air Force was equipped with their version of the B29. It was the threat, which we were told we would have to meet in battle, should war with Russia actually break out. They had developed their aircraft from those of the USAF which operated from Guam in the Pacific, and had overshot the airfields in western China, where it was planned that they should refuel after attacks on Japan. The American bombers had flown right on beyond China and had actually crash landed in Russia when their fuel was exhausted. The Soviets were certainly not going to return those wrecks. They simply took them apart and learnt all about them, then copied them with alterations that were necessary to fit their own needs. Intelligence told us how they had built up a strong strategic bomber force from that. It was all ready to be used against us.

During one air defence exercise, when I was scrambled and vectored onto a target out over the Channel to the North of Cherbourg, I found that it was a vast great Convair B36 Peacemaker. We were supposed to approach no closer than one thousand yards to this immense aircraft, as General Curtis Le May, the commander of the USAF Strategic Air Command, would not trust any British fighter pilots nearer than that to his valuable bombers. I ignored that particular rule, but the target was so huge in my sights and so much bigger than anything that I was used to, I found when my gunnery film was processed, that I had actually broken away when still really just out of range. The monstrous great bomber was an awe inspiring sight and my twenty millimetre cannon seemed puny against it. I wondered in fact, just what sort of damage they could possibly have done.

Sometimes we had exercises where the targets would be formations of Vampires from RAF Germany, or USAF Thunderjets. They were supposed to represent jet bombers, but when we met them the whole thing would break up into a great swirling dogfight with contrails twisting all over the sky; just like the summer of 1940 over Kent.

However, to us the most exiting flying that we did was the fighter versus fighter training. We would fly in battle formation, sometimes at full squadron strength, just looking for other fighters that we could bounce. Apart from other RAF Meteors or Vampires, there were the American F84 Thunderjets based at Manston and the F86 Sabres from the East

Anglian bases. Anything was fair game and we would go off on a sweep, just looking for any of these and making sure that we could not get bounced ourselves. A dogfight would develop and woe betide any of us who came back without getting cine gun film of our opponents, thus showing that we would have fired our guns and got a kill if it had all been real. We knew the Meteor inside out, we could fly it to its absolute limits and though the Sabre was certainly superior in many ways, our gunnery film indicated that we would definitely have got our share of kills against them.

During the war, a serious threat to Britain had been from the nuisance raids made by low flying Bf 109's and FW 190's. Flying at high speed right on the deck, they would come in over the coast below our radar cover and rapidly hit their targets, especially the preparations for the Normandy invasion. They never climbed until actually delivering the attack, after which they raced away, staying very low as they flew off out to sea, back to their bases in France.

This same threat was deemed to be a possibility in any future war and we trained to deal with it. When trying to intercept the raiders, we would have to fly even lower than they did, in order to see them against the sky. We flew exercises, which were known as Rat and Terrier, when we would take it in turns to be either the fighter or the target. But in major exercises, Dutch and Belgian Thunderjets would sometimes simulate low flying enemy aircraft. As we were all flying below radar cover, the target aircraft had to be tracked visually by the Royal Observer Corps lookouts. The enemy's position and direction of flight would then be broadcast on our radio frequency and from that, we would plan our own interceptions.

This was superb. We had to fly as low as we possibly could, generally at about four hundred knots, navigating very accurately and at the same time, work out the vector that would enable us to come up with our target. If we did it correctly, there would then be the prospect of a low level dogfight. Again, what more could a young fighter pilot ask for; legal low flying. 'Not Below 100 feet' would be written in the authorisation book. This we would have to sign, but nobody took much notice of that particular order. We certainly could not have been popular with the people below.

With four twenty millimetre cannon, the Meteor had what in those days, was still considered a powerful armament. It had been proven by the later World War 2 fighters, the Typhoon and the Tempest, and was not superseded until the Hunter arrived with its thirty millimetre weapons. We fired our guns regularly on exercises, both at ground targets or a drogue towed by a Miles Martinet. Later, our own Meteors were fitted with a device, which enabled them to tow large flag targets and we could operate much higher, at altitudes nearer to those at which we expected to have to fight.

Our air to ground range was close to the shore at Bracklesham Bay near Selsey. I often walk past there now, but though the place where the targets were set up is easily recognisable, the roar of the Meteors' two Derwent engines and the sound of twenty millimetre cannon is only a distant dream from the past.

Our leaders in those days were the great names, who had flown fighters during the war, and were virtually hero worshiped by young pilots such as me. Whilst I was there, the Station Commanders at Biggin Hill, were Arthur Donaldson, 'PB' Pitt-Brown and Splinter Smallwood, all of whom were highly decorated wartime pilots. Our Squadron Commander, who had taken over from Sammy Osborne was Dusty Miller, who had won a DFC flying ship-busting Beaufighters in the Mediterranean.

Our Wing Leader was one time Spitfire pilot, Ray Hesslyn with a score, I think, of twenty two. He had been shot down and had some grim stories to tell of his days as a POW in Germany. When he was posted away, his place was taken by Johnny Button of Typhoon fame. The CO of 615, one of the Auxiliary squadrons at Biggin, was Neville Duke, but he had to leave because the Hunter, which was then at its early stage of testing, took up all his time.

All the leaders in Fighter Command were such as these, and they led us as they had led their squadrons during the war. They imbued us with the same spirit that their pilots had had in those days, only a very few years before. We flew sweeps at thirty five thousand feet over the French coast, as Fighter Command had during the war, and though it was strictly against regulations, attacked anything else in the sky. We were the tops. Our comradeship was superb and we felt that we were unbeatable.

Dusty Miller was a magnificent squadron commander. He led us with from right out in front, ruling us with an iron fist and we would have followed him anywhere. He had little time for close formation work, which he called pansy formation. We seldom practised it except for publicity photographs or, as sometimes occurred, when we had to perform an official fly past. That happened in a big way, twice whilst I was on 41. First there was the Coronation of Her Majesty Queen Elizabeth 2nd, when Fighter Command performed the flypast for Sovereign's parade on the day of her crowning. For that, we formed a wing with our great rivals, Number 1 Squadron from Tangmere, doing so again a few months later, when we took part in the RAF review flypast over Odiham.

During this period, the Korean War was in full swing. We saw the current USAF intelligence reports about the fighting between Sabres and Migs and itched to take part. Much of our training was based on those reports. We had American Marine Corps pilots attached to the Squadron on exchange postings, and they had all flown their one hundred missions in Korea. We lapped up all that they had to tell us about that war, and tried to learn from anything that they could tell us.

Dusty Miller, was posted and his place as squadron commander was taken by Max Scannell. Max had just returned from Korea, where he had been flying Meteors with 77 Squadron, RAAF, so from him we got more first-hand accounts of actual combat.

Except for Sunderland flying boats on maritime patrol and the pilot secondments to the RAAF and the USAF, the RAF had no commitment to the Korean War. It was often said that a fighter wing would be sent there, but it never happened and the reason, we were told, was that there was just no airfield where an RAF wing could be based. To us this was a great disappointment and we were very jealous of the Australians on 77 Squadron with their Meteors. With our knowledge of the Meteor and our experience flying it, we knew that we would be able to put up a very good show.

In our eyes the Meteor was superb, though we did acknowledge that it was somewhat outdated and had its not so good aspects, being too slow at altitude to be a real match for the Mig 15. However, it was superior in other ways such as its ability to turn more tightly, but we would have needed to draw the Migs down to a level where the Meteor was at its best.

We always flew between thirty and forty hours on the type each month, many more than most squadron pilots get nowadays on their much more sophisticated aircraft. We were one with it, as any pilot should be with his machine, be it a 747 or a Microlight.

With the Meteor, the single engined handling was one of the supposed difficulties, but on more than one occasion when I had to land with only one engine working, I had little trouble. You just had to make sure that you had set up the last part of your final approach at a slightly steeper than normal descent angle. The whole situation had to be judged correctly so that there was absolutely no danger of having to go around, or undershoot, so having to add asymmetric power at low speed.

Also, the type did not really carry very much fuel, but we were used to that and if it was a problem, it seldom seemed to be so to us. Our flights were always planned for it.

Years later, an airline training captain, who I knew as someone who was very contemptuous about all things to do with the Meteor, told me when taking my IRT renewal, 'you Meteor pilots were on fuel emergency as soon as you had got your wheels up.' He had No Soul!

Almost all types of aircraft have a nickname given to them by their crews and the Meteor was always known as the Meatbox. But it does not seem to be remembered in the same way that many other types are, and I don't think that there is a single Meteor 8 still flying anywhere in the world. To me this is very sad. It seems now to lack the charisma that surrounds the Hunter and the Spitfire, of which there are examples galore. But the Meteor was the fighter that guarded Britain between the eras of those two and filled an important part in the Cold War defence set up of our Islands.

Many years later, I had to do a BBC interview about the Coronation Flypast. In turn, another pilot who had been on 41 at the same time, and I, sat in the cockpit of the Meteor 8 in the RAF Museum at Hendon. It was amazing. We both said how our hands knew exactly where to go round all the knobs and switches. Everything came back to us and we were utterly at home.

If the deterrent had stopped working and hot war had broken out in Europe during the first half of the nineteen fifties, the Meatbox would have born the brunt of the fighting and 41 Squadron would have been in the forefront. We would have been the 'tops.'

6.   Harvards Over Kenya

By June 1953, I had been on No.41 Squadron for two years and my tour was coming to an end. Inevitably for the last few months, I had been wondering just what my next posting would be, where I would be stationed and what aircraft I would fly. I had been told quite unofficially that I had a good chance of being one of the next batch of RAF pilots to be seconded to the USAF, flying F86's in Korea, which was exactly what I wanted. I was like an athlete at the top of my training. I was on tiptop form and wanted nothing better than to put that training into effect. Looking back, I now see that this was completely misplaced exuberance, a misguided itch though quite understandable at the time. Anyway it was not to be as luckily the Korean War came to an end at last, after four bitter years of fighting.

My next hope was to be sent to one of the squadrons in Fighter Command which had by then been equipped with Sabres, but whilst I was waiting, I was told that there was the opportunity of a posting to Kenya. Six RAF pilots were to be seconded to the Kenya Police Air Wing, where they would fly Piper Tri-Pacers. The campaign against the Mau Mau was then in full swing and these aircraft were used in support of the Army, as spotters maintaining radio contact with patrols in the forest, together with everyday, normal communication work.

It was strongly intimated that no fighter pilot, such as myself, would want to be involved in that sort of work. It would quite likely not be good for my career, and it was taken for granted that I would not be in the least interested and would refuse.

I was fascinated. I had fallen in love with Africa whilst doing my flying training there and now I was being offered a chance to return; this time to Kenya, a country which had always thrilled me, but I had only briefly visited. Also I had happy memories of all the light aircraft flying, which I had done before joining the RAF and enjoyed so much. I suddenly thought that perhaps I did not really want to be stuck so firmly in the fighter pilot role, however much I might enjoy it. Perhaps a change like this would do me a world of good, then if I felt like it I could always try to get back onto fighters when the African interval was over.

I had visions of flying again through wide blue skies, dotted with little puffy fair weather cumulus clouds, across miles and miles of never ending brown African bush, and seeing distant mountain ranges rising ahead of me. I thought of early mornings before the sun became very hot, with the bush coming to life in a manner which to me, had always seemed incredibly beautiful.

Apart from such thoughts, the knowledge that I would be on active service and flying on operations, tipped any balance that there might have been. This would be very different operational flying from anything that I might have experienced whilst on Sabres in Korea, but operational it would be. There was no real question about it in my mind. I jumped at the chance straight away.

My posting came through. On a cold November evening in 1953, the six of us met at Cliffe Pipard in Wiltshire. Cliffe Pipard was a small wartime army camp, consisting of the usual temporary wooden huts. It now belonged to the RAF, and housed those on overseas postings, who had to be accommodated overnight before flying out from Lyneham by Transport Command early the following morning. There was no transit hotel on the station in those days. The site seemed to be exposed to all the worst November weather. It was cold and wet and windy. We lit a huge fire in the mess bar and sat the night out!

The next morning, we left in a Hastings and three uncomfortable days later, after night stops in Tripoli and Khartoum, arrived in Nairobi.

When we checked in at Eastleigh, the RAF base just outside Nairobi, it was at once apparent that we were a problem to everybody concerned. The Kenyan authorities considered that the RAF were trying to take over their Police Air Wing and our posting was part of a fiendish trick. They did not want anything to do with us. I expect that they were quite right, but such politics were far from my understanding and I fretted at the necessity of having to sit and wait whilst many difficulties were put in our way. I did not like being a pawn in a political argument and I regretted very much having accepted the job. It was a very different situation to anything that I had been subject to before, or ever imagined could happen in this case.

Furthermore, we were told that there were no posts for us with the RAF in Kenya anyway, and that we would be sent to the Middle East. Horror of horrors, some sort of a ground job would be found for us when we got there. It was obvious that the Kenya Police were not the only people who did not want us. Our morale was very low.

We hung around for about ten days doing nothing. We were told to wait in the mess, so we sat on the terrace, just waiting. We wandered into Nairobi, but were unable to raise any interest in what we saw. I wondered just what on earth I had got myself into; what on earth was I doing there. It was all so different from anything that I had known before in the RAF.

At last someone did have an idea and it turned out to be a good one. About a hundred miles north of Nairobi, lay Mweiga where there was a farm airstrip. The RAF had taken this over, and six or more of the armed version of the Harvard, with their pilots and ground crew, were based there. They formed No.1340 Flight and were tasked with supporting the army in the ground attack role. The Kenya Police Air Wing was also based there. They and the RAF worked together as very friendly partners, which was exactly what might be expected with operational units and pilots, when far away from politicians or senior staff officers.

The Flight had been formed just a few months previously, the aircraft having been flown north to Kenya from Thornhill, one of the RAF flying training schools in Southern Rhodesia. The pilots who initially formed the unit were instructors from there, and they had ferried the aircraft up through Northern Rhodesia and Tanganyika, now Zambia and Tanzania. These Harvards were modified to carry 8 antipersonnel bombs, and were armed with one fixed .303 Browning machine gun, carrying 420 rounds. This was fitted in the starboard wing, so firing just outside the propeller arc.

The CO was Squadron Leader C.G. Jeffries, who had just the experience required for the post, having flown Hurricanes during the Battle of France, then again in the defence of Malta. Later in Burma he had commanded a Mohawk squadron. Following that he had gone in on the ground with the Wingate operation as an air liaison officer, far behind Japanese lines. Operating in primitive bush conditions and flying off jungle strips was nothing new to him.

It was first necessary for us to check out in the Harvard, which I personally had not flown since my own training, about three years previously. Now I remembered how at first I had been completely in awe of it, and that it had seemed to be a monster of an aircraft, presenting a learner pilot like myself with unbelievable difficulties. Also there had always been the added horrors of an instructor breathing down my neck and the threat of some test or other, which was looming up and would have to be taken in the imminent future.

In this case, I see from my log book that I had just one 15 minute dual trip, which cannot have consisted of any more than a spin and a couple of circuits, if that. It was followed by an hour's solo and then a practice formation flight, which I soon found to have been very necessary as the CO was a fanatic about formation flying.

Four out of the six of us were checked out and joined 1340 Flight, flying our first strike one very early morning soon afterwards. We took off from Eastleigh in the dark, in formation, with me flying as the CO's No 2. This was to be the position, which I was to hold for all the year that I was on the flight, but on that first occasion I was not at all popular. I spaced too far away to the side of him on the narrow runway, and during the takeoff roll, before getting airborne, I succeeded in knocking over a number of the paraffin flares that made up the runway lighting. Formation takeoffs in the dark had not been a part of any of my previous flying experience; it was a first time. But after that one, I quickly learnt exactly how it should be done and became well used to it. I had to; it was an almost daily occurrence.

After the strike, we landed at Mweiga, which was to be our future home, deep in Kikuyu Land. The airstrip was in patchy forested country, belonging to a European farm and said to be in an area riddled with Mau Mau. It was in the valley between the seventeen thousand feet high Mount Kenya massif to the east, and the chain of the Aberdares to the west, beyond which the country dropped steeply away into the Rift Valley. There we would live in tents surrounded by a high wire fence, interspersed with machine gun towers, known as sangars, which were manned by the RAF Regiment. The army was able to tell us that we had the best defended camp in the country, which was comforting. The short dirt runway stretched from this defended area, out into the bush through the wire guard fence.

This country between the ranges was the homeland of the Kikuyu people, a land of fertile black cotton soil, very broken up with small valleys and steep hillsides, covered at times with low cloud and rain. The black soil often turned to thick black glutinous mud in such weather, which made conditions impossible for aircraft operations from unpaved airstrips, such as Mweiga.

The lower slopes of the two mountain ranges were covered in dense forest, which stretched up to a belt of thick bamboo at about nine thousand feet, followed by moorland areas across the saddles between the rocky peaks. There were deep broken gorges, down which ran the fast flowing little rivers that irrigated the Kikuyu farmlands below.

The Mau Mau had based themselves in these forest covered mountains. From there they made attacks on European settlements, and infiltrated the settled areas in order to terrorise the ordinary Kikuyu people into aiding them. To counter this, the authorities had designated all these high forests as no-go areas. Anyone found there was deemed to be a terrorist. Army patrols went in to the mountains in order to flush out the enemy and fight them.

The forest was thick and virtually impenetrable in many places. The Mau Mau could usually run rings round regular army patrols, even those from regiments with jungle fighting experience in Malaya. They had built semi-permanent camps, which were almost impossible to find and they were adept at obliterating their tracks.

The job of 1340 Flight was to flush out the Mau Mau and keep them moving in ways that would drive them into army patrols and ambushes. Sometimes intelligence or air photography would locate the supposed position of a camp and this could be bombed as a pinpoint target.

Initially, these target details and the requests for strikes against them came from local ground forces with whom we worked closely and in a very friendly manner. However, as the military organisation grew, a Joint Operations Centre was set up in Nairobi. After that, almost all strikes were laid on by them, but only after the ground forces' requests had been sorted out and had been through the politics of an inter-service staff set up with all the jealous rivalry that that entailed.

The strip at Mwiega lay right at the edge of the Aberdare forest and as one took off and climbed away from it, a view of the great mountains spread out all round. I was happy, I was flying over Africa again. To the north were the vast brown plains that stretched into the Northern Frontier District, and to the south was the Kikuyu country, all green and fertile with steep little wooded valleys down which ran the small rivers that drained the mountain forests. The Kikuyu villages with the small farms, known as shambas, lay dotted everywhere in the valleys beside the streams

Climbing up over the No-Go zone of the Aberdears was fantastic. The unbroken forest appeared as a great green canopy below, with no visible gaps in it until one reached the moor land in the saddles between the peaks. Above the timber, the thick bamboo zone showed as a somewhat lighter shade of green, stretching on up for the remaining thousand feet or so. After that the colour changed once more to the contrasting purple of the moor lands. That in its turn, was bordered to the north and south by the dark grey jagged peaks, Satima and the Kinnonkop.

Running down from the moorland, were great deep gorges, each of which had a little river running over cataracts at the bottom at the bottom of it. Silvery streaks down the high cliff sides, easily visible from the air, showed where their headwaters cascaded down in long waterfalls.

Our targets could be anywhere in this huge area and naturally the maps that we carried were not entirely accurate. Navigation was not easy at first and so initially, all our targets were marked by the Tri-Pacers of the Police Air Wing, whose pilots were mostly local Kenyans, many having considerable knowledge of the country. They would drop smoke markers for us to use as aiming points. However, after a time, it was decided that we had learnt the area well enough ourselves, and were able to navigate accurately to most targets without their help. On a number of occasions, I flew with the police pilots and threw out the smoke markers, which indicated the target to the Harvards. This was exiting stuff and helped me to learn many details about the local geography.

We dive bombed pinpoint targets dropping two of our eight bombs on each attack. This was fantastic flying when we were trying to hit something deep in one of the gorges. It entailed careful consideration so that a safe zoom up could be made after the dive and a good position reached for the next attack. Also there was always the ever present danger which is common in mountain flying; unless careful, one could easily get cornered up an ever narrowing gorge and so not be able to turn back out again, or climb ahead either, because the land rose too steeply.

At other times we would be given a map square to attack. Our bombs had to be distributed over the given area with the theory that this would cause the Mau Mau to be flushed out and so move into an ambush. We would spread out in line abreast and flying straight and level, drop a bomb every second or so, in order to cover the target. This was very dull compared with dive bombing, but after dropping our bombs, we would go down and strafe the area with our single machine gun.

When you see a Harvard at an air-show nowadays as it takes its place in the line up of what are known as war birds, you get the impression of a big powerful beast of an aircraft, just as I had when I first saw the type at White Waltham. But it was never originally designed to be more than a trainer. When taking off from an airstrip at five thousand above sea level, and then climbing to attack targets in the mountains, often at over ten thousand feet, it was right at the limit of its performance with its unsupercharged engine. The Harvard was definitely under powered for the job that we had to do, but otherwise, I found it to be a beautiful aircraft to fly and enjoyed every minute that I flew it over Kenya. Without the presence of an instructor, or the threat of some check flight or other in the offing, it was an altogether different machine from the one I remembered from my training.

The under powered factor, did cause problems though, and was the reason for a number of losses. Soon after we joined the flight, one of our group of six was killed when he flew too far up a narrow gorge. He was unable to turn tightly enough and could not climb out, so just crashed into the mountain side. Later, three aircraft, climbing between ridges, found the slope of the ground steeper than their climb angle and being unable to turn back, landed together wheels up on the moorland. Luckily, nobody was hurt on that occasion. The three just belly landed in ragged formation.

In February that year, the rain drove us out of Mweiga. There had been too many times when we were grounded because the strip had become bogged. Also the domestic site was often a quagmire, and life must have been miserable for the ground crew as they waded about in thick, black cotton soil mud. However they always managed to work superbly, even under these conditions and our serviceability state was always excellent.

Life for ground crew in such a place is always dreary and these were mainly young national servicemen, who had never been away from home before and were used to a totally different existence. There was none of the excitement of flying for them and there was nowhere for them to go to off camp. This must have been a problem which the RAF had had for years in its job of policing the Empire and fighting wars in far corners of the world. But years later at reunions, when I again met these former airmen from 1340 Flight, it was very obvious that too many of them their time in the African bush was a great adventure, and the high spot of their lives.

Food was another problem. It had to be supplied by the Royal Army Service Corps. In the morning queue at their depot, the RAF were always at the bottom of the pecking order. Food was awful and there was no system whereby the airmen could buy a little more, as we could for our mess.

Our new base at Nanyuki was in dry grassland country, fifty miles further on north from Nairobi, right on the equator near the northwest corner of Mount Kenya. It had been a World War Two army camp with a large dry grass runway and there were wooden huts for us to live in, which made life far more civilised for all concerned.

In our mess there, we followed an old Kenya tradition and would lay on a party with a huge curry for Sunday lunch. A general invitation went out to our army colleagues. However, it was soon noticed that we would often be scrambled, just as the meal was ready, and would have to carry out a strike somewhere far away on the other side of the Rift Valley. Deduction indicated that this was not of the Mau Mau's doing and was no more than a clever plot. The army would eat all the curry whilst we were airborne and the troops in the forest would get a flying display.

At Nanyuki, I got my first real introduction to the CO's fanaticism for both low flying and formation flying. The long guard fence around the camp was built in a straight line on the airfield, a little way back from the runway. I was still flying as his Number 2 and inevitably, as soon as we formed up to return home after a strike, he would call us into close formation. Then he would never be happy until our wing tips were tucked in at the back of his neck, far closer than the normal wing tips in line position, which is RAF standard.

On approaching the airfield, he would get down to just a very few feet above the grass and then fly parallel to the fence. I was edged closer and closer to it, and so pushed right up against the wire which I could see out of the corner of my very nervous right eye. With the fence very nearly scraping my right wingtip and the left tight in at the back of the CO's neck, there was nowhere that I could go to get out of the way. He would then turn and grin at me, just to see how good my nerve was it seemed.

I read his expression as, 'Ha I've Got You Now,' but I wondered just what he thought of the expression on my face. I was absolutely scared stiff and it must have shown, even at that distance. Luckily, before I flew into either him or the fence, I was sent to Cyprus temporarily, on an instrument rating examiner's course.

At Nanyuki, we tried night bombing in order to keep the Mau Mau awake and to identify targets it was necessary to use parachute flares. These when released, remained connected to the bomb rack by a long cord, which streamed behind and activated the flare. It then was supposed to part from the aircraft, and drift down on a parachute. On the first occasion that we tried this, a volunteer was asked for to carry the flare. As ever, I should have known better, but stupidly said that I would do the job. I had been in the Service long enough to know better than to volunteer for anything odd like that.

We took off at about midnight, which was thought to be a good time to try and wake up the Mau Mau in their forest camps. Our target area was at the northeast corner of the Aberdears below the peak of Satima, and in a part of the forest with which we were quite familiar. We easily found it in the bright African moonlight.

The CO called me over the radio telling me to release the flare. It streamed and lighted, but remained fixed on the end of the cord, which in its turn, was still firmly fixed to my port bomb rack. It would not jettison, and I flew around, tugging it behind me, hoping desperately that the fire would not run back up the line and reach my wing. It didn't, but to say the least, that night, I was somewhat frightened.

Also, on that occasion, my airspeed indicator, as often happened, because of dust blowing back into our pitot tubes during formation takeoffs, was not working. After having nearly been set on fire, I was faced with the prospect of a formation landing at night whilst I dragged a long rope behind me. It could easily catch on a thorn tree during the last part of my approach, and that could easily cause another awkward situation to develop. An interesting flight!

When I got back from my IRE course in Cyprus, I found that here had been changes, which to me were very much for the worse. There had been a visit by a very senior person from the Air Ministry in London. He had been horrified to find this small RAF unit working away in the bush with only a squadron leader in command, and far from what such a staff officer might consider to be proper control. In his view, without sufficient supervision, it could only suffer from poor discipline and lax ways. Besides which, it operated closely alongside the Army in a practical way, and that resulted in flying operations that were not properly approved by any appropriate organisation, an organisation that was situated in an office, far away in a distant Headquarters.

There also appeared to be political reasons involved, but they all seemed rather stupid to me. The RAF seemed to be scared stiff that the Army were trying to take them over and so must show that they had a powerful organisation behind them.

1340 Flight had been moved down to Eastleigh, the main RAF station just outside Nairobi, and the RAF presence at Nanyuki had been closed down completely. Eastleigh was a large permanent base and also in those days, the international airport for Kenya. Life was now governed by RAF discipline and regulations so we had none of the freedom of operations that we had been used to.

All in all it was nothing like so much fun and not at all the life that I had enjoyed so much, though there were compensations. Perhaps Nairobi might be a good town to have locally for an evening out, but I had been happy in the bush, and to me that was the natural place to be when in Kenya.

Our airmen, who formed the Flight's loyal ground crew and had worked so very hard under difficult operational conditions in the bush, found quite a different sort of difficulty in our new home, one that they found far worse, and very difficult to get on with. Suddenly they met the discipline inherent to a permanent RAF station and everything from the way they dressed to the way they behaved in general, was anathema to that doyen of RAF discipline, the Station Warrant Officer. He persecuted them and at the least provocation, came down on them like a ton of bricks. To add further to their problems, the food in their mess was really ghastly. They were not at all happy.

Many years later, when they were in their retirement, this seemed to be their main memory of Eastleigh. It was their main topic of conversation at reunions when the subject of the move down to Eastleigh came up.

We did a lot of flying for an RAF unit and it was all flying that I loved. From my cockpit there were always marvellous views which stretched for vast distances across Africa, all with the fantastic colours of the bush and distant mountains. Apart from the operations, there was communication flying and jollies for one reason or another. When on day off, I flew south on occasion, to Arusha in Tanganyika, passing Kilimanjaro, in order to take and collect ground crew from leave. Also I flew far to the northwest, to Eldoret for that same reason. I went to Mombasa and Malindi, on the coast, in order to get lobsters for the mess.

I flew as much as I could for any reason that could be thought up. Early one month, when I added up my log book in order to enter the summary for the previous one, I found that I was just one hour short of a hundred for the period. This was infuriating as, had I known in time, I could easily have got an aircraft and soon made up the missing hour before the month actually ended. In the RAF, one hundred hours in a calendar month, on single engined aircraft would have been quite an achievement.

As expected at Eastleigh, our operations were now totally organised and controlled by the Joint Operations Centre. The Flight carried out a minimum of four strikes each day, the first entailing a pre-dawn take off in order to wish the Mau Mau good morning just as it was getting light. We would climb up in formation through two or three thousand feet of early morning stratus cloud and break out on top to see the sunrise. There, with the cloud layer all white below us, the mountains stuck out clear in the perfect visibility; Mount

Kenya's three peaks to the east side of Kikuyuland, always white with perpetual snow; the Kinankop and Sattima in the Aberdares, to the west.

The descent back down through the cloud to find the target in those mountain ranges could be interesting. I tried not to think of the solid centres, which were just waiting to catch us. I clung to the boss's wingtip, trying to trust him implicitly and hoping that he had got it right. Well, he always did get it right, but I often doubted that, had I been leading, I could have done so in the way that he did every time.

After a quick turn round, this early strike was followed by a second one, after which it was breakfast time. We would go over to the civilian restaurant on the far side of the aerodrome to eat bacon and eggs and watch the airline crews come in for their meal, whilst their aircraft were turned round for the next leg after their night flight, south to Johannesburg, or north to Europe. All the major national airlines staged through Nairobi early in the morning, and we watched Constellations, Arganauts, DC6's and Hermes amongst other types.

Through the day, we were on standby for anything that might come up suddenly, and then there were two more strikes in the late afternoon. The last of these was at dusk, and so required a night landing on our return.

Once again, the CO's fanaticism for formation flying showed up. At last light, when returning from the evening strike, usually with four aircraft, we would fly backwards and forwards over Nairobi in close formation, with the CO shouting over the radio, 'Get in tighter, tighter.' To get in steadily and to fly as tightly as he demanded, could require a lot of throttle movement. Unlike those in Britain, our Harvards had long propellers, so the tips were supersonic. The noise that we made must have been appalling. We used the Nairobi approach frequency, so in addition to our making a lot of unpopular engine noise over the city, our radio chatter cannot have pleased air traffic controllers or airline pilots.

Some strikes were out of the ordinary. Very early one morning, we were told that a gang had been found on one of the extinct volcanoes in the Rift Valley. We were to maintain a continuous attack with relays of aircraft in pairs, bombing and strafing all day, and were to hit anywhere on the mountain which looked as if it might be a likely hiding place.

When as usual, I took off in the first pair with the CO, there was very low stratus cloud over Nairobi, with a base of less than 100 feet. This was not unusual, and we would normally climb straight up through it. However, this time we remained below, and together we turned and headed west towards the Rift Valley escarpment. This took us straight across Nairobi West airport, flying right on the deck under the cloud. I still have a vivid picture in my mind of the horrified look on the controller's face through the window of the control tower there, as I passed a few feet away and just below him.

The joke was on us though. Months later, it was learnt that the Mau Mau gang had moved off the mountain during the night, before we started our attacks. Then during the day they had sat just a few miles off, watching the air show from the top of the Rift Valley escarpment, whilst we bombed the place where they had been the day before. Well, we did put on good shows and I only hope that they enjoyed this one, but they must have laughed at us.

We did a lot of low flying, and often returned from strikes right on the deck over the Kikuyu villages, the excuse being that our presence might put fear into the hearts of any potential Mau Mau, thus being a deterrent. Perhaps there was something in that, but I think that it was really an idea that the CO thought up himself as an excuse, and sold to higher authority in order to legalise our low flying!

Reading some of the things that I have recounted in this chapter, might make some people concluded that we were a somewhat irresponsible bunch, but in fact this was not the case. We had a serious job of work to do and we did take it seriously. The incidents related were isolated and we worked hard to produce the required results. We often flew through very poor weather conditions in mountains that created what could be considered extremely dangerous situations. We flew aircraft that were neither basically designed for the job nor the environment in which it took place. The skill of those leading, ensured that we continually carried out our attacks successfully and returned in one piece. But we did suffer a number of losses to both aircraft and pilots, some of which could certainly be accounted for by the conditions under which we operated.

Our work was recognised to the extent that quite a large number of decorations were awarded to members of the Flight, and some of us went on to become senior airline captains and test pilots in later life. Irresponsible pilots don't win medals or reach those positions in aviation.

We never really learnt whether we were being successful in any way in the fight against the Mau Mau and I have never had access to any intelligence summaries that might have given me an indication of our usefulness. Occasionally we would hear in passing from a Kenya Police friend that a prisoner had said that he had been bombed at a time and place that would tie up with one or other of our operations. I remember that once we got a report that a captured Mau Mau had told them that six members of his gang had been killed in one attack, but I never heard of definite proof. Such reports covered just a very few of our operations. What the strategic result was, I have no idea. The overall air effort must have been thought to be important as squadrons of Lincolns also took part in the bombing campaign and No 8 Squadron from Aden, equipped with Vampires, made a short detachment carrying out a few strikes, but they did not stay long.

As for the rest of the air effort, both Meteor 9's and 10's were detached from Middle East Airforce squadrons and used in their particular photographic rolls. These were said to be very successful in discovering the tracks made by Mau Mau in the forest and also some of their camps as well. An Auster was fitted up as a sky shouter and flown over the reserves and the forest, broadcasting messages to the people, but this did not last long, as it crashed at Eastleigh whilst landing on a day of gusty cross winds, and was written off.

The Kenya Police Air Wing, who carried out all the contact and communication work with the Army in the field with their Piper Tripacers, were superb and were based alongside us at Meiga and then Nanyuki. But when we moved down to

Eastleigh, they went back to Mweiga and the partnership was split up.

The Tripacers were fitted up with army radios and each police pilot was given the job of liaising with the army units in a particular area. Every day, he would fly over each of these and make the necessary contacts. Messages were passed and as most of the company and battalion headquarters had airstrips, he would land if necessary to hand over any mail.

The army patrols in the forest were always able to talk to him and made their reports that way. Food and other supplies could be dropped to them when needed. Air drops were made by putting what was needed in sandbags and tossing them out of the aircraft's open door, when flying very low over the patrols. The pilots had to do this themselves unless they had a helper, such as one of us, flying with them. I did so quite often and thoroughly enjoyed my trips with the Kenya Police.

All this was in addition to the job that they had of marking the targets with smoke grenades, firstly for us until we learnt our own way about, but otherwise for the Lincolns and then the Vampires during their short detachment.

My posting was for only one year and I returned to the UK at the end of 1954. For me, it was a pretty good year. I gained a great deal of flying experience, which I could never have done if after leaving Biggin Hill, I had followed the expected line and been posted to another fighter squadron. Also, it enabled me to spend another year in Africa and to get to know a part of it that was new to me, but which I had always wanted to visit. It was a marvellous part of the world and I loved it. It was a good year for me

7.   Secondment to the USAF

In December 1954, I returned to the UK after my tour flying Harvards in Kenya, and the first thing that I did was to go to Biggin Hill and visit No. 41 Squadron, my old unit, where Max Scannel was still the CO. I knocked and walked into his office.

'Hullo Sir,' I said, 'I've come back.'

Max was great. A couple of hours later, I was at thirty thousand feet flying a Meteor 8, getting the feel of the aircraft again after about a year on other types. I stayed at Biggin Hill for a few days, renewing old friendships and flying with the squadron. All this was quite unofficial and I don't expect that you can do anything like it in the RAF today.

On returning from overseas in those days, you had to report to the Air Ministry in person. There you saw an officer in a department, which was specially set up just for that purpose and after a short interview, he told you what your next posting was to be.

I found the relevant, rather dingy old office in a building off Whitehall. It looked as if it had been used for the same job since the nineteen twenties at least, when officers had returned by sea after a tour on Vernons or DH9a's, policing the Empire in Mesopotamia. Or perhaps it might have been India, where they could have flown Bristol Fighters or Wapitis on the Northwest Frontier. I was told that I would probably be posted to RAF Pembrey in South Wales, where I would be an instructor on the Vampire Operational Conversion Unit, which was based there. However he seemed rather doubtful and I was not quite sure why. I wanted to get back on a squadron, but it was not to be.

I was vaguely disappointed with this. I had only flown the Vampire on a couple of occasions and thought that it could not, in any way, compare with the Meteor in performance. Fighter Command was soon to start re-equipping with Hunters, and all fighter pilots were starry eyed about them. That definitely included me, so I had hoped for a posting to a day fighter squadron, which was due to get them soon; but it was not to be. I was told to go home and wait. I would receive official details after I had been on leave for about a week.

The person who had interviewed me in the Air Ministry, phoned a few days later. I expected him to give me the date when I was to report to Pembrey, but it was to tell me that there was another posting open to me. Four RAF pilots were to be seconded to the USAF at Furstenfeldbruk, an airbase near Munich in Bavaria. He didn't quite know what the job would be, but he said that it sounded like pilot attack instructor work on F84 Thunderjets.

'Would I be interested'

'Oh yes, certainly I would be.'

This really did sound interesting; it was quite out of the ordinary and again would be something new for me.

I was not a PAI, a Pilot Attack Instructor, but never mind about that. I was confident that I would learn and get along easily enough. There was a catch however. I had to be current on jets and my last posting had been on piston engined aircraft. He said that the Americans would not accept me unless I could do something about it. Well, I had. I was able to tell him about my flying at Biggin Hill during the previous week. All was well.

One day early in January 1955, I met the other three RAF pilots with whom I was to spend the next two years in the United States Air Force. We were on Liverpool Street Station about to join the boat train to Harwich and would cross to The Hook of Holland that evening. After the crossing, we would continue on a British military train. A number of them left from The Hook, with destinations all across Europe and ours was known as the White Train. It would drop us off in Munich whilst on its way to Austria, which was then under Allied occupation. I found that the others knew no more than I did about the job to which we were heading.

At about three the next morning, we were turned out of the train in Munich, and found about a foot of snow on the ground with a temperature far below that which we had left behind in England. We waited. There was supposed to be transport to pick us up, but it had naturally gone to the main central station in the city, whilst we were at another one which was little more than a halt, and far off on Munich's outskirts. Dropping us there had been much easier for our through train, which was not actually destined for Munich itself, but bound for Vienna.

The railway staff were helpful and phoned the base, but it took an hour or more to sort everything out, and for the driver to actually find this small out of the way place and collect us. Luckily the waiting room was good and warm.

At about five in the morning we were dropped outside the Bachelor Officer Quarters (BOQ) at Furstenfeldbruk, or Fursty, as we soon found that it was always called.

It was amazing, there was organisation, we were expected and accommodation had actually been reserved for us, but everyone was surprised that we had not arrived in the only sensible way, by air. Who had ever heard of travelling by train when you were a member of an airforce that operated airplanes and could supposedly fly anywhere across the world. I rather agreed with that outlook, but the British military were still train bound.

We might not have got to bed until after five in the morning, but we did not get much of a chance to sleep in. Soon after nine o'clock we were woken by somebody who wore a Major's rank badges, said his name was Dorris and that, as CO of the 7330th Student Squadron, he was in charge of us. Why had we not reported in. We were supposed to be in class right then. Well, that was interesting.

'What class?'

The Major looked surprised. Didn't we know?

We professed ignorance. He was even more surprised, but when we asked what our job was to be, he gave us a run down on the whole thing. It was nothing like anything we had imagined.

Fursty was the home of the 7330th Pilot Training Wing. The task was to convert pilots from MDAP nations onto jets. Many of them had only flown pistons before and if they had flown jets, they would have been British types, not American.

The whole thing had to be Americanised as American types were on the way to them.

What was MDAP?

"Mutual Defence Assistance Programme", he said.

Well, I had never heard of that, but apparently we were part of it. The students came from the many countries, which were opposed to the Eastern Block and formed part of NATO, together with other such treaty organisations.

We were to join an instructor's course that was starting that morning. It seemed that the Air Ministry had not been quite right when they told me about F84's and pilot attack. We would be working as Jet Transition Instructors and flying Lockheed T33's. This was straight forward instructing, not my world at all. My heart dropped. I would rather have been at Pembrey on Vampires.

It was this business of volunteering. I had done it for my previous tour when I left No. 41 Squadron. Then it had been to volunteer to fly for the Kenya Police and that had not worked out. Whilst in Kenya, volunteering had resulted in my flying around in the middle of the night towing a great ball of fire on the end of a rope behind my aircraft and into the bargain, not having an airspeed indicator. Now I found that this time, the volunteering was just going to get me into the back seat of a training aircraft. I did not want to be in such a place, even though it might be an American one, and in what for me, would be an entirely new and probably interesting environment. Would I ever learn to keep quiet.

Fighter pilots of my generation considered instructing and instructors to be a lower form of life, far beneath them. I did learn better in later years, but the learning had not started by that time.

We staggered out of bed, got dressed and made our way, cold, hungry and on foot to the ground school block, where we arrived very late for class. Compared with the RAF stations that we had been used to, Fursty was a huge place and it took some time to find our way about. One thing that struck us about it straight away though, was the central heating. In the grip of a central European winter when the temperature was well below zero, it was good to find that it was well up to American standards.

The class that we joined was made up of a number of American pilots as well as ourselves. We were to be the next batch of instructors forming the staff of the 7330th Pilot Training Squadron. Everything here was 7330th and the course that we were on was a straight forward flying instructors' course.

As time went on, I could not help comparing this with the RAF, Central Flying School instructor's course at Little Rissington, about which I had naturally heard all sorts of ghastly rumours, but never yet actually faced. Here we found that the American ground school was nothing like so comprehensive and only took place every other day. It lasted for little more than three weeks and had very easy exams at the end. We passed with hardly any difficulty, as by then we had managed to learn the American aviation phraseology, but soon began to realise that there was a wide difference between the British and American ways of operating.

Our introduction to the T33 took some time. The weather clamped solidly for a week or more, with heavy snow and thick, low cloud. It was a typical Central European winter state, which later would change to very cold clear skies with hard snow and ice on the ground. However, before that change of weather, there was no chance of a straight forward general handling flight to start the ball rolling. After a number of wasted days, the instructor who had the job of converting me onto the type and turning me into a T33 jet transition instructor, got bored with waiting and said that we must get started somehow. He put me straight into the back seat under the instrument hood so my first flight in an American jet was an instrument ride. Oh!

Now the instrument layout in American aircraft is very different from the standard RAF panel, which all British aircraft had at that time. The instruments themselves were also somewhat different in appearance and compared with us, the Americans had quite different techniques for using them. Their instrument flying exercises were nothing like the ones that I was used to and I had not the least idea what was meant when my instructor, Kent Rabbit, told me to do something, or to carry out some procedure or other.

Also the Americans did not use anything like our system of bad weather instrument let downs. I was used to calling for a QGH and being given headings to steer, then being told when to descend or level off as necessary. In the RAF, we followed a system where everything was worked out with the aid of sophisticated equipment in Approach Control. The USAF did everything by using a radio compass in the aircraft and following published let down procedures in the standard ICAO, worldwide fashion, which was utterly different from anything used by fighters in the RAF. It was something that I had absolutely no experience of.

At last it was time to return and land, but that only produced more difficulties still.

It was a classic case. There was I, in cloud, under the hood, in the back seat of a strange aircraft with what seemed a complete muddle of an instrument panel in front of me. In the front cockpit was an instructor who had no understanding whatever of RAF procedures, what I was used to, or where my knowledge ended. I was being told to fly the aircraft, get out the let down book, find the page, read the let down procedure and call for a jet penetration and GCA. Then I had to follow procedures all on the chart for Fursty, make the penetration at a given time and put us in a position for the instructor to take over and land visually. Oh!

Naturally all this was utterly strange to me, but Kent had no understanding, and told me to get on with it, being surprised when I asked what on earth he meant. I just had not got a clue what he was talking about and I was having much too much trouble anyway, just trying to fly steadily, without bothering about anything more that was totally strange to me. But oh, I had to learn. It was the only way of getting down.

That first flight of mine with a totally strange American instructor, in a totally strange aircraft, flying totally strange procedures, was I remember, just a disastrous hour and a half.

It took me sometime to fully understand the American instruments and master the techniques of using them, but when I did, I found that it enabled me to fly far more accurately that I ever had before. The system of using published procedures out of a let down book was also something that I came to appreciate. Just as in civil aviation, one could go anywhere in the world, to any airport, and make an instrument approach by following the procedure as published in the let down book.

The T33 had power assisted ailerons, which were very light and had an entirely different feel from that of the Meteor with its manual control. The Meteor was much heavier in roll and any pilot, who was used to that sort of feel, started rocking a T33's wings as he overcorrected in bank, right from the moment that he took off. The Americans used to watch and laugh as a wing waggling T33, being flown by some pilot who had just come off Meteors, disappeared into the distance. It took two or three flights at least before that difficulty was overcome.

That first flight of mine at Fursty was one that I shall never forget. I made a complete hash of it and certainly got off to a bad start. Also my instructor, having no understanding of the difference in aircraft types or procedures, was of little help. As he knew nothing of the procedures that I was used to in the RAF, and was somewhat contemptuous of them, there were numerous difficulties to overcome. But in time, they were overcome and it was not long before I was teaching it all myself to the MDAP students from many different nations, then later on to other American pilots themselves.

Because of the strangeness, and all these difficulties which had to be overcome, the T33 which was known as the T-bird in the USAF, ranked low in my estimation of aircraft, for quite some time. I was slow to get used to it, but as time went on and I built up hours on it, I radically changed my opinion. Developed from the F80 Shooting Star, just as the Vampire T11 and the Meteor 7 were developments of the original fighter versions, it was a superb aircraft, beautiful to handle, with light positive controls and a roomy, comfortable cockpit. As any aircraft that you fly regularly should do, it eventually became part of me, and I now look back on it as one of my favourites. Another thing in its favour was the ample fuel load, which it carried; so different from a Meteor.

Other things which we had to learn, were the American rules and regulations that applied to all their flying. In fact, these were very similar to the international ICAO rules that governed all flying, but in those days, especially on fighters, the RAF operated entirely in its own way and really ignored all such rules and regulations. All that I learnt, and the way that I had to operate with the USAF, gave me a very good grounding when later I came to take a civil instrument rating and understand the laws governing civil aviation the world over.

In the USAF, we had to file an instrument flight plan if there was any chance of entering cloud, which was in complete contrast to the RAF manner of just ploughing straight though, however claggy it might be at any time, in and out of cloud if it happened to be there. Also it was necessary to stick to many other rules, such as weather limitations and landing minima, which I had never heard of in Fighter Command. In fact, fighters in the UK air defence system could not have operated if they had had to work under all these regulations. I was in a totally new world and having to learn a great deal, but when I had got over the shock, I found it all very interesting and saw the sense in it, even though it would never have done for RAF fighter operations.

At first though, it did seem rather complicated. To stick to the regulations, as we had to, an IFR (Instrument Flight Rules) flight plan had to be filed in order to climb up through cloud and carry out whatever exercise was planned. Then to be able to actually carry out that exercise, we had to change to VFR (Visual Flight Rules) On Top, before going IFR once more for the descent. At first, it all seemed to be very ponderous, but it worked out well enough in practice when you understood it, and got used to it.

In the USAF, we had to learn to fly an ADF (Automatic Direction Finding) approach, which we had never heard of in the RAF. It entailed using the aircraft's radio compass to position over the airfield's NDB (Non-Directional Beacon) at twenty thousand feet and then carrying out a jet penetration, as the descent through cloud was called, in order to feed into the GCA. All this was following the published pattern, as laid down in the airfield letdown chart, and with no help coming from the man in the tower.

Except for the initial overhead height of twenty thousand feet, which was necessary for military jets, it was exactly the same system that was used by civil aircraft, and any pilot with a civil instrument rating would be quite familiar with all of it. In later life, when I became an airline pilot, it would be only too familiar, as stacked up in a queue, I waited for my approach time. However, in those days it just added to my confusion.

Nevertheless I did learn to fly on instruments in a much better way than I ever had in the RAF where, at that time we were simply taught to have a very rapid scan of our flight instruments and read them all as quickly as possible. There was however, no thought as to how the readings from each instrument individually should be interpreted and reacted to. On the other hand, the USAF taught a very good, well thought out method of doing so and using it, one was able to control the aircraft extremely accurately. Once I had mastered the method that they used, I found that my flying improved by leaps and bounds. However I did feel that all the rules and regulations made flying somewhat hidebound, and lacking in the operational freedom that I now realised we had had in Fighter Command.

There had been a feeling in the RAF that the Americans' ability to fly in cloud was not of a very high standard, but now I was learning better and thought that in some ways they were definitely ahead of us. Years later, when I was an instructor in the RAF, I tried to teach my students the American method of using their flight instruments. I hope that they benefited, though I think some people tried to have me locked up in the Tower of London for treason.

The course consisted of about forty flying hours, and as well as the instrument flying, covered rear seat general handling and teaching technique, though as with the ground school, it was nothing like so comprehensive as the RAF

Central Flying School instructor's course. The cross-country flying was all on airways and all navigation was by the use of radio aids on the ground, which were then just NDB's. The civilian airport at Munich even had an old radio range, which could only be used in the audio mode. I was always got lost when trying to fly it, and used to take about forty five minutes doing a let down. As yet there were no VOR's in Europe.

All this was another totally new experience for me and had to be learned from scratch. Not only had I never seen a radio compass before, but I had to learn how to put in a wind correction and track to and from a beacon, maintaining a centre line, not just putting the needle on the nose and homing. We seldom if ever looked at a topographical map, only using airways charts and generally flying in a manner that was completely different to anything that I had known in the RAF.

This was in the days before jet airliners so we did have the upper airspace to ourselves. Viscounts had only recently been introduced by British European Airways, and we would hear them on the radio sometimes. Flying at about twenty thousand feet and working the same controlling authority, they were the nearest aircraft to us.

When the course was complete, we were moved from the 7330th Student Squadron and put on the strength of the 7330th Pilot Training Squadron alongside the Americans instructors. We graduated with the title of Jet Transition and Instrument Instructor. I felt very grand.

Our boss was no longer Major Dorris, who had dragged us out of bed on that cold morning when we had only just arrived and told us that we should be in ground school. It was now Major Nickerson, the commander of the Pilot Training Squadron, for whom I soon developed a great respect and liking. We were in the proper working world of flying, not just students under instruction.

The first students that I was given, were from the Pakistani Air Force, which was about to re-equip with F86 Sabres after the retirement of their first jet type, the Supermarine Attacker. These were two of the four Pakistani pilots, who were at Fursty in order to learn American ways and my two were a

Squadron Leader and a Flight Lieutenant, whilst I was only a Flying Officer, though locally I was known as a First Lieutenant (UK).

This did not work out very well at all. They did not want an RAF instructor; they knew all about our ways. They complained to their government and some months later, after they had completed their course and gone home, the complaint filtered back to us. It was obvious that they had not liked having me, and that I had not produced the Americanisation which they thought that they should have had. However, the Americans did not bother much about it and told me that as far as they were concerned, they were happy with my work. My next students were a series of Norwegian, Belgian, Portuguese, Greeks and Iranians. Some were on jet transition courses, some on instrument flying courses.

In all, during the two years that I was at Fursty, I flew with, and taught students from fifteen different airforces, even Yugoslavian and Turkish. From that point of view, it was a tremendous education for me and now I will never say that some nationalities can fly better than others. I met some very good, and some not so good pilots from every one of those countries and learnt that whatever the background a person might come from, his ability as a pilot was a totally individual thing. Also, as far as my getting on personally with a student went, this again had nothing to do with race or nationality, but was just a natural thing between any flying instructor and his student

After about a year I was moved to a flight where the job was to teach instrument flying and procedures to USAF pilots, who had recently arrived from America and as yet had very little experience in European conditions. Remembering the difficulty that I had had at first to master all the instrument procedures and the American methods, I could not help having a little chuckle about the work. These pilots were mainly from fighter squadrons, which were based all over the European Theatre of Operations, which extended from Turkey to the UK, taking in North Africa on the way. I really enjoyed this job, as it enabled me to work very closely with the USAF and learn more of their ways. Also being with fighter pilots and talking their language, was just what I liked.

After a few months doing this, I was finally assigned as an instructor to the flight which put brand new American Second Lieutenants, just out of flying school, through the instructor's course. They then joined the staff at Fursty, becoming instructors themselves.

Once the course was complete and I was working on the line, I soon found that all the differences that I had first encountered with the American ways of flying just disappeared and I fitted into the system with no problems. After a while I suddenly realised that I no longer noticed that my uniform was of a different shade of blue to that warn by my American colleagues; I was just one of the crowd, which was great. One thing that I did notice though, was that they seemed to me to be professional pilots, who were working for the Airforce. In the RAF I had often thought, some officers only flew as a part of their duties, however good they might have been at it, but first and foremost, they were airforce officers, and considered flying as just one of their duties. When I came back into the RAF, I found it very difficult to settle down, and realised in fact, that I was far more professional pilot than service officer.

There was another part of the flying at Fursty, which was totally different to the RAF. The USAF firmly believed that aircraft were meant to take off from one airport and unless they had some particular exercise to carry out, land at another. Airplanes were for going places, so cross countries were naturally part of the course, both for instrument work when the student would be under the hood in the back, as well as normal general handling jet conversion. Except for a local round robin at night, they all entailed landing away at another airport, often in another country somewhere across Europe.

Apart from those laid down exercises, it was normal to be allowed to take a T-bird for a weekend cross country. Weekend cross country destinations could be anywhere within the Theatre of Operations, which took in the NATO countries across most of Western Europe, plus parts of North Africa. In theory, such a flight was supposed to be a student training exercise and a course member was meant to be taken along after a request form had been submitted, but in fact that was seldom the case. We just asked the Major for a T-Bird, and went off to the other end of Europe after work on the Friday, returning on Sunday evening. Having been allocated a particular aircraft, we would go to Base Operations in the normal pre-flight way, file a flight plan and get airborne.

Now that is exactly the way aircraft should be used at the weekend, but it's not quite the system that I had known as normal in Fighter Command. However, Fighter Command could never allow its operational aircraft to be scattered about, all over the place when there might suddenly be a threat and they would be needed in earnest.

My first introduction to the weekend cross-country culture occurred very soon after I had graduated and become an instructor. The Wing was invited to visit the Spanish Airforce, as there were a number of Spaniards at Fursty doing the course in preparation for their re-equipment with F 86's. So on a Saturday morning, thirty six T-Birds in mass formation led by the Base Commander, Colonel Mark H. Vinzant, flew from Fursty to Getaffe, the Spanish Airforce base just outside Madrid. We were royally entertained there and all flew back on the Sunday afternoon.

It was this flight that really brought home to me the fact that the T33 carried so much more fuel than comparable British jets. We could cruise easily for three hours at forty thousand feet and then have plenty of reserve fuel in case of a problem at our destination. I did approve of that.

This flight was then considered as a qualification for me to go anywhere that I might wish to go to in Europe, civil or military within reason. All that I had done though, was absolutely nothing more than to just sit there, flying as one of the huge formation. I did not really feel that I had learnt very much. But Major Nickerson seemed to think that I now must know enough to be let loose and I did not argue with him about it, neither did I tell him that we did not actually do that sort of thing in the RAF. I was just as much in the dark as any American pilot, who had only recently been posted from the

States. Possibly more so really as operating procedures outside the RAF were something right out of my ken.

The next weekend, after explaining to the Major just how I was going to go about it I shot straight off to Biggin Hill and showed my new aircraft to my old squadron. I had to buy them a lot of beer for the privilege.

The idea of Malta as a weekend destination soon crossed my mind. There the weather was likely to be fine and warm, I would see more RAF friends and visit places that were part of RAF history. The flight there from Fursty worked out very well as the US Navy had a base at Naples airport. We could fly over Austria as it was still occupied by the Allies and land at Naples for fuel. That meant that we would then have sufficient to get to most of the places that we might want to round the Mediterranean, and still have plenty of reserves. Horizons that I had never deemed possible before, opened up for me.

I had an old friend who was a flight commander on 249 Squadron based at Amman in Jordan. Middle East Airforce did allow weekend cross-countries sometimes, just for official training purposes, so he could also get to Malta and bring a flight of Venom 4's to meet us there. I would organise a bunch of my American friends, who were only too keen to meet the RAF at home. We would take a flight of our T-Birds to Luqa, the RAF station which is now Malta's International airport. There, our two groups would have a weekend together, fly each other's aircraft, talk shop about each other's jobs and generally have a great deal of fun. Apart from the fun, it was of course a very good way of getting the two airforces together and really getting to know one another in an unofficial manner.

I'm sure that neither RAF nor USAF officialdom would have been at all happy if they had known about the flying that was going on, but nobody at squadron level, who knew what we were doing ever questioned our plans. Neither do I suppose that anyone would be able to get away with that sort of thing now, but it was an easier world in the Services in those days and there was more chance to have fun. We made the most of it

Once or twice, I took a bunch of my American friends to visit my old squadron at Biggin Hill for the weekend. The resulting parties were memorable! Occasionally, I would fly back to the UK, just for a quick visit to my parents. Apart from such 'jollies,' there were official weekend visits to other airforces, like the Spanish in Madrid. Another was to the Turks in Istanbul.

I remember that I was given the job of leading a flight of four aircraft to Istanbul. Major Nickerson told me that this was because I must know all the procedures that were used in that part of the world. Well, I had never been there and had not got a clue about procedures, but the Major would not listen to my protestations. Luckily all went well in spite of bad weather at Naples where we refuelled en-route as usual.

Nearly one hundred T-33's made up the strength of the 7330th, far more aircraft than one would find at an RAF flying school in those days. There were also the base support aircraft, amongst them a number of C47 'Goony Birds,' the type that we know as the Dakota. I was able to get a few flying hours on that wonderful old machine, but I wish now that I had managed a full conversion onto it, which would have been possible for me. It could easily have been done during my time off from instructing, and would have been no trouble. However, at that time, I had become entirely jet minded and was not interested. What a pity, it's one of the things that I always regret not taking advantage of when the chance was there.

Two years went happily by and my tour came to an end. Early one cold December morning, just before Christmas 1956, I got a lift to Manston in a Gooney Bird. Together with the other three RAF pilots with whom I had travelled out, two years before, I was dumped out on the tarmac by Base Operations. The co-pilot asked if I wanted to my name on the Form 1 so that I might log the flying time.

I had sat in the back doing nothing and feeling a bit sad, I had not earned flying time.

'No thanks' I said, but it was a lot better way to travel from Munich than by the British military train.

From there, I made my way to London and checked in at the same dingy Air Ministry office, in the way that I had done when returning from Kenya two years earlier.

My local aviation museum has a T-bird. A Meteor 8 is parked beside it. They are kept outside and together they seem miserable and neglected, as they stand, sadly rotting away in the rain. I go to look at then sometimes and mourn.

Tiger Moth G-AIRK on which the author had his first flight, White Waltham, 1948.

Club aircraft at White Waltham, 1948.

Varsity, 5 FTS Oakington.

Javelin 9, 25 Squadron, 1961.

Author on secondment to the USAF, in the cockpit of a T33, 1957.

Author in instructor's seat of this T-Bird.

Author in cockpit of a Harvard, 1954.

41 Squadron Meteor 8's.

41 Squadron pilots, winter 1951/52 (Author standing far right).

41 Squadron, 1952 (Author seated, with mouth open). [Gloster Aircraft Company]

Javelin 7s, 25 Squadron, 1960.

Harvard 1340 Flight, Kenya 1954.

Meteor NF14, 153 Squadron, 1958.

USAF T33's, Germany, 1957,
7330th Pilot Training Wing.

Dan Air 748.

GBEJE, used on oil support work after the Author had ferried it from Argentina.

Dan Air 1-11, 300 Series.

Dan Air Comet 4c.

Author with Easy Raider, Popham 2002.

Author reunited with Tiger Moth G-AIRK, Cranfield 1998.

The author, cockpit of HS 748, mid 1970s.

Dan Air 1-11, 500 Series.

On holiday in Spain, October 2000.

The Thruster Sprint.

Gliders at Long Mynd, Shropshire.

8.   Posted to Night Fighters

I did not know the person in Air Ministry Postings who wore civilian clothes, and sat behind the rather grubby old desk in front of me. He must have been a squadron leader as they were the people, who were responsible for dealing with flight lieutenants such as me, and I had been directed to his office when I checked in at the entrance. He would have been a General Duties Officer just as I was, posted to an Air Ministry desk for a ground tour far from any flying, so unless he was a really keen, career minded person, he would hate the job. When I looked at him, I thought that to be given such work myself, would be the absolute bitter end and I could not possibly have coped with the life. However, he greeted me quite cheerfully and asked if I had any preference for my next posting.

'Fighters please,' I said, 'I would like to get onto Hunters.'

He just said 'No'

'Venoms,' I said, 'In the Middle or Far East.' He looked at me pityingly

'Bomber Command, Canberras,' I suggested, but it seemed that there was a seven month waiting list for a course, so that was ruled out.

I felt that it might be time for me to prepare myself for a possible future as an airline pilot and said rather keenly, 'Right, how about Transport Command.'

Beverlys were soon to come into service, and I was excited by the thought of flying the huge great transports into jungle airstrips in Malaya which, though it might be very different from any airline work, seemed to be something that would definitely interest me and would entail a conversion onto big aircraft. I was told that a posting to Transport Command was not possible. No reason was given.

I realised that I had arrived at the end. I could think of nothing more that particularly appealed to me, so I just came up rather drearily with a suggestion.

'Night fighters,' I said and was told that that was where I was going anyway.

The whole interview seemed to me to be rather a waste of time and a bit of a farce.

When I had been a day fighter pilot during the early 1950's, a posting onto night fighters was considered to be a great insult, almost as bad as being posted to the CFS course at Little Rissington in order to become a flying instructor. I had always considered that night fighters were just not for me. However the RAF had realised what their future needs would be and the policy now was to sow the seeds for the all weather fighter force, which in years to come would take shape and do away with the old concept of day and night fighters.

It would not really come into being until the Phantom was in service, but then in 1956, such an aircraft was hardly even a dream. Meanwhile the RAF had to build up a strength of crews, who could go straight into an environment where neither day, night nor weather mattered, people who could fly aircraft that were equipped to make interceptions and fight in any conditions. The description *all weather*, rather than *night fighter*, was just coming in, but as yet I did not have any real understanding of what that meant.

The backbone of the night fighter force at that time was the latest version of the Meteor, and to my mind it could not really operate in any worse weather than could the old Meteor 8 that I had flown before.

I was posted to No. 238 OCU, the Night Fighter Operational Conversion Unit at North Luffenham in Rutland, where I would learn the rudiments of the night fighter trade and fly the Meteor NF 12. I felt strongly that it would be a step backwards for me to fly Meteors again. It was three years since I had flown them on a squadron and it had then been the day fighter version. They had been obsolete at that time, so this definitely seemed a bad move for me. I should be going ahead onto some more advanced type.

I drove to Luffenham on a miserable dank grey day in January 1957 and found myself in trouble straight away. I was interviewed by the Chief Instructor, a very distant and haughty Wing Commander, who obviously had no intention of being at all friendly towards any OCU student, whatever their background or experience might be. He asked me where my last tour had been and I told him that it had been a secondment to the USAF, where I had been instructing on T33's. He presumed that I must have done a refresher course on Meteors and obtained an RAF instrument rating on that type before getting posted to Luffenham. When I told him that my current instrument rating was American and that I had only occasionally flown a Meteor during the last three years, he told me that I certainly could not come on his course. I would have to go to Training Command and do a refresher, learning to fly Meteors there, and getting an instrument rating before I would ever be allowed near one of his aircraft.

This was very different from the keen and friendly, go ahead attitude that I had known in Fighter Command when I had been on day fighters. It was a straight laced peacetime way of going about things and the whole spectrum seemed to have changed during the three and a half years since I had left 41 Squadron.

I argued as well as I knew how, saying that I had a lot of experience on Meteors and had been an IRE on the type. I asked that I be given a chance to fly with one of his instructors and take my instrument rating with an examiner there and then. He would think about it, he told me, but I left that interview with my morale even further down the scale than it had been when I went in. It was not at all a happy way to start a new job.

The next day I was reprieved. I was tested and given a chance. I flew with an instructor in a Meteor 7 trainer being given a general handling check first and then completing an instrument rating as a second test. All went well and I was told that I could stay, but I was definitely unpopular and remained so throughout the course. I had beaten the system and that was an unpardonable sin.

A new experience was waiting for me, as an ex-single seater pilot. I now had to crew up with a navigator/radar operator, known as a nav/rad. We would work together as a single entity through the course and then be posted to an operational squadron as a crew. Almost all of the navigators on the course were just out of training school and were about to start their first tour. We mixed together and fixed up partnerships. I was lucky, I met Paul Rundell and we got on well together.

When I got to know a bit about it, the nav/rad's job in the back seat of a night fighter seemed to me to be incredibly complicated. He had to operate his airborne interception radar, known as AI, and from what he could see on his screens, work out an interception path which included following all the evasive manoeuvres that a target might make. To do this, he had to give directions to his pilot in a manner, which could be followed, and that entailed anticipating just how the particular pilot with whom he was flying, might react to all those instructions.

Naturally standard phrases were used for the instructions, which related to the various angles of bank and rates of climb or descent that might be required, but one pilot would naturally react just a bit differently from another. A nav/rad had to allow for all this and talk his pilot into a position, close behind the target, where a visual sighting could be obtained in the night and an attack might be made with the fighter's fixed forward firing guns. It was the system that had been worked out during World War Two with Beaufighters and then Mosquitos, and though the radar had been improved considerably since then, the manner of using it was still the same. Our Meteors were also a considerable improvement over those wartime types, but by now, they too were obsolete. The Derwent 8 engines, which powered Meteor NF 12's, ensured that we had a performance that was superior to that of the earlier NF 11's and the Mk 8, which I had known so well, but it was by no means enough.

Apart from all his interception work, the nav/rad had to cope with the ordinary navigation, which usually consisted of being asked for a course to steer, just when he had his head in the AI set or was busy with one of his many other tasks. Having been controlling an interception, he would have no idea where he actually was at that moment, so he had to rapidly switch his whole attention to his navigation aids and quickly come up with an answer to that question.

There was a lot to do and it all had to be done at once, often at a time when fuel might be getting low, so causing even more pressure. Paul was great and as we gained experience together, he became one of the best nav/rads in our group. I couldn't have asked for a better one.

I surprised myself; I found this course both interesting and demanding. The feeling that I had had about night fighters soon beginning to disappear. There was a great deal to learn, and working as one of a team with somebody in the back who shared in the operation of the aircraft, was an entirely new experience for me. There was just a little cine gun work, but almost all the flying on the course was tied up with the use of the radar and practice interceptions.

I was introduced to the normal procedure that formed the standard every day, every night, exercise, which was carried out on night fighter squadrons, practice interceptions known as PI's. Two aircraft would go off together as a pair and on reaching their operating altitude, would be split up by the fighter controller in his underground radar station. One aircraft would be given the task of acting as target, whilst the other, acting as the fighter, would be given vectors in order to make an interception. As soon as the fighter's nav/rad had picked up the target with his AI, he would take over from the man on the ground and talk the pilot in until he had obtained a visual and could make an attack

A pilot and his nav/rad had to work hard at it until they could reach and maintain the required team status. Teamwork was essential and each had obviously got to know exactly what the other would do under any circumstances and then react as needed.

It took me a long time to get used to creeping up in the dark behind another aircraft, which I couldn't see. My night vision was not very good at the best of times and I had to work hard to do Paul justice after he had done his best to put us into a close enough position for me to visually identify the target and make an attack with my forward firing armament. He became very skilled at his job and I soon learned to trust him implicitly, as more often than not he would get us into just the right place.

The course lasted for about three months and then it was time for a posting to an operational squadron. By now, the early marks of Javelin were just being introduced into the first squadrons to convert, so Paul and I having done reasonably well, hoped to be sent to one of those units, but it was not to be. We were, though, given what we were told was about the best possible posting that was available to us, whilst remaining on Meteors. We were sent to 153 Squadron at West Malling, near Maidstone in Kent. West Malling had the reputation of being the home of night fighters and there were three squadrons based there, No's 25, 85 and 153.

I was going back to Kent where, whilst stationed at Biggin Hill, I had learnt the fighter pilot's trade. This was great and in spite of missing out on Javelins, I couldn't have asked for any better posting at the time. It was a form of home coming for me after three years overseas and when Paul and I arrived there in the spring of 1957, I felt that life had a chance of being pretty good after all.

West Malling had night fighter traditions going back to World War Two days, just as Biggin Hill had day fighter traditions. The joke was that during my time at Biggin on 41 Squadron, we had always looked down from our hill top airfield at the night fighter station below us with the over confident superiority that day fighter pilots often showed to their night colleagues. Now I was one of the latter!

The three Squadrons stationed at Malling, were all equipped with a mixture of Meteor NF12's and 14's, the only real difference between these two types being the form of cockpit canopy that was fitted. The 14 had the much improved clear bubble, whilst the 12 had the same old green house affair as the Mark 7 trainer.

There was no difference in performance between the two, but the night fighters also had the original Meteor, long span wing and that, combined with the extra engine power, enabled us to operate at rather higher altitudes than any version of the Meteor that I had flown previously. It did not however, increase the top speed, which was of course, governed by the airframe drag and limiting Mach Number

153 was a fine squadron with plenty of spirit. The CO was Wing Commander "Togs" Melish, a high scoring wartime night fighter pilot, and one of the best CO's that I served under. He later rose to very high rank in the RAF. West Malling was a happy station, where they knew just about all there was to know about night fighters at that time. I soon made friends and fitted in, realising that the night fighter world was not as bad as I had thought it would be and that I had a good chance of enjoying my time in it.

The flying that we did was split about equally between night and day, though even on a night fighter station in those days, the RAF still considered that after flying all night, crews should have no more than the following morning off. Also it was the rule that a pilot had to carry out what was known as an NFT, a night flying test, before flying in the dark. It only consisted of a short flight where you tested your radar, but I considered this to be ridiculous, and worthy of 1930's thinking. A night fighter pilot should be well used to flying in the dark anyway, and certainly should not need to fly in the daylight first.

After I had been on the squadron for a little while and become part of it, I suggested that we should change to the American system, whereby you either worked for a full night and did not come in at all during the day, or otherwise just did an ordinary day's work. Half the squadron would be in for day work, the other half for night work, the routine being to rotate between flights on a weekly basis.

This system was not considered at all appropriate at the time, but about a year later it was adopted by the RAF, and work on night fighter squadrons followed that pattern. The change did seem sensible to me, but I don't think that it was because I had suggested it!

Every night, the three Malling squadrons launched their Meteors into the skies over Southeast England and East Anglia for the usual PI exercises.

To get good results when making any interception, be it a set practice exercise like these, an exercise against RAF or American bombers simulating an enemy raid, or a real raid in wartime, a third person had to join the team of pilot and nav/rad. This was the Ground Controlled Interception, GCI, controller, who worked deep underground in one of Fighter Command's air defence radar stations. It was absolutely essential that he manoeuvred the fighter accurately into a place from where the nav/rad could pick up the target and take over control, continuing all the way to the firing position. Our regular PI's were as much practice for these people who operated from deep underground, or down the hole, as it was known, as they were for us and were something that had to be continually worked at. If ever we suddenly had to go to war, the whole team needed to be at the peak of perfection in order to counter an enemy attack.

This meant that the vast majority of the exercises that we flew were just PI's and to me, this tended to become rather boring. The fact that we would probably have to fight in daylight, as well as during darkness, meant that day tactics would have to be used when needed. It would be suicide to creep up straight behind a bomber in broad daylight, as we did. The gunners would easily shoot you down long before you could do any damage to them, but this seemed to be totally ignored in the night fighter force. Besides, there would always be the chance of being jumped by escorting fighters, which made me feel that there should certainly be some training in day tactics as well.

We did however carry out some gunnery training, which helped to make things more exciting. This was the standard air to air firing exercise where the target was the usual banner, towed over the sea on one of the ranges off the Sussex coast. I found that the night fighter version of the Meteor was a good steady gun platform and rather better I thought, than the Meteor 8. Certainly my average score was an improvement on the efforts that I had produced when I had been on 41 Squadron. That pleased me as much as any improvement should.

We did not practice the cine gun quarter attacks that I had known so well on day fighters, but when closing to firing position during our day time PI's, we took cine and our film was processed to make sure that we would have got a kill.

During this period, the squadron's designated war station was Valley, the RAF advanced flying training school on Anglesey in North Wales. Should there be a war scare, we would have to up sticks, move there at short notice, and operate straight away. It was expected at the time that Russian bombers might come down out of the north and penetrate into British airspace from the Atlantic. It was our job to stop them.

In 1957, the main annual air defence exercise came in May, which was somewhat earlier than usual. I had always remembered them as taking place in the autumn when the weather had begun to deteriorate. By then, Paul and I had been on the squadron for nearly two months and were considered operational, so we were part of the show when the order came to deploy to Valley for the week that covered the exercise period.

I remember that week as just about the most enjoyable that I had during the whole of my time on night fighters, a period of long hot summer days and nights during which we lived right beside a beach and flew hard. We were given a lot of work to do as the air defence system seemed to be testing the theory about the possibility of the Russians attacking from that direction. Night fighters we might be, but during that exercise, we were scrambled at any time during the twenty four hours, being used as any interceptors should be, and naturally were when the all weather force really came into being.

We were based on the far side of the airfield, with our own offices and hanger, away from the main Training Command operations. There our aircraft were parked on an isolated ramp right beside a small beach on the shore of the channel between Holy Island and Anglesey.

We were fed by a mobile kitchen and so became almost self sufficient. Though we had the chance to go across to the mess and sleep in rooms there when off duty, many of us did not bother, but just lay down on the sand where we were, be it day or night. I did more flying than I had ever done on previous defence exercises and thoroughly enjoyed it.

Unfortunately, we really learnt how outdated our Meteors were by then. The majority of the targets were Canberras and they came in, flying well above forty thousand feet. We took the underwing fuel tanks off our aircraft, in order to give them a better performance, but it was not enough. We could climb to forty thousand fairly successfully, but were slow and of little use anywhere much above that height. The Canberras came in over the top of us laughing and the squadron did not get a single successful interception throughout the whole period. It was extremely frustrating, apart from being rather worrying. How would we be able to cope, I thought, if we really had to go to war.

Paul and I did have one success though. We were scrambled one evening and told to climb to forty thousand feet as usual. The controller was superb, and put us in just the right position for Paul to get a contact on his AI and work us in behind the bomber without a stern chase. I don't think that anybody believed us when we landed and claimed a Valiant.

I remember that time at West Malling as an on going period of long summer days and nights, but those happy times on 153 in Kent could not last. Togs Melish was posted and his place was taken by a navigator. We were the first squadron in Fighter Command to have a navigator CO and the whole character of the unit changed completely.

Next, we were told that Malling was closing as a night fighter station, and that we were to move to Waterbeach, near Cambridge. There would be winged up with two day fighter squadrons, No's 56 and 63, as it was Fighter Command's policy that this set up should be the strength on each of its stations. What's more, we were to loose half our crews and be combined with 253, a squadron that had been flying the night fighter version of the Venom, a type which was then being withdrawn from service.

In September 1957, we moved. The squadron took on a new face and character with the addition of the new crews and the departure of many old friends, who we had been with at Malling. Also, not long after the move, we changed our number. We were no longer 153, but became 25. None of this helped the squadron spirit, which is so important on any operational unit.

Waterbeach was basically a day fighter station and, in spite of having a station commander who had been one of the top wartime night fighter pilots, was not geared for night fighters in any of the ways that we had taken for granted at Malling. Our wants were neither understood nor catered for at all. We were definitely the poor relations. With our navigator CO, flying became very stereotyped, PI's becoming almost the only exercise that we ever carried out. There was very little of the air firing or other exercises that we had done before, and which provided the more lively element of our work.

I wondered about the whole practicality of the attack procedure that we were expected to use against Russian bombers. They had tail armament and it was pretty certain that their guns would be controlled by radar in just the same way as those in American aircraft. It seemed to me that we would be dead ducks as we crept up behind the bombers and closed in to about 200 yards astern of them, before opening fire visually.

During the time that I had been seconded to the USAF, I had been involved with a squadron of F86D's. These were the night fighter version of the famous Sabre. They were armed with a clutch of unguided rockets, which they fired like a shotgun burst, using their radar to make a beam attack as they flew on a collision course at right angles to the bomber. This made them pretty well immune to any defensive armament that the bomber might have had.

The Americans practised this attack with the F86D pilot flying on instruments under the hood throughout the whole manoeuvre, working entirely with his radar, and picking up his target after being given the usual headings by a GCI controller. There was none of the business of slowly closing in from dead astern.

On one occasion when the F86D's were on armament practice at Wheelus Field near Tripoli, working with live rockets, I had flown in a T33, as chase plane on the fighter. The job was to make sure that the large banner target being towed behind a B29 was what the fighter's radar was locked onto and would thus be the target for his rockets. Otherwise it was quite possible that he might lock onto the tug and shoot that down, a disaster which had occurred in the States on one occasion.

This manoeuvre though not at all easy to position for and fly accurately, was I thought, the best way in which to make attacks against a bomber with tail guns, and a great improvement on our system. When I suggested it to senior RAF people, I was once again pointed at the Tower of London, with the prospect of only ever leaving there through the Traitor's Gate on the way to Tyburn Tree.

The Meteor had obviously come to the end of its days as an operational interceptor long ago, and a replacement that could deal with the threat of modern high flying jet bombers was urgently needed. It had been lucky that war had not broken out when it was the only fighter available to counter night attacks, but now the Meteor's replacement, in the form of the early marks of Javelin was starting to come in. We eagerly awaited our turn on 25 Squadron to convert to it and re-equip.

One crew who had been on the same course as Paul and I at the OCU at North Luffenham, had been posted onto a squadron with Javelin 4's, but were disappointed. The pilot told me that their performance was in practice, though not on paper, little better than that of the Meteor. However, 25 was lucky; we were told that we were to get the first Javelin 7's, armed with four thirty millimetre cannon plus the Firestreak air to air missile. This really was a great advance, as the Mk 7 had much more powerful engines than its predecessors and in consequence, a vastly better performance. Also, these first British missiles to reach the squadrons, would enable us to keep well away from the dreaded tail guns. We were to convert in January 1959 and felt that we would then have an aircraft, which was far more able to take on any threat that might be thrown against us at the time.

I had never followed the development of the Javelin with bated breath, as I had that of the Hunter. It looked to be a great ugly monster of an aircraft, and in spite of its delta wings, just spoke of drag in almost all its aspects. But, compared with anything that we had been used to before, it did give the impression of being a big powerful, and very capable machine. Its two huge Armstrong Siddley Sapphire engines did nothing to belie that impression, but pilots soon named it the Dragmaster.

Fighter Command's Javelin Conversion Unit was based at West Raynham in Norfolk, the home of the Central Fighter Establishment, but it was mobile in its operation, moving round to each squadron as required. The dual controlled version of the Javelin, the T Mark 3, had not yet come into service, but the conversion team brought with them what they called a simulator. In fact, it was little more than a rough mock up of the cockpit of an earlier mark of Javelin, but even so was very useful indeed. In it we were able to learn the drills, the checks and the emergency procedures.

The new type of AI radar, the Mark 17, which equipped the Javelin 7 had been installed in Valettas, so turning them into flying classrooms. Our navigators did their airborne conversion in these. So, in order to see what went on, I flew as co-pilot in one whenever I could, and when I actually stood behind them and watched over their shoulders, my respect for the nav/rads increased by leaps and bounds. I was even more convinced that I could never have sat there in any aeroplane, looking at a very odd radar screen, interpreting what it showed and controlling an interception.

As we approached Waterbeach at the end of one exercise, the pilot said, 'You land it then.'

Never had I landed an aeroplane of that size or weight before so I did wonder if this chap was quite in his right mind. He knew nothing about me, but I took over the controls, got settled and did manage to pull off a just passable arrival. I felt pretty pleased with myself and logged up another first in my type hunting career.

Then one day, we were told that our first aircraft would be arriving in a couple of hours. Our excitement was immense and we asked Air Traffic to let us know when it was on the way in. We would be on the tarmac to welcome it. Work stopped as soon as the word came through and the whole squadron, air and ground crew plus many other station personnel turned out to watch it land and taxi in.

The noise that it made was fantastic, a deep hollow, booming howl and a very different note to the roar of our Meteors, but I soon learnt that the Javelin meant unpopular noise. That booming howl, which might be music to me, could be heard many miles away, far across the Cambridgeshire fen country, and at night, complaints from the farms were unfortunately to become common place.

At that moment, I only noticed the noise in passing, I was staring at this huge monster and wondering just how I was going to cope with it when it was actually strapped to me. I had flown a number of types with larger dimensions, but nothing that at first glance, looked so vast and formidable. Allan, my navigator at the time, was standing beside me and though he did not say it, I am sure that he was wondering just the same thing.

The ground school course that we went through lasted for about two weeks and between sessions, we continued to do our normal flying on our Meteors. But then came the day that had been in my mind all the time and the thought of which, had caused not only lots of excited anticipation, but also not a little apprehension. I had to climb up into the beast, get strapped to it and fly it. Though none showed it outwardly, I expect that in fact, all of us must have felt a similar apprehension. We all knew that it would be very different from the staid and steady old Meteor that we had been flying for so long.

Naturally I had spent quite a lot of time in the cockpit going over everything and trying to remember all the drills, even though I had learnt them in the procedure trainer. That was different and without the life of the real thing. Now it was time to turn it all into reality.

Allan and I climbed up the ladder and found our way into our cockpits. We were both rather silent and I noticed that Allan had a rather more serious expression on his face than usual.

However much time you have spent in a simulator, or practised sitting in the aircraft on the ground, new cockpits are always strange and not easy to get settled into. The straps are never in the right place and it takes ages to find and adjust them. Something sharp digs into your back and it's impossible to get the rudder pedals into any position that suits you. Just don't flap, spend plenty of time getting it all worked out and settle yourself in comfortably. Then, quite soon, after just a few flights, it all becomes totally familiar and you wonder how you had ever thought it difficult.

After what seemed an age, both Allan and I were ready to start. The ground crew pulled out the ejector seat safety pins, showed them to us, stowed them and climbed down the ladders. We were on our own.

About two and a half years before, I had climbed into a Hunter after a quick look at the pilot's notes. I had been briefed by a friend, who had then leant over the cockpit combing and pointed various things out to me. He had shown me how to start the engine and I had flown the aircraft away with no trouble. I don't remember that being at all difficult, but this monster did seem rather imposing. Here I seemed to be perched at a vast height above the tarmac and out in front of me there stretched a huge nose full of radar. But suddenly I realised that all this had given me a magnificent feeling of power, and I knew that from then on that all would be well.

In those days in Fighter Command, there was no reading of printed checklists. We memorised them and just went through them, working from left to right across the cockpit. That was now what Allan and I got on with as soon as we had each managed to overcome our initial feeling of being in such an unfamiliar place.

Then it was time to start the two massive Sapphire engines: Both Throttles Closed, Low and High Pressure Cocks Open, then press the first starter button. That fired a cartridge which ignited a metered dose of a fluid called Avpin. The Avpin's explosion turned the engine and so initiated the run up to self sustaining speed.

The Avpin was extremely flammable and if the burn was not properly controlled, it could easily blow up the whole aircraft including the crew, we were told. That meant us, so it was with some trepidation that I pressed the button for the first time. However, it worked correctly, and did so on every subsequent occasion that I started a Javelin's engines. First there was a loud hiss, which rapidly changed to a rumbling roar as the engine started to rotate and the fuel ignited. The roar soon changed to the droning Javelin howl as the revs settled down to idling.

Taxiing was easy with toe brakes; a vast improving over the Meteor, and making the steering easy along the taxiway. As we moved slowly round towards the takeoff point, the feeling of power just continued to increase and I realised that I was already beginning to fit in with the monster.

At the holding point we continued slowly and carefully to go over all the checks, but on a first flight such as this, you do tend to get things right. It's later on when you think you know it all and are over confident and rushing, that you make stupid mistakes.

When I opened the throttles for takeoff, the feeling of power and the push against my back, was incredible. The Mark 7 had the best thrust/weight ratio of all the Javelin clan and, once again, compared with the Meteor, it seemed awe inspiring on that first occasion. There was an immense heave forward, first on the ground and then in the air as we continued to accelerate towards climb speed.

The next awe inspiring moment was when we reached it and I pulled the nose up into the climb attitude. When I first converted onto Meteors after getting my wings on Harvards, the increase in speed and climb performance had seemed fantastic. It became one of the topics of bar conversations for a long time amongst us students, but here in the Javelin 7 after the Meteor, it was just the same again, if not more so. Awe inspiring is a fitting description.

Above thirty thousand feet the Meteor's rate of climb and performance rapidly dropped off, even in the NF 14 with its uprated Derwent engines, but not so at all in this aircraft. We just went on climbing like a home sick angel. Later in fact, I found that the Javelin 7 would operate quite satisfactorily above fifty thousand feet and was the version of the Javelin with far the best high altitude performance.

A night fighter needs to be a good instrument platform, and here again the Javelin excelled. She was very steady and stable, thus enabling her pilots to fly very accurately, either under the nav's direction whilst making an interception during a dark night, or recovering down a GCA approach in foul weather.

Throughout this first flight, I had naturally wondered just what sort of a mess I would make of the landing. I dreaded making a fool of myself in front of all the onlookers, who would be watching hard for anything that they might criticise, but it turned out to be easy. The beast just sat down firmly and stayed there.

One of the exercises in the series of conversion flights was to exceed Mach One. This entailed climbing out over the North Sea, under radar control to forty five thousand feet, then rolling over and putting the aircraft into a vertical dive at full power. If you got it right, you could reach Mach 1.08 indicated. However, it did feel to me as if there was some sort of massive barrier building up in front of that huge nose as we hurtled down. Some spoilsports said that there was really a considerable instrument error and that you did not actually go through the sound barrier at all in a Javelin. I preferred not to believe that, but it was very different from the Hunter, which I remembered had just slipped easily past Mach One in a shallow dive.

The Javelin was soon an everyday part of our lives, the Meteor becoming just a memory. Though the exercises that we carried out were very similar, we operated at well over forty thousand feet, instead of round about thirty five. Also our radar had a much better range and we felt that we would now be able to intercept any of the threats that might be expected to attack Britain at that time.

All aircraft have some trick that they can play on you; something that you must be aware of all the times and be ready to deal with, should it occur. The Javelin was no exception. The delta wing stalled at a much higher angle of attack than did a conventional wing. Also at this high angle of attack, about thirty degrees, the great slab of the wing shielded the tail plane, so causing the airflow from the trailing edge to pass a long way below it. The elevators became completely blanked off and were thus useless. There was no chance of recovering from the stall in the normal, time-honoured way.

Naturally enough stalling the aircraft was not allowed. If you did happen to stall, the prescribed recovery action was to put the beast into a spin, if you could. Then the laid down spin recovery was to put all the controls hard into the forward corner of the cockpit, which it was hoped, would convert the spin into a spiral dive. The recovery from that was actually normal. This whole procedure used up at least fifteen thousand feet of sky. Hard luck if you started below that height.

I take my hat off to the Boscombe Down test pilots who worked on this manoeuvre and came up with the method of recovery which we were instructed to use, should we ever actually have the misfortune to find ourselves in such a situation.

The problem came to be known as the deep stall and was a killer during the test flights of some air liners with rear mounted engines, such as the Trident and the BAC 1-11. When in service, in order to keep you well above the danger speed, these aircraft had stall warning devices and stick pushers. Years later, long after I had left the RAF and was a 1-11 skipper, I was glad of all that the Javelin had taught me about the problem.

However, the expectation that we might have to fight in daylight conditions, did worry me for one reason which would be obvious to any day fighter pilot. Should you inadvertently get mixed up in turning fight with an enemy, you would be handicapped by the Javelin's stall problem, and would not be able to pull round just as tightly as you possibly could, almost right on the judder, and so turn inside him. By doing so you might avoid being shot down yourself, and with any luck, be able to get into a position to shoot him down.

There was still no thought of ever practising day fighter tactics and I firmly believed that this was an error, which urgently needed to be rectified. Many of our pilots had no day fighter experience and would have been mince meat for Migs, but our navigator CO had no understanding of the danger. The problem was never rectified, but we never had to go to war against enemy fighters in the Javelin.

In fact, one day I did get into a bit of a mix up with F100 Super Sabres. Turns did not develop and I found that I could certainly out accelerate them initially, and then easily out climb them. They got away because they were supersonic in level flight and could pull away from me as soon I reached my maximum level speed, which was well below there's.

In the course of time, some of our Javelin 7's were exchanged for Javelin 9's. This was virtually the same aircraft, but it had extra power in the form of reheat. It was though, a very simple form of reheat, and only gave extra power above ten thousand feet. The fitting caused a lot of extra weight, to such an extent that in order to maintain altitude, it had to be kept running all the time above about forty three thousand feet. However, it did enable us to carry out a new form of attack, which would keep us well away from any defensive armament that a bomber might have, be it guns or missiles.

Basically we had to position well below any target, usually at about thirty five thousand feet, accelerating at full power as we did so. Then when just in the right place, we would pull up into a steep zoom to where the Firestreak missile would lock on and could be fired. We would then wing over and dive away, well clear of any defensive armament. That was very satisfactory, I thought.

Apart from the normal practise interception exercises, we would often get the chance to operate against Bomber Command or American aircraft simulating enemy raiders. This came to a climax once a year with the big annual defence exercise. One of these really brought home to me the fact that the Javelin 7 was good weapon, which could do the job that it was supposed to do, a far cry from the Meteor.

By then, these big exercises were becoming far more realistic than the ones that I had experienced some years before on 41 Squadron. In this case, as the battle progressed, some stations were deemed to have been obliterated by nuclear attack, others to have become unusable due to fallout. Their squadrons, if airborne at the time, would be diverted. If their fighters were on the ground, they were put out of action and written off, so no longer being part of the defence force. Some squadrons were moved round the country at short notice, in order to counter an expected threat in a different sector.

Thus one evening after meeting a raid, Javelins from two other squadrons recovered to Waterbeach. We were then told that another raid was expected, so after they had been re-armed and refuelled, all aircraft were brought to readiness. Each squadron consisted of twelve aircraft, so we now had thirty six Javelins ready to be thrown into the battle.

Paul and I were crewed together again by now, which was great. We had started together in the night fighter world and had got on well right from the start. Though we had each flown with many other people since then, we still found that together, we made a first class team, so when at about mid-night all Waterbeach aircraft were called to cockpit standby, I could not think of a better nav/rad to have flying with me.

It had long been expected that any radar and radio control would be completely jammed out, and swamped in the event of a real attack, so to counter that, each interceptor was given a predetermined position and height out over the North Sea, to which he had to proceed when the order to scramble was given. Thus as the raid approached there would be a great arc of fighters positioned, and waiting to be unleashed at it on a reciprocal heading, exactly when the defence commander deemed the time to be right.

From our cockpits, we were plugged by land line into a telephone system linking us to Sector Operations. As each crew checked in, they were given the position to which they were to proceed to and hold, as soon as they were scrambled. A commentary followed, telling us what to expect. A raid was building up over the Baltic and it looked as if it would head for the UK. Then, as it crossed Northern Germany, we were told how it was being engaged by fighters from RAF 2nd TAF; then those from the Low Countries.

Now came the order, which fighter pilots will tell you, to-tally electrifies them: "Waterbeach, Waterbeach, start up thirty six Javelins. All aircraft, as briefed, Scramble Scramble".

Now, in those days, the layout of most fighter airfields had changed very little since the end of World War Two. Waterbeach was like that with a narrow, poorly lit, winding 'peri-track,' leading to the runway threshold. When you were scrambled, you did not taxi slowly in the way that you had been taught to do at flying school, you opened the taps and got down to the takeoff point, just as quickly as possible. You did not wait for air traffic to give you takeoff clearance. You just judged it as best you could and hurtled off into the night. Daylight scrambles were more organised as you could see what was happening. Day fighter squadrons tried to move in the order in which they were to pick up battle formation, so everybody had his place and tried to get into it right from the start.

That night there were thirty six of us hurtling round the bends and rushing into the air, all working as individuals. How there were no taxiing accidents and everybody managed to get away safely, I have no idea, but it worked. Years later, during the brilliantly controlled rush hour situations at Heathrow or Gatwick, I was never worried. I had been part of far tighter situations.

Later we heard that this was the largest raid of the whole exercise and that Fighter Command had reacted with every available night-fighter, including Fleet Air Arm Sea Vixens from Yeovilton in Somerset, but I have no idea what the total number of aircraft ranged across the North Sea amounted to that night.

We were held for only a short time before being unleashed eastwards, head on towards the raid, and soon Paul called, 'I have a contact at one o'clock, fifteen miles, slightly high.' Then a moment later, 'I have three more contacts.' Then again, 'They're all over the place'

He began giving me instructions that would bring us round behind, and put us into a firing position astern of one that he had picked out. First we made Firestreak attacks, but the rules said that we must get visual identification, so we then closed in to simulate gun attacks.

Quickly we picked off three Canberras, which were flying at about forty five thousand feet. They would have been impossible for us with Meteors, but now with our Javelins, they were easy meat

Then Paul suddenly said, "I have another contact, very high, do you want to go for it".

"Yes, straight away, let's go"

He turned us in, saying, "Climb as hard as you can".

Up through fifty thousand feet we went, and continued to climb well beyond that. But the Javelin 7 could easily cope, with Paul bringing us in neatly behind the bomber. There, silhouetted against the stars, was the huge great shape of a mighty Vulcan. We got him, but with that, our fourth kill for the sortie, it was time to head back home. Our fuel was getting low.

The Bomber Command tactics were now obvious to me. All the Canberras, flying at around forty five thousand feet, were just expendable decoys. The main strike force consisted of Victors and Vulcans carrying nuclear weapons. Flying well above the decoys, they generally avoided interception, but we had been successful, we had got one and later at debriefing we would tell the story.

After that, Paul and I were on top of the world. We knew that with the Javelin 7, we had an interceptor that was the best. Perhaps it may have seemed a bit odd aerodynamically, and was obviously the 'Dragmaster,' but it could do the job that it was designed for superbly and before the day of supersonic bombers, could deal with any threat that might be thrown against us.

9.   Varsity

Some people have told me that the Varsity was a dull and dreary aircraft without character. That's rubbish, she was an absolutely magnificent old aeroplane. She might have been rudely nicknamed the Pig, but she was a very fine old porker.

She was the type that I flew during my last tour in the RAF before taking the plunge into civil aviation, and I have very fond memories of the lumbering beast. She was great.

First though, the inevitable happened to me, as I knew it would, sooner or later. At the end of my night fighter tour, I was posted to a ground job. To me, it was unthinkable to be put into such a position. However, it is what the RAF does to you in the interest of your career; though by then I had realised that a career on the RAF promotion ladder was not the best for me, and civil aviation was what I should aim for.

Years before, when I had told my mother that I intended to join the RAF, she had said that I would never get anywhere in the Service as I would not be able to cope with the inevitable indoor desk jobs that would come my way. Now I realised what she had meant and that this was just another sensible thing amongst many others that she had told me and I had ignored at the time.

To really rub the problem in for me, this posting was to a one of the RAF's technical training schools where boy entrants, mostly only fifteen years old, were indoctrinated into various trades such as nursing orderlies, office typists and telegraphists. I was told that aircraft never came into the picture on such a station, and much of the indoctrination was done on the parade square, by bullying drill sergeants. Naturally, none of this was my scene.

Not yet having anywhere to live, I said goodbye to my family and in the depths of despair, drove off across the country to my new station, where I checked into the officers' mess.

The whole station seemed to be built of old wartime huts, laid out in straight lines and covering many acres of land. Which particular ones were to be my work place for the next two years, I had no idea. I could not face the thought of reporting to my new boss, and so just sat there in the officer's mess, allowing my misery to work itself out for a little while. However, whilst doing so, I was greeted by someone else who wore pilots' wings and was I found, in the same boat as myself, working as a flight commander with the boy entrants. This person saved me when he told me that there was actually a small airfield on the station and that a flight of Chipmunks was based there. These were used to give the boy entrants air experience and it was the job of the small number of pilots, such as ourselves who were stationed there on ground tours, to fly them.

I rushed across to the flight offices at once and being current on Chipmunks, got to work straight away. Having flown one detail, I put my name down on the next day's programme and told the flight commander that I would try to get across to the airfield and fly for him every day.

The sun shone once more and I felt able to check in for my job as the commander of 'A' Flight in the boy entrants' Initial Training Squadron. My squadron commander was an ancient secretarial squadron leader, who had been an officer in the Czech cavalry and one who obviously thought that flying was just a sideline in the Service, not of any real importance. I had known him in different circumstances in the past and then had had a great liking and respect for him. He had escaped from both Germans and Russians on more than one occasion and his stories about those times were fascinating. In his present position however, things were quite different

'Mike,' he said, 'How nice to see you again, but I must tell you this straight away. You will hear that the boy entrants are given air experience in some aeroplanes that they have here. These are flown by pilots like yourself, but you are not to take part in any flying. You are to remain in your office, except for the times when you go out to watch your flight being drilled by your sergeant on the parade square.'

That was just too much. 'Sorry Sir,' I said, 'I have just been flying and will be doing so again. I am on tomorrow's programme and intend to fly on every occasion that I possibly can.'

I did just that. Those Chipmunks saved my sanity and during that two year period, I achieved over four hundred hours on them, which must be as near a record as any for a ground tour. However, it was quite obvious that with my reply to the squadron leader, I had totally dashed any chance that I might have had of ever getting any more promotion in the Royal Air Force.

This I found, did not really worry me at all. Professional flying was the career that I should follow during my life and as far as the RAF was concerned, it had given me a superb start and I was very proud to have held a commission in the Service. However there was not really anything more for me there. Besides, I had also come to realise that I was not actually the sort of person that the RAF wanted as a future senior officer. It was time for me to leave, move on and join the big world outside.

As the end of that miserable two year period approached, I applied for the flying instructor's course at the Central Flying School and was accepted. A final tour as an instructor would neatly take me to the age of thirty eight, when I could leave the Service and start civil flying. In fact it all worked out very well for me along those lines.

The CFS course was one that I had always studiously avoided, and as I had often said; with my ingrained fighter pilot's outlook, instructors and I were hardly on the same wave length. However, I now needed all the flying qualifications that I could get and this seemed the best one to try for in the time available.

The Royal Air Force Central Flying School was, and still is, the very heart of flying instruction. People came there from the airforces of many nations in order to learn the art, or science, of teaching people to fly. The methods used now, in almost all civil and military flying training organisations world wide, stem from the wisdom imparted by CFS. Their tradition of teaching, together with the methods used, had started at Gosport during World War One, and now the unit was based at Little Rissington near Stow on the Wold in the Cotswolds.

For many years that station had been the home of CFS, and the name had always sown dread in the hearts of everyday pilots like myself. Apart from the instructor's course, CFS harboured the Standards Squadron. From that dark corner, there emerged people known as trappers, who visited other units in order to carry out flight checks on the pilots and make sure that they maintained what CFS considered to be the proper standards and were not picking up any sloppy ways. These trappers could make life very difficult at times, for normal aviators like myself.

Before I could start the CFS course, I had to do what was called a flying refresher course, which was always a normal thing for people coming back onto a flying after a ground tour. In my case it consisted of the usual week or two's ground school, which was followed by thirty flying hours on the piston engined Provost. This I found was very much of a steady old gentleman's aeroplane, when compared with the Harvard, which it had replaced as the RAF's advanced trainer. However, after my two years on Chipmunks I enjoyed flying it. It was one step up in power and performance and I always felt comfortable when I sat behind any big radial engine.

In its turn, the Piston Provost had now been replaced in the flying training schools by the Jet Provost, which was the type that I would have to fly during the basic part of the CFS course. That started as soon as the refresher course was complete.

I was most surprised, and of course very pleased to find that Little Rissington was a really happy station and the staff there, who were reputed to eat pilots like me for breakfast, all turned out to be friendly and helpful. This naturally made the whole course much more interesting and caused my morale to go leaping up. It needed to after the previous two years. But then, perhaps any flying station would have been happy after a session such as I had had in Technical Training Command.

The refresher course had made me get some order into my standard of flying, which after two years doing only air experience work in Chipmunks, probably had become really sloppy. But now at Little Rissington, I really had to do it all as CFS considered that it should be done. Their high standard of flying soon showed up my slaphappy ways and it was obvious that I had a lot to learn. However, I found it all fascinating, which surprised me. Learning to fly in the manner that they required, together with reciting the instructional patter at the same time, was I found, not only very interesting as far as I was concerned, but a challenge as well. I hadn't expected to develop this attitude at all, so it came as another surprised for me. The CFS course was a happy time for me.

At that time, basic training in the RAF was carried out mainly on the Jet Provost Mark 3, known as the JP3, together with the JP4, which had a slightly more powerful engine. The Gnat was just starting its service career as the standard advanced jet trainer and was about to replace the Vampire T11. Otherwise, the Varsity, which had taken over from the trainer version of the Wellington, held the fort in the multi-engined pilot training roll. It was also the flying classroom for navigator, signaller and air electronics training. Then there was the Chipmunk, which was used in the University Air Squadrons.

I had no desire to go on the Gnat and as I seemed to get on all right during the first part of the course with the JP, I expected to be channelled into working as a basic flying instructor. However, I was a bit apprehensive as I thought that the people who decided such things, just might look at the Chipmunk experience which I had picked up over the last two years, and send me down that channel. I felt that I had had quite enough of Chipmunks for some time and the thought of being posted to a University Air Squadron, horrified me. Though flying, it would be similar to my last job, and just not really my world at all.

I certainly did not expect to go on Varsitys. For that roll I was sure that you had to have come from Coastal or Transport Command. My multi-engined experience had been mainly on Meteors and the multi-piston time in my logbook was mainly on Oxfords and Ansons. This was flying accrued in the days when they had been our squadron hacks; not one might think, a good basis for someone who would have to teach people destined for Beverlys or Shackeltons.

Towards the end of the basic part of the course though, they asked for volunteers to go on the Varsity and I jumped at the chance. After what I had been flying, I looked upon the Varsity as a large aircraft, though it was nothing of the sort really; just a very good training lead into them. Whatever, it would be something entirely new for me and act as the lead-in which I needed for the future. However I still thought that I was not really the right sort of person to be picked for the job. Much to my surprise, possibly because there were only two other volunteers anyway, I was accepted and so continued with the advanced part of the course on a totally new type of flying. I became completely absorbed into what I found was a very interesting environment and, as time went on, found that I did seem to fit into it all reasonably well, which was another pleasant surprise.

The first thing was to convert onto the Varsity and learn how to fly it in the correct and accurate manner, the manner that was approved by CFS. Any pilot with reasonable experience can, they said, get into an unfamiliar aircraft and bumble it around the sky in a totally unprofessional way. That was not at all what was required of us. We had to operate as near perfectly as might be, and fly the aircraft exactly as they taught. This being what they called the correct manner, the one they told us, which we would then be able to pass on to our students in the future.

Learning how to handle the two big Bristol Hercules engines, each producing over two thousand horsepower, was important and another thing which had to be perfected. They were magnificent engines and ones that I soon came to have absolute faith in. In the training role they were often handled abominably, in ways that were never really intended by the designers, but they never objected. Big, round radial, piston engines are definitely my favourites.

In fact I found the aircraft very easy to fly, so after a while I was able to try to concentrate on the elusive, correct part of the requirement. To a certain extent, I did seem to satisfy the two instructors with whom I flew, which again surprised me. They were Allan Rudd, who years later, came to DAN-AIR, when I was a pilot with that airline, and Vic Stanton who went to Gulf Air when he left the RAF. I'm grateful to both of them. They made me progress from perhaps a somewhat wild ex-fighter pilot, to one who could just manage in the world of larger multi-engined aircraft.

On fighter squadrons, we always used to say that Qualified Flying Instructors, QFI's, at CFS, never flew a Meteor on two engines. They had the reputation of always closing one down and flying on asymmetric power in order to show how clever they were, we said. I found that that was just about the way things were with the instructors on Varsitys, here at Little Rissington, but it certainly was not just to show the clever side.

Asymmetric flight is probably the most important thing that has to be taught when converting students onto multi-engined aircraft, and later when I was working, I found that it was one of the most interesting things to teach. During the course, learning the method of teaching it correctly was another thing that had to be mastered perfectly. But first it was necessary to learn how to deal faultlessly with an engine failure at any time during a flight, and then continue safely down to a landing in the asymmetric configuration.

I had previously had a fair number of engine failures when flying Meteors, and now wondered how I had ever managed to cope with them successfully, landing safely without crashing when only one engine was working. I soon learned that I had been doing everything wrong and that I must now learn how to do it all as it should be done. This showed up an interesting fact, I thought. When I converted onto Meteors in 1950, the RAF did not really fully understand the science of asymmetric flight, and certainly did not teach it very deeply in the way that I was learning it in 1963. This must partly account for the huge attrition rate on Meteors that existed in those days.

Now on the Varsity, we practised dealing with engine failures on every flight, regardless of the actual exercise which happened to be the main purpose of it. Apart from that, we had to understand and discuss exactly what the forces were that acted on an aircraft when an engine had failed, and how they could cause loss of control, followed by a crash at any time. Our students would ask us about it all and we would have to give detailed and easily understandable explanations

Now I was able to realise just how totally wrong were many of the drills that had previously been the order of the day in aircraft such as Beaufighters and Blenheims, and why so many pilots had died as a result of engine failures. It explained why such types as the Mosquito did not have a very happy reputation when it came to asymmetric flight. There was nothing to be afraid of if you understood just what was going on, carried out all the drills properly and handled the aircraft correctly. At Little Rissington they made sure that we knew all the theory, exactly what to do when it happened and that we were one hundred percent capable of coping with the practical side; then teaching it.

An instructor would simulate an engine failure at any time, probably when the student least expected it. But then, when it's a case of the real thing, that is just when engines do fail. Engines were actually shut down completely by closing the fuel cock. The full drill had to be followed, the checks covered and the propeller feathered. There was no simply throttling back to a zero thrust position in order to represent an engine failure, and then going through the drills by touch whilst the engine remained running with the propeller windmilling. You had actually lost it, and were genuinely flying on one. The single engined landing that followed had to be right and you jolly well learnt to do it correctly. The benefits of working through such a situation, day after day, were enormous.

I've been grateful for this ever since. It was what we had to do later after we had graduated from CFS and were instructors ourselves. I hope that our students then, felt the same way about it. You only have to read general aviation accident reports on light twin crashes, to know just what happens so often to many of those who have not had the benefit of such training.

You just had to get it right every time, but since then, such thinking has been ignored and those in favour of this exercise have been overruled. In almost all training establishments the system has been altered and the engine, which suffers a simulated failure is no longer shut down. It is left to idle with a windmilling prop, set at zero power. It seems to be considered that the risk of a crash when training, overrides the benefit from the confidence and the experience gained. That is utter rubbish.

Anyone who has been through pilot training knows how the whole thing is divided up into a sequence of exercises that cover the whole process. Each of these exercises has a set form of patter, which the instructor has to real off to the student at the same time as flying the aircraft and demonstrating just what he is talking about. The basic patter has to be thoroughly learnt and understood for each particular one of those exercises, as does the sequence that has to be flown at the same time. The two have to be co-ordinated perfectly, so the student can understand exactly what is being talked about, and at the same time see it going on. He can then practice it himself; first under supervision, but then solo.

Years of experience have shown just what should be said and how all these prescribed exercises must be taught in order to get the best result by bringing out the many points, which a student has to understand and master. That sounds complicated and to begin with, it certainly can be for anybody who is trying to learn it all. It is very tricky at first and I was soon tying myself in knots, getting completely muddled, flying very badly and talking utter rubbish. Well, situation normal.

We were divided into pairs and having covered a particular exercise with an instructor, would fly with our partner and take turns giving the lesson, or acting as student. My partners were usually either Don McKen or John McAllister, who were both more experienced than me. I expect that though they never admitted it, they soon got completely fed up with having to listen to the rubbish that I came out with all the time.

By the end of the course, I was really pleased with my decision. I had become very interested in the Varsity and the syllabus that evolved round it. Both had taught me a lot about flying and that was just the way that it should be. Had I been channelled as a basic instructor, I felt that the Jet Provost would soon have bored me. On the advanced jet side, though neither the Gnat nor the flying that was entailed, really attracted me, I would like to have just flown the aircraft in order to see what this supposedly super new type was actually like.

On the instructors' course in the past, there had been what was known as type flying and I had hoped to have the chance of flying a Gnat under this scheme. CFS students flew as many different types of service aircraft as were available, which at one time had ranged through everything from Lancasters to Spitfires. Unfortunately by the time that I got there, that part of the syllabus had been discontinued. This was very disappointing, and the only non-course type that I got to fly was the Anson, which was not at all exciting and a type that I had collected some hours on anyway, when they had been station hacks.

The Commandant of CFS at the time was Air Commodore Bird Wilson. He was an extremely experienced military pilot with a fine war record and, as far as I could see, spent only the minimum of time in his office. He could usually be seen somewhere on the flight line, either talking to any of us or flying the Mosquito which he had managed to have based at Little Rissington as his personal aircraft. He was approachable and easy to talk to, so one day I asked him if I might have a go on the Mossie. Unfortunately though, it seemed that he was the only one who was allowed to fly it. He told me that he was very sorry, but the powers that be did not permit him to let any other pilots get their hands on it. Oh Well!

Then one day, a couple of Royal Navy pilots brought a Swordfish into Rissington for an afternoon visit. It was one which the Fleet Air Arm kept flying at Yeovilton, and on arrival had been parked not far from our crew room. Suddenly I noticed that there was a queue of our pilots standing near to it. In turn they were being strapped in and shown over the cockpit by the FAA people. Then they themselves were actually taxiing out, getting airborne and flying a quick solo circuit.

This was it, this was something that I just couldn't miss. I dropped what I was supposed to be doing and rushed across to stake a place at the back of the queue. I was incredibly excited, I was actually going to fly this wonderful old aircraft.

No luck. When it came to my turn, the naval lieutenant, who was looking after things said that he was very sorry, but it would soon be dark and they had to get back to Yeovilton. Oh dear, that's another disappointment, which I have never really managed to get over. What a thing that would have been, to have actually flown a circuit in a Swordfish.

At the end of the five month course, having graduated as a QFI, Qualified Fling Instructor, there was a chance of either working at RAF Strubby in Lincolnshire, where refresher flying was carried out for those who had been on ground tours and were coming back to flying duties, or to be posted to No 5 Flying Training School at RAF Oakington, near Cambridge. Lincolnshire did not appeal to me at all, neither would I have been the least interested in teaching people on refresher courses. But I was lucky, I got exactly what I wanted and was posted to Oakington. That meant working with students who had just got their wings on Jet Provosts and had been channelled onto heavies. It was straight forward advanced instructing, which now held a lot of interest for me. Besides, Cambridgeshire was a part of the country that both my wife and I knew well, and liked after our years at Waterbeach, so we were very happy to return there. Things were working out in a much better way than I had ever imagined they could do, and I was eager to get started.

I arrived at Oakington in February 1964, and being welcomed into the fold straight away, I soon realised that I was on another happy station. Here the atmosphere was totally different to the one, which I had lived through during the previous years at Cosford. At once it seemed to me that all the people there, from the station commander down, were cheerful, happy and friendly. It was the way that I remembered things to have been years before at such places as Biggin Hill and West Malling, and of course is the way that RAF stations should be and usually are.

The Station Commander was Group Captain Burt Ambrose, of wartime fighter fame. I had known him distantly when I was a new pilot officer on 41 Squadron at Biggin Hill. He then was 11 Group Weapons Officer and one of his duties had been to visit all the squadrons in the group, but I was amazed when he recognised me and greeted me as if I was an old friend. Well, I think that in reality he just kept tabs on all officers who were posted to his station, and noting my past service on 41, was able to pin me down, however, his welcome was another thing that really made me feel at home.

The Chief Instructor and Wing Commander Flying was Wing Commander Stanislau Wandzelak, one of the Poles who had stayed on in the RAF after the War. He had also been a topline wartime fighter pilot on Mustangs, but for some years had been in Training Command, mainly teaching on the advanced jet side of things. It was his third tour on the station and he had previously instructed there on Meteors and Vampires. Everybody liked him and had tremendous respect for him, so with all those tours in the one place he had earned the nickname of 'Mr Oakington'

I always think of him as just about the best Wing Commander Flying that I ever served under, and had I been in any fighter wing which he led, I would have followed him anywhere. When he was posted eighteen months later, we put up a formation of twelve Varsitys in a fly past to bid him good luck and farewell. He was superb.

After about a week of check flights, being shown the ropes and the local area with the Station Standards Flight, I was put on the line to work and earn my living. Our students were newly commissioned Pilot Officers, some being graduates of the Royal Air Force College, Cranwell, whilst the others were short service, having been through the usual FTS scheme of things as I had done nearly fifteen years before. With their newly acquired wings and all that that meant, they were very confident and raring to go. Ahead of them, on completion of their Varsity training, lay the prospect of a posting to either Coastal or Transport Command.

The syllabus, which I now had to teach, started with a straight forward conversion onto the aircraft, and the exercises which that entailed are familiar to anybody who has gone through basic pilot training. They start with effects of controls and continue through straight and level flight, turning and stalling, to circuits and bumps, then going solo. The form of these exercises was just the same as any student, whether he be military or civil, must endure today when first starting off in a Grob Tutor or a Cessna 150, whatever the type may be. To learn to fly an aircraft that is new to you, you must start with the basics; only then will you become totally familiar, and as one with it. It was very necessary that our students should achieve that relationship with the Varsity.

After having only flown single engined aircraft during their training up till then, the next step that our students had to face, was something totally new to them. They had to learn all about asymmetric flight and it was now up to me to teach my group of four how to recognise an engine failure, control the aircraft, carry out the drills and then fly it down to a safe landing on only one engine.

Basically there were two exercises, which covered this and I was always enjoyed teaching them. The first covered recognition of an engine failure, identifying which one had failed, and then controlling the aircraft. When that had all been worked out, the second part of the exercise consisted of teaching the student how to determine exactly what his critical speed might be; the critical speed being that below which he could no longer keep straight and control the yaw caused by the asymmetric power situation. He had of course, to get his personal critical speed as low as the design of the aircraft would allow.

This exercise entailed flying at the height where the supercharged Hercules engines produced their greatest power, then with one windmilling at idle power and the other at full throttle, reducing the speed steadily by raising the nose until it was no longer possible to keep straight with full opposite rudder. There was always a bit of a competition with that one, and getting right down to the recognised minimum critical speed for the Varsity required practise, with inevitably more than one attempt.

The loss of control was of course, due to there being no longer sufficient airflow over the rudder surface to provide the force necessary to keep the aircraft straight, even with full deflection held hard on. In the normal manner at that point, the aircraft would start to yaw, then roll in towards the dead engine, before entering a spiral. It was a very sedate and gentlemanly operation, just like everything else with the Varsity, but had to be perfectly understood and carried out correctly. If it should happen when low down on the approach to land, or just after take-off, it might be fatal.

Because they were supercharged, the engines gave their best power at about six thousand feet, so that was the height where we carried out the exercise. This meant that there was plenty of sky below us after control had been lost, in which to lower the nose, gain speed and recover back to straight and level flight.

A pilot also had to learn just what would be the lowest point during an asymmetric approach at which an overshoot could be commenced when the airspeed had been reduced to its final reading. Below that, the initial sink caused by the inertia of the aircraft, before its flight path was changed from the descent to a climb, would cause an unavoidable and most unpleasant meeting between it and the ground. This was known as the decision height, and below it one was committed to continue, and land ahead whatever might happen.

Throughout the years that I was a flying instructor, these were the things that I most enjoyed teaching and found most interesting, even more so that doing circuits and bumps, then sending a brand new pilot off on his first solo.

After leaving the RAF, I worked at the College of Air Training where we taught the same exercise using Piper Apaches followed by Beech Barons, both with un-supercharged engines. They gave their full power right on the deck where any situation involving engine failure would be most critical anyway. I used to take my students out over the Channel, south of the Isle of White, and do the exercise as low over the water as I thought was safe. That was far more exiting and needed a much more rapid recovery action when directional control was lost.

The second asymmetric exercise which had to be taught, covered the emergencies such as fire drills and actually feathering the engine; also of course, how to use the rudder trim and to keep the ball in the centre, maintaining balanced flight.

The flying instructor's mantra, 'Come on now, keep the ball in the centre,' really meant something under those conditions.

After that you could start ramming home the asymmetric training; so on completion of the planned exercise during nearly every flight, you would simulate an engine failure on the way home. The student then had to carry out the drill correctly, shutting down the engine and feathering the propeller. After that, a circuit, approach and overshoot was required, which was followed by another circuit and full stop landing on just the one good engine.

Well, that was something that certainly could not be allowed to go wrong, but would give any student enormous confidence after he had done it successfully on a number if occasions. It never was got wrong, so when an engine failure happened to them for real, as it was sure to do at sometime in the future, they had no qualms in dealing with it all and landing safely.

Another aspect was the way that the Varsity gave students an introduction into flying as a crew member. With a minimum crew configuration of two pilots, when a student went solo it was not so in the strict sense of the word. He would not be alone in the aircraft, but would be accompanied by a second student, who acted as his co-pilot. Thus both would start learning how a crew must work together as a team, reading the check lists, using the call and response system, and giving the necessary briefings.

A further useful thing was the Varsity's ability to carry a fuel load that enabled her to keep the engines running throughout the whole working day. Each normal training detail was scheduled to last for one hour and thirty minutes airborne time, and each aircraft would normally operate four of these during the day. The first crew, instructor and student, who were detailed for each aircraft, would miss met briefing and do the pre-flight checks, start the engines and get airborne before 0900 hours, whilst all the remainder of the crew changes after that throughout the day, would be made with the engines running. There was no need for a refuelling stop until the end of the afternoon when the aircraft were got ready for night flying, or for flying the next day.

The RAF logged flying time just from take off to touch down. Taxiing time was never counted as it is in civil aviation, so all of the one hour thirty minutes detail would be spent in the air. Up to half an hour was allowed for taxiing in between flights, plus all the business of crews changing over, getting strapped in and doing the checks, whilst the engines were kept running. This system worked well and four details fitted neatly into the working day.

Cross countries might last for six hours if three students were carried, or just four hours, if there were only two aboard. These could provide lots of variety, not just going from 'A' to 'B' in a straight line, as was the case in basic training. Part of the exercise might be flown at about twenty thousand feet, so operating on oxygen; then part would be airways training below ten thousand feet. There was always low flying, some of it out over the North Sea, and the remainder along pre-scribed routes in East Anglia. Low flying was an important part of the RAF's operations.

Generally on such flights, except for landings and takeoffs I would stand behind the pilots' position with one student in the captain's seat and another in the co-pilot's. Like that, I would try to teach them how to work together as a crew. On flights where we carried a navigator I would send the third student back to work with him. They would all be rotated every two hours.

As the flight progressed, we would make touch and go landings at RAF airfields near our route, anywhere from Leuchars or Macrihanish in Scotland to St Mawgan in Corn-wall. There was plenty of variation and it was all very interesting and enjoyable. Though I hope the students thought so too, I don't think that I was a very easy instructor to fly with!

Overseas cross-countries would be to RAF bases in Germany or to Gibraltar. These would be flown on airways and of course, were eagerly looked forward to. Berlin was my favourite destination and I was able to get a number of flights down the corridor into Gatow. The city fascinated me during those years when the Cold War was very much alive and German unification was not even a vague consideration. Years later when airline flying, I was often based there for a week or two, as the company that I was with had many routes in and out of the city. As time went on, I was able to regularly watch the progress of rebuilding, which was slowly but steadily getting rid of the war damage, but it always remained a fascinating place, entirely surrounded by the Soviet occupation.

To begin with, the flight in there along the Berlin Corridor was always a bit of an adventure. When airline flying, I got to know it well and it became routine, though of course different from everyday work, but then in my Varsity days, it was all new to me and exciting. With airliners using the flight levels above us, we had to fly too low to be able to maintain proper radio contact with the Allied air traffic control authorities. That always caused a few problems as they needed to be very positive. Our radio navigation equipment was rather basic, not really being very helpful at times. The way things were at that time during the Cold War, meant that we were virtually over enemy territory. Below on the ground along the corridor, you could see Russian and East German airfields with masses of military aircraft and helicopters parked on them.

Another task that we had with our Varsitys at Oakington, was to act as a standby transport unit. When there were exercises, or periods of tension, which entailed the dispersal of the V-bomber force to their war stations, we would be called out, and have to carry their ground crew. These flights were in total radio silence and often entailed low flying. I remember one during which I crept at low level across the Irish Sea to Ballykelly, all the way in pouring rain under a low grey cloud base, carrying ground crew to a Vulcan that had positioned there, and was on standby, waiting to be scrambled. All that sort of thing added some excitement to a normally routine life.

Also at times, we had to meet the ground crews belonging to fighter squadrons, which were returning home from Cyprus detachments on Transport Command aircraft, and had been dumped off at Lynham. Without us, they would then have had to face a long, uncomfortable bus ride to their station, which might be a couple of hundred miles or more away, across the country. We met them at Lynham, piled them into the Varsity and took them home to their base.

Passenger safety together with weight and balance seemed to be ignored on such jobs, as our aircraft had only the minimum of seats down the back. The space was filled with racks for various kinds of equipment that would be needed for the Varsity's other training roles with different aircrew categories. The passengers were just piled in and had to sit anywhere on the floor. I never heard a grumble about this from any of them, though I remember one flight sergeant being a bit doubtful about the whole thing. They must have thought that the alternative journey by road, lasting hours in an uncomfortable service bus was a worse option. Nobody ever came to any harm.

The Varsity had never been intended as an aircraft to carry passengers so it could not really be blamed for having nowhere for them to sit. It was superb for all the jobs that it had been designed to carry out, and that was what counted.

One such trip when I carried ground crew to Coltishall, earned me a ride in a two-seater Lightning T5, which was the nearest that I ever came to flying anything more advanced than the Javelin, my last operational type. I flew with an American pilot who was on exchange, and so qualified for a ten ton tie, but I was somewhat amused to find that I was no longer anywhere near at home in the cockpit of a fighter. It showed me just how far I had drifted from the corner of the flying world where I had started operationally, and at times still thought of as home. The Lightning's cockpit seemed cramped and uncomfortable, whilst the aircraft bounced all over the place. Maybe if I had been posted to them, I would soon have got used to them, and it would have been quite different.

If I had ever admitted this to any current fighter pilots, they would certainly have called me an old dead beat. Perhaps though, a couple more trips would have settled me in and I actually might have felt that I was back home. Well, I never got the chance.

The Varsity, a development of the Viking and Valetta, was the aircraft, which took student pilots right out of the basic environment, in which they had previously been flying prior to getting their wings, first on Chipmunks then Jet Provosts. Because of its size and power, and in spite of being neither turboprop nor jet, but an old piston engined type, it did give them a fair idea as to what any aircraft that they were likely to fly during their future careers might be like.

Well, that's what training is all about. Also, though still students, they worked as operational co-pilots on the transport flights that we had to make, and that, I'm sure gave them confidence, and made them realise that they were getting somewhere at last.

Sometimes the navigators that flew with us on these occasions had just graduated at the end of their course at a nearby Navigator's School. I remember that the one who came with me on the flight to Ballykelly, when I had crept low across the Irish Sea, was absolutely thrilled to be doing the job of a full crew member for the first time. He kept telling me so and it was good to hear it.

The Varsity's ability to carry ice showed up well on some of these flights. She was fitted with an alcohol anti-icing system with enough fluid to last for forty five minutes use. If it ever looked as if you would have to fly through cloud where icing was likely, you started the system going and de-icing fluid oozed from numerous small holes on the leading edges of the wings and tail plane. It then flowed back over the upper surfaces, forming a film and so stopping any ice from forming at the critical points.

I've flown with various anti-icing systems that didn't work particularly well, but this one was fine until you had used up all the fluid. That had a habit of happening during long flights on airways just when, because of other traffic you could not climb or descend as you would have liked to, in order to get out of the icing levels. If you looked out at the wing, you then saw that it had become white and was now a totally different shape from normal. At the same time, more ice was coming off the props in lumps and battering the fuselage by your head. You wondered how she could possibly keep flying, but the Varsity did so, seemingly with no trouble in spite of the extra drag, weight and misshapen wing.

I spent over two years on this job at Oakington and thoroughly enjoyed all my time there. Unlike many flying jobs in the Service, we actually did plenty of flying and I can't remember being given any those infuriating secondary ground duties, for which the RAF is renowned.

Later in the airline world, there was another pleasant thing, which often happened as a result of that tour instructing at Oakington. I often met my erstwhile students, who had also left the RAF by then, and were civil flying. The thing that always surprised me about these meetings was that in spite of the way that I had treated them when they had had to endure my rather wild efforts at instructing, they greeted me as a friend. One became a training captain in the same airline and I did a number of routine base checks plus an instrument rating renewal on the simulator with him. Not once did he fail me. Well, that never ceases to amaze me!

10. An Apprenticeship

It was obvious that there was a great deal which I had to learn about civil aviation before I took the plunge into it. People who had left the RAF ahead of me and were struggling to get their licences and to find jobs, spoke of the civil aviation blues and seldom seemed at all happy with the way that things were going for them. Others were out of work after the airline in which they had managed to get a job, went bust. However, one important thing that I always did hear was how there were superb salaries to be had when you did land the right job, in the right place. At the time, the great thing to aim for was a Boeing 707 command in one of the main airlines, but it entailed a lot of time, hard work and patience in order to climb the seniority ladder and reach that position.

I needed to find out for myself, tread carefully and if possible, start off in a job somewhere where I could settle and make a good home and base for the family, one that I hoped might be permanent. After that I would be able to look around and see what actually might suit me.

Going through the CFS course and so gaining its qualifications, was a very sensible thing to have done and gave me opportunities, which I needed to start with. Having managed to climb that ladder a little way and reach A2 instructor standard, to which I could add my American flying instructor experience, I felt that I had at least some chance of landing a job in a top civil flying school.

During the two years before I actually had to face it all for real, and hoping that the RAF would never find out, I tried to get some part time civil flying work with any small companies, which operated reasonably near to where I was stationed. This consisted of taxi work, ferrying, crop spraying and club instructing. To go airline flying during my time off was obviously impossible, so all that remained a bit of a mystery. However I kept my ears open when I was amongst civilian pilots and tried to pick up all the comments that people made.

First I learnt that club instructing was definitely not for me, and anyhow, a flying instructor was right at the bottom of the pecking order in civil aviation. He was rewarded with a ludicrously small salary for working all the hours that God gave. However, by working part time in a club during weekends, I gained experience in basic instruction, which was something that I had never done in the RAF. But as a permanent form of employment, instructing at a club was not an option as far as I was concerned.

Apart from that, crop spraying was fun, but very hard work. I tried it for a week, flying a Super Cub and bouncing over the sugar beat fields in the Fen Country. I enjoyed it, and good money could be made, but it meant going off for seasons to such places as the Sudan, where you spent day after endless day in impossible heat, bouncing over the vast cotton fields by the Nile and logging up to two hundred uncomfortable flying hours each month; no thanks, and not so good for a family. Besides, it was not exactly the safest sort of flying and pension schemes naturally did not exist. I had come to realise that the latter were an important factor. Crop spraying was another non-option.

Then ferrying was another penniless occupation unless you could get in on transatlantic operations. But I did not think much of piloting single engined aircraft on those very long flights across the never ending ocean. The ferrying that I managed to get, just consisted of the odd delivery flight to destinations in Europe.

It was obvious in fact, that big salaries only came in big airlines, with commands on big aircraft and the more engines that those aircraft had, the bigger the salaries were. Furthermore, you had to be in a line of work where BALPA, the pilots' union held a lot of power, and that meant the well established, main airlines. Without experience in the RAF on large aircraft, it seemed unlikely that such an airline would snap me up and give me a job, unless at some critical moment there was a shortage of people with the background, and experience that they really wanted. I was sure that it would not be easy for me to find the right job.

However, much of civil aviation continued to remain something of a mystery and so it did seem that my plan to find a job which would give me a good basic start, and from which I could get a much better view of the whole picture, was the best path to follow.

The answer to that seemed to be one of the approved flying schools, which taught ab initio students to Commercial Licence standard for professional flying. There were just three of these at the time; one at Perth in Scotland, but I did not want to move up there, one at Oxford, and thirdly the College of Air Training at Hamble, near Southampton.

Another big obstacle loomed up and had to be overcome. It was obvious that the business of getting a pilot's licence figured very largely as one of the main causes of those civil aviation blues. I determined to create some sort of a basis to work from and so made sure that I obtained an ordinary Commercial Pilot's Licence a couple of years before I left the RAF, and went out into the cold hard world. It would not get me much of a job, but it was a little money in the bank and I could use it for the work, which I intended to get in order to test the water whilst I was still in the RAF at Oakington.

The Commercial exam was not really at all difficult, but just needed a good deal of swatting, mainly to learn exactly what answers were required for standard questions. It was interesting to see that the Civil Aviation Authority often wanted one answer whilst the ARB needed another one. In the RAF there had sometimes even been a third, which they considered correct for some particular question.

One example was the reason for using flaps on the approach; each organisation required a different answer to the question and they were all correct to a certain degree. You just had to know who wanted what and you really did have to keep your sense of humour, which was something that some people obviously found difficult. It appeared that a number of the questions in the exams, were left over from the 1930s way of thinking.

I started with a correspondence course from the old London School of Air Navigation in Kensington. It was all in a rather tatty blue paperback book, with the pages bound in the wrong order. I then spent a few days there, doing my best to learn how to exactly pass the exams.

The classroom was in a dark and grimy basement, and the instructor was someone who, at the age I was then, I considered to be well past it. He wasn't actually so, but had been a pilot during the thirties and still held a licence. How he still passed the medical, we could never make out, as he appeared to be just about on his last legs. There was hope for us yet. He wheezed loudly as he shuffled round the room from student to student, moving with great difficulty in a floppy sort of way, whilst on his feet were a grubby old pair of warn out carpet slippers. As he flopped about, he repeatedly told us how he had ferried an Aero Commander across the Atlantic and how he liked neither the American compass nor the instruments. But he did teach me what answers were required for many of the exam questions; and that was what counted and was what I was paying for.

What I did see there were people who had recently come out of the RAF. They had no licence, so no job, and were spending their gratuities just to live and pay for the course. You could feel the tension when you spoke to them; no wonder they talked of the civil aviation blues. Naturally enough, no airline would even give you an interview unless you could put a current licence there on the table in front of them.

Then there was the Instrument Rating, which I had no fear of initially, in spite of all the rumours that seeped down from those who had worked for it and been through the mill. Without it, no licence was really worth anything except for such things as club instructing or crop spraying. It had to be faced, but after all, I was an Instrument Rating Examiner in the RAF, and currently taught instrument flying on the Varsity. I had also done so in the USAF and did not expect too much difficulty. How wrong I was. Also it was all very expensive and that could only add to the problem.

The test with a CAA examiner would have to be taken at Stansted where the Examining Unit was based. Luckily that was not far from Oakington and I heard of man there who operated a Twin Comanche, and catered for people such as me. I booked up with him, but found that he was not an instructor and was actually of little help. He just sat there beside anyone who had hired his aircraft, acting as safety pilot and, as in my case, letting me make masses of mistakes as I struggled through repeated practice attempts at the Stansted let down pattern and ILS, together with the set routes on the local airways.

Every pilot has some type of aircraft, which is his favourite, and another which he likes least. I have found that the operation on which I have flown any particular type, and what I associate it with, has a lot to do with my feelings for it. I hated that Twin Comanche and ever since, I have looked upon the type as a really horrid little aircraft. But I did manage to pass my civil instrument rating test on it. I have loathsome memories, which have carried my feeling of intense dislike to all Twin Comanches, but that's purely my personal opinion. Most other Piper aircraft that I've flown have been superb.

After that I went for my Airline Transport Pilot's Licence, which did mean a lot of hard work and study, but I was given really magnificent backing from my bosses at Oakington; plenty of time off to attend school and take exams. When, very unexpectedly one morning, a real live licence came through the post after my first attempt at the exams, and I realised that I had actually passed, I was amazed and on top of the world. I had managed to beat that side of the blues.

The station commander congratulated me one day and said, 'Well, now you're a proper pilot.' But I hadn't quite thought of it like that.

Now all I had to do was to get a job. I decided on the College of Air Training as the first choice. It was then jointly owned by BOAC and BEA, and operated solely to train their own cadets, who had passed through their selection scheme.

It sounded as if it was the most secure of the three schools and the Hamble River area seemed to be just the place for the family to settle and call home. A full year before my discharge, I went for my first interview there and was naturally told that they could not guarantee me a job as far ahead as that. Never mind, I had got a foot in the door and managed to keep it there by making further visits as time went on. Because of discharge leave allowances, I was able to start work with them a whole month before the RAF stopped paying me, which seemed to be a good omen. My plans were working out.

The culture at the College of Air Training was definitely not far removed from that of a stuffy version of Training Command in the Royal Air Force and there was only one instructor employed there at the time, who was not either ex-RAF or Fleet Air Arm. Some had trained or worked at Hamble as civilians in the 1930s, when it was AST, but all of those had been in the Services during the war. The crew room conversation was very similar to that in an instructors' room at an RAF Flying Training School, except that there were many more open grumbles about pay. Also BALPA, the pilots' union was often mentioned, and most people were members. Well, there was a good reason for that; the pay was very poor, less than that of a Viscount first officer in BEA, and did reflect the low status of a flying instructor in civil aviation. When it came to being paid roughly by the size of the aircraft that you flew and the number of engines that it had, Chipmunks came out with a pretty low rating

The Principal was a retired Air Vice Marshall, who remained totally aloof from us all the time. In fact, I only saw him once or twice during the four years that I worked there, and then just very distantly; certainly never to speak to. However, the CFI was someone who I got on with straight away and greatly respected. Though he had been in the RAF during the War, he was fundamentally a pre-war airline pilot.

Right from the beginning though, one thing was obvious; apart from the unsatisfactory pay, this could not be a good steady job for life. The two airline corporations were never sure whether or not they wanted to keep the place going and our security of employment naturally depended upon their requirement for new pilots. With a low seniority number, an instructor at Hamble could be made redundant and sent out into the cold at any time. I kept ears and eyes open in my ongoing search for what might just be the right place for me in the wide world, but aimed during the first two years at The College, to become nicely settled, get my legs well under the table and enjoy the work.

In fact, I did enjoy the work, especially teaching airways and instrument flying, first on Piper Apaches, then on Beech Barons; the latter most of all, as it was a good powerful aircraft for a light twin. Teaching asymmetric exercises on the Apache could be rather tricky; the type did not exactly have much of a performance on one engine and I always felt that we were on a pretty shaky knife edge when doing single engined circuit work with one feathered. I missed the Varsity with its big powerful Bristol Hercules radials.

Initially, Chipmunks were the type used for the basic part of the training and naturally, that was where I first had to teach. The Chipmunk was just beautiful, but not quite what was thought to be the best way of introducing people to flight deck management and all the things that were necessary for an airline pilot's operation. I loved flying it though, especially doing circuits and bumps. A perfect three point landing on grass in a Chipmunk, always thrilled me, but there was I felt, one big catch to the aircraft. I instructed on them throughout my first winter at Hamble and without a heater, under a heavy cold grey sky, I was often chilled through and through. That was one of the reasons why I was very pleased to be moved onto Apaches, where I taught the advanced side of the course, a civilianised version of the one that I had taught on Varsitys, and again consisting of asymmetric and instrument flying.

The Chipmunks were replaced by Cherokees, an aircraft that at first did seem to me to be totally dreary and characterless, but was obviously very much better for the initial training of students who were to be airline pilots. Right from the word go, an element of flight deck management came into the operation. The happy Chipmunk with its tight little cockpit, minimum of instrumentation and radio, plus a tail wheel undercarriage, could never do the job as well as the Cherokee with its side by side seating and far more sophisticated instrument panel.

This then was the atmosphere in which I began to learn a little about working as a civil pilot. It was probably not the best place to do so, because of the strong ex-service attitude and culture, but I did manage to get some ideas about what went on. Amusing insights into the world of civil aviation also came from local contacts.

We had a wonderful old Scottish family doctor, whose husband had been an Imperial Airways flying boat captain and later, still on flying boats, a captain with Aquila Airways. Dr Janet had a pretty wide knowledge of the ways of civil aviation. She had learned the hard way.

One Sunday I damaged a rib whilst working up a tree in my garden and went to her in agony the next morning, expecting all sorts of wonderful treatment plus a sick note for my employers. I had never damaged a rib before.

When I walked in and told her about it, Dr Janet just scowled up at me from behind her desk and growled, 'If y'don't fly, y'won't get paid. If y'don't get paid, y'can't buy food and y'children'll starve. Awa w'ye, to work and get airborne.'

Well, she wasn't quite right, we did have sickness benefits by then, but I learnt a bit more about flying from that. I got airborne, and accepted the pain of the broken rib. Also, on two later occasions in my life, when I had damaged a rib, I did not bother to go sick, I just got on with it and went on flying.

Crewroom talk about the pros and cons of the various independent airlines, plus listening to the views of pilots who had been instructors at Hamble, but had moved on as I intended to, seemed to indicate that British Eagle was the one to try for. A friend and I applied and were soon called for an interview. Together we went to the small office which we found in a hanger at Heathrow. However, the whole show was a non-event and a bit of a farce really. We saw the personnel manager, who just asked us about our previous flying experience and when we would be able to start work with Eagle. He told me that I would be going on BAC 1-11's, based at Liverpool, which was not what I wanted. We saw none of the pilot management.

Having listened to our replies, he then picked up the phone to the chief pilot saying, 'I've got two for the 1-11.'

I had not been asked what aircraft I wanted to go on, but had I been, I would have opted for Britannias based at Heathrow, and flying long range. I certainly did not want to move up to Liverpool.

Whilst still on the phone he handed us papers to fill in and sign. My friend and I looked at one another, shook our heads and walked out. Not long after that, British Eagle went bust and ceased operations. I decided that it was best to stay at Hamble and think about it all for a bit longer.

A year later though, it became obvious that it was time to try again. There was much talk about the College of Air Training closing; BOAC and BEA needed fewer new pilots and I found that my instructing was not what it should have been. I had really had enough of it. I did not relate properly to my students anymore and I would easily loose patience with them and perhaps bully them. That was bad.

At the same time, it seemed that apart from myself, a number of the instructors had come to the same decision about leaving, and we often discussed just which airline we actually should try to join. They all seemed to be recruiting just then so we reckoned that we might have a fair chance of getting a job. Besides, it also seemed that Hamble instructors were well thought of by the airlines and with their experience and qualifications, could be considered as future training captains. Privately, that amazed me.

There was little point in us trying to go to either BOAC or BEA where the conditions and pay were by far the best. They wanted younger pilots and the promotion was very slow. Besides, we would be junior to our own students and at our age, with the slow movement up the seniority ladders, we would be unlikely to ever get commands. It seemed to boil down to a choice of two independents, British Caledonian or DAN-AIR. I picked DAN. Together with half a dozen others I was interviewed, properly this time, and offered a place as a first officer on their Comet fleet, based at Gatwick.

The group of us left Hamble towards the end of nineteen seventy and later I realised that that was the moment when I started what was really my apprenticeship to commercial flying and the airline world. At Hamble, I had just been filling in time and looking around. Now I found that I was in an entirely unfamiliar environment. I had masses to learn and soon realised that during all my previous flying there had been very little that might really prepare me for operating a Comet on airline work, even as a lowly co-pilot in the right hand seat. But having decided that that was where I was going, I found that I was keen to learn, and do a good job. I just had to knuckle down, work hard, watch what went on, learn in every way that I could and get on with it.

During the interview, one of the points made by the Fleet Manager who conducted it, was that a command would soon be available as the Company was expanding. I was even shown what my seniority number would probably be and how I would move up with the airline's expansion plans. But it did not take me long to realise that though I had the flying hours, I was a long way from having the standard of experience that was required of a captain in that company. I recognised the Comet fleet manager; he and I had been at school at Pangbourne Nautical College together, which was probably why I got the job. He had been very senior to me then and now it was exactly the same again.

All except one other of my colleagues from Hamble were accepted and the first thing that we had to do was to get the Comet on our licences. Straight away we started the ground school part of the course which was conducted near the railway station at Horsham, in a big old warehouse. This had been converted by DAN into the company training centre, and was crammed full of classrooms built all along the sides, with the middle taken up by a mock up escape slide and the Comet simulator. Together with many other pilots, I would grow to intensely dislike that simulator, which had been the original one owned by BOAC when they first introduced the Comet 4.

The ground school course which would lead up to the ARB exam, was run by one of the current company flight engineers. He was a character and told us mainly about the people who we would meet, those that should be avoided and those who were friendly and helpful, the captains who were good to fly with and those who had the opposite reputation. To this was added a vast amount of company politics, culture and gossip. Also of course, there were blow by blow details of his conquests amongst the cabin staff. He had a sense of humour, his stories were always good to listen to, often with useful points to remember, but apart from that, he did manage to teach us something of the technicalities of the Comet. However, these usually left me totally muddled. I had never before had to deal with the intricacies of a large four engined aircraft, and found this one incredibly difficult to understand. In fact, judging by the remarks made by the others, when we swatted together in our cheap pub accommodation, I think that all of us on the course felt just as I did.

All the ARB exams that I taken before, in order to get an aircraft on my licence, were for much smaller types and though swatting was certainly required, there was never any real difficulty about it and I had become imbued with false sense of it all being very easy. Here, with DAN, the Comet was difficult.

I have often heard it said that the degree of complication which goes with any type of aircraft, varies considerably from operator to operator. You can make any aeroplane complicated, if you want to. That I think, was certainly so with the Comet. Subsequently over the years, I listened to many pilots who had flown it in some form or another in various different organisations, both civil and military. Across the spectrum, their opinions differed very widely, some describing it as an easy, simple aircraft, others as a very complicated one. I think that DAN's old, deeply imbedded training hierarchy did tend to lean heavily towards the complicated side of things.

In the RAF one tends to think that the way a particular aircraft is operated is the only way to do so. In the RAF's case it has all been worked out before release to the Service, when the testing takes place at Boscombe Down, and that's that; there is no other way to operate it. Not so in the civil world; all the various owners have their own way of doing things, their own standard of flight deck operation, and these can differ totally from one company to another with the same basic type of aircraft.

A number of us had managed to find a dormitory room in a pub near Horsham, where we were able to live uncomfortably, but reasonably cheaply. Because I was going to be based at Gatwick, the company would pay me no allowances as the training set up was all in the local area. I knew nothing about airline allowances at that time, so had no clues as to how I might fiddle anything. I paid the pub rates and chuckled at being in a dormitory for the first time since I had been a cadet pilot in the RAF, on initial training over twenty years before.

All of us it seemed were pretty much bewildered by the Comet's various systems, but we had to learn all about each one of them and know them perfectly for the exam; more so of course, in order to enable us to operate the aircraft afterwards in a way that would satisfy the trainers. The electrics floored me; other people were having terrible difficulties with the hydraulics, which were the easiest as far as I was concerned. Every evening we sat round in circle on the floor in our dormitory and discussed what we had been unable to understand. Then we asked each other questions and thrashed out the answers.

This worked for us and paid off. We managed all right, far more so than if we had studied on our own, but with us was a pilot from British Midland who was trying to switch airlines. He found the standard that was required to be all too much for him, and soon dropped out completely, having to ask his previous employers for his old job back. He went through a bad time for some weeks, but eventually managed to rejoin them. I was learning more about civil aviation all the time. DAN-AIR required a very high standard, and the airline world was not all honey and roses. I wondered about my own future.

All of us did pass the ARB exam on the Comet, though two of my colleagues only got partial passes on their first try.

The next phase of the course was the simulator training. The monster sat just outside our classroom and because of the stories told about it, for me at least, had formed another of the many objects of dread, which had to be faced on this course. Its presence could never be ignored. When in operation, it creaked and groaned all the time and had provided a continual background noise to our classroom work, whilst the course ahead of us were being put through that part of the syllabus and line pilots endured one or other of their regular six monthly checks.

When DAN bought the aircraft, they acquired the simulator from BOAC as well. As far as simulators went, it was a marvellous antique and worthy of a place in any aviation museum. Unlike modern simulators though, it had to be operated without any movement. A movement system worked by vast great cranky pistons was built into it, but this took so much electric power that on the one occasion when it had been tried, it was said to have fused the whole electrical system in Horsham town, so creating an unpopular power cut.

I think that we had about a dozen sessions in the simulator and the first two or three were quite an adventure without much stress, as they were really just familiarisation. The stress, for me, built up in a great wave after that, and was always there when instrument rating renewals and other checks had to be taken on it later. Though normal airline routine, I did feel it as something of a dark cloud that hung over life on the Comet fleet.

Whatever it may be, big or small, fighter or airliner, the cockpit or flight deck of an aircraft that you are just beginning to convert onto is a complete mystery, but must soon become totally familiar so that you know exactly where everything is and can reach out and operate any control or switch when blindfolded. Certainly not so to start with; at that point it's all a bit of a muddle and you have absolutely no idea where anything could possibly be. Also, if you are like me, you don't really understand just what it's all about anyway, when you do operate it. Well, that is one of the things that simulators are for. You can get to know exactly what and where everything is and how to work it, plus all the many drills and emergency procedures that go with the operation of any aircraft. This must happen before you actually have to face it for real and the company has to carry the cost of non-revenue training flying. Naturally enough any airline's accountants loath flying that is non-revenue.

The Varsity had been the nearest thing to a large aircraft that I had faced before and the Javelin the most complicated, but their operation and cockpit layouts seemed basic and simple compared with the Comet and its systems. I was taken unawares by the Comet and the attitude of the training captains, who I had to face. The whole environment was utterly different from anything that I had experienced in the RAF. I had to sit back and take a hard look at things and work out just how I would cope with it all. It was also obvious by now that my age did not make things any easier for me in this completely new environment, and that I took a great deal more time than I had in the past, when trying to learn and assimilate anything that was strange to me. I found things were difficult, and I knew that I had to face a lot of hard work through the rest of that Comet conversion course. Tests were not easy to pass and generally that was the way that things tended to remain during the two years or so that I was on the Comet fleet.

By now I had sorted out the hydraulic system in my own mind and it had started to make some sort of sense, but the electrical system continued to be completely beyond my understanding. We were each given a schematic diagram of it and this had to be carried whenever we were flying or in the simulator. Electrical emergencies came thick and fast; training captains loved them and when they happened, the diagram had to be got out, interpreted and the fault diagnosed and corrected. I did not enjoy those sorts of situations at all.

At the end of the allotted hours on the simulator, the training captains reluctantly decided that I could graduate to base training on the aircraft itself. That was a great relief as I felt that I had come nowhere near reaching the sort of standard, which I would have considered acceptable, had I been in their shoes. In fact, I think that they just gave me up as a bad job and looked with great pity upon any captain that I might have to fly with on the line, if I did happen to graduate at the end of the course.

The Company base training was carried out at Teeside Airport near Darlington, which I had known years before as RAF Middleton St George. I had very happy memories of the place from the days when I had done my Meteor conversion there in 1950. I felt at home, but all that happy feeling was soon shattered when I was actually face to face with the Company's Comet training set up there.

The team, which I would have to face was led by the much respected, but profoundly dreaded, fleet chief training captain. Whenever he had been spoken of by any members of the training staff that I had met so far during my few weeks in the system, I had always noticed that his name had been mentioned with utter awe. He had been an airline pilot during the thirties, some said with Imperial Airways, others said that he had been with the old British Airways. My bet was with Imperial as he had that air about him. During the war, he had been with BOAC. He fitted into the picture that I had formed from what I had read, and what I had heard when people described Imperial captains and their attitude to lesser mortals in the flying business. I knew definitely that I was by a long way, a far lesser mortal.

Apart from all that, I was going through, what to me was a fantastic experience. For the first time I had got my hands on a large four engined aircraft and was learning how to fly and operate it. I was actually getting four engined time in my logbook, and was proud of it, even though I did find that the whole procedure was something that had a side to it which I had never really expected or in fact, seriously thought much about.

My brain was slow and when emergencies were thrown at me, I was slow to deal with them. There were so many things to remember. The fuel system was complicated, and trying to remember the sequence in which to use the various tanks whilst booster pumps were failing was to me a major operation in itself. Then, when training captains were creating emergencies there were the workings of the impossible electric system, and the ins and outs of the hydraulics, all of which had to be dealt with at the same time as trying to fly the aircraft round the circuit or through the instrument pattern.

It all made me feel that I was very much a beginner, a sprog again and not a reasonably experienced pilot in my own right. I felt very small, but I coped and was deemed fit to go ahead to the next phase, which was line training.

Not all of us made the grade. Two of us did not satisfy the trainers and were given their marching orders. They were out without a job, and having failed such a course, it would be unlikely that they might be accepted by any other leading airline. One was a very experienced flying instructor, who had been a colleague at Hamble. He had a disagreement with the chief trainer over some point or other and was quietly taken aside and told that it was obvious that airline flying was not his bent. I quailed in my boots and expected to be told the same thing at any moment.

I remembered Dr Janet's words, 'If y'don't fly y'won't get paid and y'can't buy food.

But somehow I was accepted.

In fact, years later when I was a 1-11 skipper and was positioning an aircraft up to Teesside one early morning, I carried some Comet trainers and course students, who were led by that same ex-Imperial Airways pilot who I had been so much in awe and dread of some years before. He came up onto the flight deck and chatted away to me in a very cheerful, friendly manner, completely as an equal, one captain to another. I was amazed. It was a side to him that I had never imagined, but then I was not in the fleet which he had responsibility for and my operation of the BAC 1-11 was not something that really concerned him directly.

It was a nasty winter morning with low cloud and snow on the runway, plus many other problems which had to be dealt with. Luckily, judging from his attitude, it did not seem that I was committing any ghastly sins in his eyes.

Line training was the fourth and final phase in the Comet training. This was it, now I was flying on the routes, but flying with a training captain, whose job it was to teach me all that a first officer had to do. There was masses to learn and to do, and naturally to begin with, I was quite unable to get it done in time and most of what I did get done, I got wrong in some way or another.

For the first three or four flights, an experienced first officer supervised my flight planning, and the way that I carried out the masses of checks. He then sat in the right hand seat for the take-off and landing whilst I had to occupy the jump seat behind. During the cruise, he stood behind me and endeavoured to teach me what to do. During the turn round at our destination, an airport which might be in some far corner of Europe or North Africa but was most often in Spain, he would take me round, showing me all that had to be done, such as checking the return flight plan and getting the met. Of course, at that stage there was nothing like enough time to do it all. Everything seemed to be a muddled rush from the moment that I reported to crewing at Gatwick, to the moment that I went off duty after the flight.

When visiting the met office, all that the met man had to say about the weather had to be assimilated and later passed on accurately to the captain. The return flight plan had to be checked in the flight planning office and sometimes a new one had to filed as the original one that had been filed at Gatwick had not got through, had been lost, or had to be altered. Then all the pre-flight checks had to be completed, so that everything was ready when the captain came onto the flight deck and took his seat. We carried a flight engineer on Comets and happily the outside check was in his department, otherwise that would have been my job as well.

By the time that we got clearance to start engines, and then had the business of going through all the checks that were linked with that procedure, I would usually be in a complete muddle. After that, as we taxied out, there would be the pre-takeoff checks and the business of reading back the air traffic clearance, word for word. Not only that, but it had to be understood perfectly and the route noted correctly from the charts, with the relevant beacons tuned in and set up on our radios. Any sort of mistake, however minor could cause danger, and was just not acceptable. It could lead to some ghastly accident.

It always seemed to me that line training captains had a pretty difficult time. They not only had to do their own job perfectly, but they had to keep at least half their attention locked on whatever it was that the first officer under training had to do, making sure that he did not miss anything and that everything that he did do, was correct. I'm sure that I must have caused quite a lot of problems at that stage, but I did not know enough about it to realise just how much of a problem I might have been. However, at last I must have been considered acceptable and was put up for my final check, which I somehow managed to pass. I was let loose on the line.

When you all meet up in the briefing room before a flight, if the captain does not know the first officer and has not flown with him before, he will obviously ask this person who is going to sit beside him in the right hand seat for the coming day or night or whatever it may be, all about himself.

From my own experience later when I had a command, I know just how the unfortunate captain must have felt that morning, when I told him that it was my first unsupervised flight, that I was a complete new boy, and had only just been let loose on the line as a qualified first officer. His heart would have crashed down to his boots somewhere. He would never be able to totally relax and trust me. He would always have to keep at least one eye, and half his attention on everything that I did, when he really needed to give his full attention to what he himself had to do.

It was now the early spring of 1971 and the holiday season was just starting. There was a never diminishing hoard of holidaymakers to be piled into the back of our Comets and flown south to the sunshine. They flew to Palma in their masses, to Alicante and Malaga, to Barcelona, Ibiza, Gerona and the Canaries. There were also those whose holiday destination was Athens, Rhodes or Crete, or perhaps Rimini or Corfu. A few went to Tunis, Tangier or Yugoslavia. Other destinations were in Romania and Bulgaria, where we had to operate under Eastern block regulations after crossing the Iron Curtain.

These people left from Gatwick, from Newcastle, from Birmingham, and from Manchester, plus Teesside, Glasgow or Bristol at all hours of the day or night.

Then the company had a contract to carry forces families to and from Cyprus. These were almost always night flights and the longest straight, there and back flights that we made on the Comet fleet. They were long never ending nights which dragged and dragged; about five hours flying either way.

I came to know all those airports equally well, their departure and arrival routes, their layouts and where to find all the necessary offices such as met and flight planning; which of the met forecasters would give a good estimation of the coming weather en-route and our destination, or which ones to ignore. I learnt who were the helpful people in flight planning offices or traffic offices, and who were the ones that you could expect nothing from.

Most important; I got to know and to make friends with the company staff on the ground, both in the UK and overseas, the engineers, the station managers, the traffic officers, the check in desk people, anyone there who might be of help one day and could give me tips on how things ran on their patch. I made genuine friends with many of them and realised that the old RAF culture of relationships and barriers, officer/other rank, aircrew/groundcrew, was totally artificial. In fact you were all on the same side, working for exactly the same goal and it was stupid to create differences between you. Again, later on when I was a captain, I found that these friendships that I had made, really paid off and helped my work all along the line.

I also learnt just what the various airport hotels were like, where to eat, and how best to pass the time before the next flight, if possible without getting involved in the inevitable aircrew parties. These seemed to run continually in all the hotels where we stayed and I saw how the booze habits, which had sometimes been part of life in the Services had ruined a few people.

You could be greeted at the desk, when checking into some hotels for a stop over by, 'Hullo Captain, nice to see you again. The aircrew party seems to be in Room 123.'

There you would meet pilots and crew members from many of the charter airlines, sometimes old RAF friends, who you had not seen for years. But with the next flight in mind, I soon learnt that you had to mind the booze angle and be sensible, so I avoided being dragged into such sessions.

Throughout the summer, we would generally be rostered for flights which covered long weekends, and would have to work out of one or other of the of the airports round Britain where the holiday flights originated. Usually we would travel to our starting point on the Thursday afternoon, be it Glasgow, Tees Side or perhaps Bristol; then be ready to take over an aircraft when it arrived sometime during the night, or the next day.

Sometimes we would start the ball rolling from Gatwick and hand over to another crew in the middle of the night at Newcastle, or perhaps Manchester on our return from such places as Palma or Alicante.

Sometimes we would operate through a series of different airports in Britain and so spend the various rest periods between flights in a new hotel each time. This would sometimes be for just for one day between night flights, sometimes for part of a day or night, but hardly ever for a normal night's rest. Whatever time of day though, we would have to try and sleep and be fit for the next effort. Regardless of our roster, we always carried our night stop kit with us and never left it in the hotel. There might be weather diversions, unserviceabilities, or sudden changes to our roster. You never knew for sure; you had to ready for any change, and to go anywhere. On one occasion, a sudden change resulted in me ending a duty period in Djibouti, French Somaliland, after routing through Rotterdam and Athens.

The two crews, one arriving, the other taking over the aircraft and departing, would usually meet in passing and then after normal greetings, there would be a standard conversation.

From the departing crew: 'How's the aircraft, what's its serviceability like.' 'What are the delays like in Palma.' 'What's the thunderstorm situation like round Alicante.' 'Where are you going next.'

From the arriving crew: 'Where are you off to. There's a large group of thunderstorms blocking the way into Gerona. Number three engine is running slightly hotter than the others, but well within limits. Needs watching. Malaga had bad delays, but they seem to be thinning out as the evening goes on. There was congestion and we had an en-route hold over France.'

There would inevitably be long delays in the daytime. These were especially bad in Palma where sometimes twenty or thirty aircraft could be waiting for clearance to start up for their destinations in Britain, Germany or Scandinavia. It was normal to be delayed for at least two hours, so everyone's temper was strained to point of bursting.

You had to board the passengers in case you suddenly got clearance to start at once, but the girls had no way of keeping them amused and the cabin of the Comet, with no air conditioning, could become unbearably hot. The cabin crew could not serve the one meal that was carried. If they did, it was sure to mean that suddenly you would be told to go. Everything would have to cleared up and secured in a rush, so passengers would be furious when their unfinished food trays were grabbed from them and dumped in a rubbish bag.

Some captains made fools of themselves by being very rude over the radio to the Spanish air traffic controllers. The delays were not their fault and they could do nothing about them. I developed a great respect for Spanish ATC, and vowed never to grumble at them when I had a command.

After these weekend wandering periods, we would normally get back to our main base at Gatwick on the Monday or Tuesday, sometimes bringing an aircraft in there, sometimes travelling the length and breadth of Britain from where we had completed the last flight of our schedule. We then had two days off at home, but our days off were very seldom at weekends, which was difficult for families. That was when people wanted to travel on holiday, so that was when we worked. This was an entirely new sort of life to me, one that I had never really envisaged, but I coped and began to learn just how to be an acceptable first officer. I got to know the various captains and what they would expect me to do and just what I might expect from any particular one of them.

Most of the Comet captains were very senior in the company and had been with it for a long time. They differed very much one from another. Some were unapproachable and overbearing. Some treated you as an absolute menial, just wanting you to tune the radios, read the checklists and raise or lower the undercarriage, never giving you a leg to fly yourself. Some expected you to buy them gallons of whiskey during stopovers. One or two expected you to do everything, flying and co-pilot work, whilst they slept or sat at the navigation table reading their newspaper. Some were superb and worked as one of the team, giving you leg and leg about. Some became good friends. From all of them, I learnt a lot.

From the friends I learnt a great deal about company culture and what a captain really had to do behind the scenes. I learnt about the funds which he carried and just what they had to cover. I learnt what perks the captain had and what fiddles would be accepted, how to fill in the accounts forms that were needed for each flight, and how to make them balance. I learnt all the things that a captain needs to know but are not taught officially, though are very much a part of the system.

However, one thing became obvious to me. It was most unlikely that I would ever get a Comet command. I did not fit in to what was required by the hierarchy, but I had no intention of remaining a professional first officer all my life, as I saw some people do. I needed somehow to find a fleet where I could put into effect all that I learnt whilst on Comets, maintaining the very high operating standard and flight deck management that had been instilled in me whilst flying them. I could then take stock of things and again work out what was best for me.

After about two years on the line on Comets, it all fell into place. I was offered a command on the HS 748, which was considered by many to be beneath consideration. 748 captains hardly rated as members of the captains' hierarchy and such people were not really to be noticed, certainly not to be treated as members of the club.

That did not worry me. I grabbed the chance and went for it without a second thought. I got onto the captains' ladder with a captain's number.

But I looked back at the Comet fleet with great respect. It was there that I learnt what was meant by being an airline pilot and what it really entailed; how one must continuously maintain a very high standard of operation and be totally in control of all that might go on, thinking far ahead, and being ready for anything that might occur. I learnt just what flight deck management meant and everything else that was part of an aircraft's safe operation. I tried to put all that into practice for as long as I went on flying.

11.   The Islands, the Link and the Oil

I quickly became part of the 748 operation and I felt on top of the world in the new job. As it was just a twin-engined turbo-prop, I received only a minimal pay rise over that of a Comet first officer, but it did not bother me at all at the time. Most important, I was now on the captains' seniority ladder. In the airline world that is always an important place to be, and means that in years to come there is the chance of a much higher salary as you progress through different types.

The 748 and I fitted together straight away. Here was a good working aircraft, which handled well and was powered by two superb Rolls Royce Dart, turboprops. The Dart was virtually a development of the Derwent in its basic design; a pure jet engine which I well remembered from my Meteor days. A number of alterations had been made, which con-verted it to a turboprop, but basically the works were the same; the power that it produced was just transmitted differ-ently.

The conversion work was easy. The Comet had taught me what was required on such a course as run by an airline, so I had no difficulty in learning all that was needed, and under-standing the systems. There was no simulator, which cheered me, and the flying was all well taught and interesting, with a good training captain who was easy to work with. I enjoyed the whole thing.

DAN-AIR used the 748 for scheduled services round the British Isles, having a number of bases to cover the various routes that were operated about the country. Initially I was officially based in Newcastle, a long way from home, but the service from there connected with Bournemouth, which made travelling either way, easy enough. Whenever I needed either to go home or back to work, I would just hop on the next aircraft which was going in the direction in which I wanted to travel, and cadge a ride. Then, after just a few months, I managed to switch my base to Bournemouth, at the southern end, so that problem was solved anyway.

The service, which we flew between Newcastle and Bournemouth airport, Hurn, was known as the Link City, and each early morning and evening at times suitable for business commuters, an aircraft departed from either end and bus stopped its way up or down Britain. There would usually be three sectors and depending on the day of the week, the stops would be at Birmingham, Bristol, Cardiff, Manchester, Liverpool or Tees Side. Scheduled time on the ground was always just ten minutes. Until one got on top of the situation and learnt all the tricks of the trade, these short sectors, short turn round times and a very necessary reputation for always being on time, meant that the whole thing could be something of a rush. I soon found that when I had learnt the tricks, the operation all fitted together neatly and became just routine.

From Newcastle we would often carry on to some scheduled destination in Norway, usually Kristiansand, but otherwise, depending on the day off the week, Bergen or Stavanger, before returning to Newcastle, ending our duty period and flopping half exhausted into the airport hotel. Then after an off duty rest period, we would operate it all in the opposite direction, ending up in Bournemouth once more.

At the Bournemouth end, there were of course, the Channel Islands, Jersey and Guernsey. Especially over summer weekends, the flights to them, seemed to form something like continuous motion; backwards and forwards, backwards and forwards, all day long, flying to and fro' across the Channel.

Many pilots have told me that they would find short haul work like this to be nothing less than deadly boring, and initially I expected to feel a little like that myself in many ways. I had wanted to get into an aeroplane and fly for hours, watching the world slide by underneath; then to arrive at a destination in some distant country, preferably on the far side of an ocean. I wanted a continual variety in my destinations, certainly not the same ones day after day. Bus stopping flights, usually much less than an hour in duration, were not really my idea of how flying should be, but now that I was actually operating those short sectors; the same ones all the time, I did find a fascination in it.

At each of the places where I landed, I would see familiar faces standing and waiting every time that I taxied up to the ramp and stopped my engines. Then they would wave and smile, before coming up onto the flight deck, bringing a cheerful welcome and the latest news, as well as all the paper work. They soon became individual people, who then often became real friends. These friendships remained firm for all the five years that I flew those routes on the 748. Then later, when I was on the 1-11, and landed at many of the same airports, they continued to remain just as firm.

As for the flying, it never really bored me. Over the years I came to know every trick of the weather at the various airfields and just what I might expect in practice when I read a forecast. When a weather state was reported to me, apart from the official code that they all came in, I could link it to the office or person who was making it and I learnt to understand exactly what the figures would mean in practice. I could ring the agent's duty officer at a destination such as Jersey and know exactly what he was thinking when he looked out of the window and assessed the weather. His years of experience on the spot would tell me all that I needed to know when it was marginal.

'You've got a chance Mike, get going as soon as you can,' or, 'No it's no good, pointless to try.'

The verdict from the local, who knew just how the weather moved, meant more than all the official reports and forecasts which came to the office.

Flights to the Channel Islands were easily my favourites, and on a summer Sunday I would sometimes land at Jersey three or more times during the day's work. Out of Bournemouth, it was usually about forty minutes from chock to chock; slipping out to sea past Christchurch, and then picking up the airway in order to cross over Alderney, before heading, perhaps for Guernsey, perhaps for Jersey. I can't say that I was able to look down and recognise the individual waves in the Channel, but I knew all the streaks showing tidal movement near the coasts

Apart from the sunshine which the Channel Islands are always associated with, I remember Guernsey for its howling crosswinds in pouring rain and turbulence, with cloud right down to the minimum legal base. With only a step down radar approach available, getting in there could sometimes be very like hard work.

As a contrast, the main problem with Jersey that sticks in my memory, was the thick sea fog in the spring. It would come rolling in off the Atlantic and put an impenetrable blanket over the whole island, which could keep it below landing minima, sometimes for days on end. This was when the locals' knowledge was especially useful. They knew just what in the way of slight windshifts or slight alterations in its density, might indicate a move in the fog blanket. The phone would go in our Bournemouth ops room.

'Get airborne right away. You've just got a chance, but it'll clamp in again in an hour or two.'

There were always numbers of aircraft waiting on mainland airfields for the fog to clear, so you had to get overhead the Jersey radio beacon as soon as you could. If not, you would be a long way down the line, sitting in a holding pattern whilst others ahead of you landed. By the time it was your turn to make an approach, the fog would often have rolled in again. Too bad; back to Bournemouth with the passengers getting more and more fed up, and having a wasted a lot of company money because of the flying time and fuel, all for nothing.

As time went on, the Link City routes became more and more well known to me and the countryside over which I flew was as familiar as a back yard. The whole operation was one of teamwork and I felt that I was almost part of a family. There were not many of us doing the job, Bournemouth was just a small base, so we flew together as crews time and time again, also becoming good friends. We had regular customers, who the cabin staff would welcome aboard as familiar people, not just as a bunch of holidaymakers bound for hotels in Spain. The whole operation had a point to it and we felt that we were doing a good job. What is more, we always flew with high passenger loads, and that is something that is cheering for airline crews. Flying empty aircraft around is a miserable business. The whole operation was useful and I was happy doing it. But I was soon to become involved in something very different.

At that time, the search for oil in the North Sea was just starting to get properly under way and the huge support operation, which would be needed to maintain it, together with the production that would result, was beginning to take shape. I did not know it right away, but this would open up entirely new flying experiences for me and make my life on the 748 fleet far more interesting.

The base for the exploration was Aberdeen and already the associated masses of oil related industrial development was starting to change the face of the whole area. DAN-AIR management sensed that there would be a lot of money to be made there and they were keen to get into the oil scene right at the beginning. Opportunities of which they could take advantage, would keep opening up as the industry expanded, and they wanted to be on the spot and ready for them whenever they appeared. Other airlines had similar thoughts and there was a rush to get any contracts that were available. I had already flown a number of oil related charters between Aberdeen and Stavanger in Norway, but that was only just scratching the surface of the whole thing.

The initial contract that DAN-AIR landed, was with Conoco, one of the first of the oil companies that were starting to drill in the North Sea. Their rig crews had to be flown into Sumburgh, the small airport at the southern tip of the Shetland Isles, which soon became a major forward base with a seemingly ceaseless flow of aircraft movements. From there they would be taken out by helicopter to the drilling platforms and likewise, after the helicopters had made the swap, the returning crews would be flown back from Sumburgh to Aberdeen, so returning them to dry land at the end of their two weeks stint on the rigs.

Masses of helicopters were based in Aberdeen and operated directly from there out to the closer rigs, but their range was too short for them to be able to reach the more numerous platforms that were situated far to the north. A forward base was required for the northern operations and Sumburgh fitted the bill. From there, helicopters could reach even the most distant of the rigs. These aircraft were mainly S 61's, the civil version of the Naval Sea King, but a few Wessex were also used when smaller parties had to be moved. Bristows and the helicopter division of British Airways were the companies that first came north and set up that side of the operation. They were the ones operating when I first came on the scene.

Such an operation was a completely new aeronautical experience for airlines in Britain at that time, and little was really known about the ins and outs of it. People soon learnt however, and it was not long before it became the main core of the huge oil related flying support work, which went on ceaselessly in the north.

To operate the fixed wing part of the contract, aircraft had to be based at Aberdeen airport. This was Dyce, which had in the past been an RAF station, as well as the regional airport for that part of Britain. Initially the place was swamped with more aircraft than it had ever seen before at one time, and more movements than it had ever dreamt of having to cope with. It was a happy little country airport, very like Bournemouth in those days, where everybody knew everybody else and worked together as friends. Apart from the British Airways schedules to and from London, there were the Logan Air flights which covered the Highlands and extended to the Western Isles. Then there was the usual flying club, which in this case seemed to be a thriving operation, their Cessnas always going round and round the circuit. As far as the RAF went though, there was just the Aberdeen University Air Squadron remaining. The Auxiliary squadron which had been based there with its Vampires, had suffered the axe, and been disbanded a few years before.

Now what had been a small country airport, was to become a seething mass of helicopters, oil flights into Sumburgh, business aircraft from across the world and vastly increased schedules. Somehow it coped.

The type of aircraft that could do this work in the North had to be rugged, and able to take off and land on short runways in cross wind conditions far higher than were normally found during line flying operations in other parts of Britain. The forty eight seat, Avro 748, was the type that came nearest to being the ideal aeroplane for the job. Also there were a number available in the UK at the time and later, DAN-AIR bought seven more from Argentina.

Another type that came to the North was the ancient DC 3. This was another place where that evergreen aircraft could play an important role and where there was plenty of work for it supporting the search for oil. The Handley Page Herald, under the colours of British Midland also put in an appearance, and naturally, the magnificent Viscount was on the scene as well, being operated not only by British Airways, but also by Alidair.

In October 1974, DAN-AIR's involvement started and our fleet training captain took a 748 to Aberdeen. He began the flying with just the one initial aircraft that was required for the contract with Conoco and in so doing, first checked out the route and then covered the normal line captains who would work there, on their first flight into Sumburgh. At Bournemouth we had been told that we would not become involved as we were fully occupied with our every day normal work and that was it for us. However, for no apparent reason, things suddenly change and I did become involved.

Just as it was getting dark, one misty autumn evening, I was in our ops. room at Hurn with another skipper, George. Together with our crews, we had just finished a routine day's work going round the Channel Islands and up and down the Link City. We were about to go home, when the phone rang. As was often the case, it was Nobby our crewing officer, and he asked for the other skipper. I was all right, I was not getting a roster change; there was nothing for me to bother about, I thought.

George spoke into the phone forcefully, "No certainly not, I'm never going there".

I heard Nobby's answer, which was equally forceful. "Yes you are, a line captain has to go there straight away, be checked into Sumburgh, and take over from the training captain in order to start the operation rolling".

There then followed the sort of discussion that often occurs between crewing and pilots when a roster change is required. It was obvious that George had no intention of letting anybody send him to the far north, for whatever the reason might be or however short the length of time. He was happy to be well dug into the everyday, routine life that we led at our Bournemouth base.

I sensed that there was something new in the wind and as ever, I was stupid enough to volunteer for the unknown. I never really did learn to avoid volunteering like that, and in consequence, regularly got myself into difficult situations.

I grabbed the phone from George and said, "I'll go Nobby".

"Right", he said, "Passenger to Newcastle on the Link in the morning, then on to Aberdeen by train".

24 hours later, the train stopped on the approach to Aberdeen station in the way that trains, for reasons best known to themselves, often do just before reaching stations. The smell of the kipper smokeries in the still, cold foggy, evening air was a smell that I'll never forget. It's now the smell that reminds me, above all others, of Aberdeen, but I still like kippers.

Aberdeen airport was a few miles to the North of the city. The Skean Dhu, a new hotel, whose owners hoped to take advantage of the oil rush, had just been opened there. I took a taxi out to it and checked in. Even in the dark it looked new and prefabricated, and had that unfinished, impermanent appearance that buildings put up in a hurry in such places and under such conditions often do. I think it always remained like that, but I stayed there many times over the years and ceased to notice that kind of detail. It could never be a home from home, but it became the next best thing. It was full of pilots working on the oil, and remained so as long as I knew it. I met old friends, some of whom I had often not seen for many years and then perhaps in far distant corners of the earth. Parties soon develop under such circumstances. They did that night.

I was supposed to report to John, the training captain, but he had not appeared in the bar that evening, and by the time that I remembered, he was well asleep and not at all pleased to be woken by a knock on his door in the middle of the night. He told me to meet him at some ghastly hour in the morning, out at the portakabin which served as our ops room.

I did so. I remember a cold, clear autumn morning, which was just starting to show the first signs of the dawn, but there was none of the sleet or snow, which I later came to know so well in that part of the world. John was not particularly friendly when he arrived for work, but I had not really expected him to greet me with open arms. It was very early in the morning and I had woken him up at a very uncivilised hour the night before.

Our passengers were led out to us across the ramp from the wooden airport terminal building, and came aboard, up the steps. They looked dreadful, and the massive hangovers that accompanied them, were only too obvious. They reminded me of merchant seamen who had just been signed on to a particularly hard ship and had made the most of their last night ashore before going away for a two year voyage. That of course was just the background from which many of these rig workers actually came. Many seemed to me to be the descendants of the old merchant seamen who had worked the great windjammers round the Horn, and whose fathers had been the targets of the U-boats in the Battle of the Atlantic. Now they had just signed on in Aberdeen, only this time it was to work for two weeks, out on an oil rig in the North Sea, not aboard some tramp steamer bound for the ends of the Earth.

I acted as John's co-pilot on the flight North into Sumburgh, so that I could learn about the route. He was rather silent throughout, but I could hardly blame him for that. As soon as we had unloaded the rig workers, we took off again and I flew the aircraft, doing a few circuits and familiarising myself, under John's guidance, with the place and the local area round about.

My efforts seemed to satisfy him, so we landed again and had breakfast in the shack, which served as a terminal building. There we waited for the helicopters to return with the rig crews that we were to take back to Aberdeen. They would sign off and have time ashore until they had to sign on again for their next work period. Their pay on the rigs was said to very good.

The moment that we landed back at Aberdeen, John said, 'that's it lad,' and shot off into town to catch a train home to Bournemouth. He had had enough of the north, it was not his sort of place, and so with just my first officer I was left alone for a day or two. We held the fort there until Nobby worked out a roster and we were relieved, so ensuring that some organisation fell into place. But, we were the first line captains working for DAN-AIR on oil support in the North, and I have always been a bit pleased about that.

It was not long before the company set up a base and stationed crews permanently at Aberdeen. That never happened to me, I was never posted there permanently, but for the next three winters I was quite often sent there on detachment from my base in at Bournemouth, usually for about a week or ten days at a time.

I never went north in the summer. I've never seen the Shetlands except when they were receiving the full blast of winter. It seemed to me that the pilots who were actually based there, were no fools. They always took their leave and went away during the times of the year when the northern weather could be atrocious, and because of it, those such as myself who covered for them, often flew during the worst periods. I could not really blame them, but it never seemed to bother me.

I just made the most of it on the occasions when the weather was wonderful, as it had been on that morning when I first flew into Sumburgh. It had that fantastic clarity that you only find in the north, where the air is absolutely free of the least little bit of pollution and there sometimes seems to be a peculiar light, which you only ever find there. I always felt that it requires the presence of distant ice fields before the necessary reflections come into the sky. The Shetlands are a long way from any ice but when the light is like that, it is easy to imagine. You can see forever and the colours are brilliant.

Straight away, I succumbed to the fascination of the north, whilst enjoying the excitement of the flying, and the gold rush atmosphere that went with the early oil exploration. The 748 was superb for the job and, except for what I considered to be the mere pittance that you got paid for flying it, became one of my favourite aircraft. So, working under these circumstances, I was happy. There was a challenge that was totally absent from my normal everyday tasks down south.

Behind me in the cabin, were two DAN-AIR stewardesses who were normally based in Newcastle, and I did worry about possible nasty situations that might arise when they had to deal with any obstreperous oilies, as the rig workers were called. When these people had just spent a couple of weeks out on a drilling rig in the North Sea, there were some amongst them, who could easily cause trouble. They would be very different from the commuting business people, who flew with us every morning and evening on the routes in the south, most of whom the cabin staff had got to know quite well. But there was no need to worry; DAN girls could cope. If charm did not keep the cabin in order, a clip round the ear would. They were superb.

On the aircraft maintenance side, we had just three engineers when we started the show in Aberdeen. They also had previously been stationed at one of the southern DAN-AIR bases. The leader of these three engineers was Eddie Seagrave and with him were Bud and Ken. They were a wonderful trio, the sort of aircraft engineers, who worked for DAN and together with the aircrew, formed an unbeatable team on the line. Away from the artificial rank barriers in the RAF, DAN engineers taught me just what the relationship between pilots and ground crew really should be. We had no hanger and these three worked in the open in all weathers through the winter. They were often frozen and soaked to the skin, but our aircraft was always ready and fit to fly on time. I wonder if the DAN-AIR senior management ever realised just how much they owed to them, and to all the others like them, who worked on the company aircraft and kept them flying.

Our station manager was Noel, an American. Where he popped up from, I never learnt, but he rapidly became a firm friend. He was a little guy, whose father had been one of the old mail pilots in The States. Noel's flying career had come to an early finish when, as a new co-pilot, he had fallen off the wing of a DC 3, and in so doing had smashed his head. After that, he could no longer pass the medical for his pilot's licence. Noel looked just like Snoopy and could draw hilarious Snoopy cartoons, almost worthy of Shultz himself. Unfortunately his paper work did not come up to the standard that DAN head office required of their base managers, so he did not last very long.

When the airlift into Sumburgh first started, the airport there had not changed since it was first hurriedly built as a wartime fighter strip. Its use had been as a forward base from which to mount shipping strikes, and from where fighters could hunt the Focke Wulf Condors as they passed on their way to and from the Battle of the Atlantic. It had been described to me by a friend, who had been based there for a time, flying Hurricanes during World War Two. His description of the place was pretty much the same as I found it to be in 1974. Very little had changed

Right from the start, the whole business provided me with something of a challenge. We were told that under the contract which DAN had with Conoco, the oilies just had to be got there and back at the designated times. There seemed to be no let out, which would allow for the impossible weather that could occur in the north. No delays were acceptable and I always wondered what would have happened if the weather had ever been really impossible. Aberdeen airport, could be closed by heavy snow falls and Sumburgh, being right on the shore, was prone to the sea fog that sometimes completely blanketed the North Sea, especially in spring time. This was known as the Harr, and when it came in, the visibility at airfields that were affected by it would drop well below minima, then they would stay that way until something such as a change in wind direction, moved it away. On the line, we did our best to comply with the contract, and I wouldn't say that we threw the rulebook out of the window, but at the beginning, we certainly interpreted it in ways to suit our individual selves.

For those pilots, who have never ventured north and away from the mainline airports of the world, Sumburgh as it was then, would definitely appear as something 'different.' Situated behind Sumburgh Head, between two narrow bays, or *voes* as they are called in Shetland, and with hills nearby, it consisted of two, not very long runways, laid across a rough bit of land which was only a foot or two above the high water level of the spring tides. Apart from its use as an airport, this land had for years formed the local, somewhat wild golf course. It still did so and golf balls which suffered from a nasty slice could easily have been a hazard to aircraft.

The two runways were orientated about east-west and southeast-northwest. The southeast end of the latter ran straight into the rising ground at the base of a six hundred foot high hill which then, as a ridge, led on up to Sumburgh Head where there was a lighthouse high on the southernmost point. There was also a VOR with an NDB on the hilltop. About three miles away to the northwest, more high ground rose up, and this could cause a hazard in poor visibility. The east-west runway had better approaches, but was the shorter of the two and had no overruns as both ends were right on the sea's edge. This meant that it could be quite interesting when you were trying to stop your landing roll on icy winter mornings.

The VOR and the NDB had been positioned there as over-flight navigation aids, not as approach aids for the airport, but a published VOR cloud break procedure had been worked out and could be used for a descent over the sea. Circling minima allowed a cloud base of four hundred feet, but I forget what the minimum allowed visibility was then. Anyway, that was usually of little consequence, as either the vis would be well within limits or completely zero in fog. In the latter case, there would be no question about it. However even in rain or drizzle, there would seldom be much of a visibility problem, but high winds and heavy rain rolling in off the Atlantic were common. A low cloud base went with that, but because of the Gulf Stream, even in winter, temperatures were seldom as low as might be expected for that latitude. It was common to have to fly through sleet or snow, but on the ground it soon melted.

In order to help the oil related operations, radar was soon set up on the airfield and a step down approach, which came in from over the sea, was possible when landing on the westerly runway. This runway was the shortest and often not the best to use for landing, so I always had visions of simply rolling on, straight off the far end and into the sea.

A map of the islands showed up well on a 748's weather radar as we flew up from the south. Then, by continuing to use the radar on the way in from the open sea past Fair Isle, we could get down below the cloud, whilst still well out over the water. After that it was not difficult to join the circuit and set everything up for a landing.

All this formed a completely different world from the main airline operations that I was used to, and just the sort of change which really suited me. But, I always wondered just what the hierarchy on the Comet fleet, with their ridged minds in far away Gatwick, would have thought of it all.

If you were landing on the north-westerly runway, you flew north in approach configuration to join the base leg by the hill top. You tucked well into the slope, and slid your starboard wing tip past the lighthouse keeper's office, descending all the time. Then at the right moment, you turned left to line up with the runway and land, touching down near the Sumburgh Hotel, a large imposing, iron grey building which stood at the edge of the airfield

Taking off in the opposite direction was exiting as the six hundred foot hill was straight in front of you. As soon as you were safely airborne and had gained sufficient airspeed, it was necessary to bank hard to the right and climb away, leaving the high ground on your left. It was much steeper than a 748's angle of climb, and you would have had no hope of clearing it if you had flown straight ahead. I think that in later years, the CAA stopped 748 takeoffs from that runway, because of the danger in the event of an engine failure. Ridiculous; I really enjoyed those takeoffs. It was like being on fighters once more.

In really nasty weather, it became possible to do a step down radar approach to the westerly runway, and see the threshold through the rain because of the breakers on the shore. Then, if because of the wind direction, you had to land on the southeasterly runway, you could fly straight ahead after you had broken cloud, and wait until the ADF needle had swung to the left and shown you that you were past the hill. At that point, it was safe to turn left through ninety degrees and fly across the airport below the cloud, then to follow a line of skerries to the south until reaching Horse Island. A right turn there would put you on the downwind leg and you could carry on to Lady's Skerry, at which point, the curve of a bay on the coast appeared through the rain ahead of you. It was easy to recognise, as there was a house with a radio mast right on the beach. You just turned right and followed the shore for the base leg, before sliding inland over a large pond. At that point, there in front of you the runway threshold would appear through the rain. Great, you were down.

Having landed and managed to stop in time, you could see some battered old wooden shacks standing at the south side of the airfield, just as they had during the war. They formed the terminal, but there was never room to park in front of them because of all the aircraft ahead of you, which were also trying to put down and pick up their rig crew passengers. You found a slot and parked way out on a runway that was not in use, which usually meant a long walk in to the shacks, probably in the wind and rain. Inside, I remember it as always being soaking wet, but very warm and steaming, packed full with oil and airline people.

All through the day, a kind of steaming hot, greenish soup was dished up in huge bowls from a food counter at the side. Just what species this soup might be, was difficult to determine, but it was always exactly the same and no other was available. Outside was a large blue metal tank, which was said to contain many years supply of it. I wondered if it was perhaps a left over from the pea soup that was dished out from the galleys on the old windjammers.

During the nineteen eighties, all this was done away with. The whole airport was modernised, and great new permanent buildings created. The gold rush atmosphere became a thing of the past. What another ghastly loss for British aviation heritage.

As an accompaniment to everything at Sumburgh, there was the ceaseless roar and clatter of helicopters going to and from the rigs. On two occasions, I took my life in my hands and got a jump seat ride in a helicopter out to one of those rigs. It was an experience that I would not have missed for anything, but it certainly did not give me an urge to fly helicopters in that work; rather the opposite perhaps!

It usually took about four hours for a helicopter to take your passengers out to their rig and return with the lot that had been relieved. This meant waiting around. If you had two helicopter loads, there would often be a gap between them and so there would be passengers waiting; all adding to the seething mass in the terminal shack.

Booze was strictly forbidden to the oilies from the time that they signed on in Aberdeen to the time they returned, and signed off there two weeks later. The rigs were dry so they headed straight to the nearest bar as soon as they could when they reached land. The bar at the Sumburgh Hotel was just a short walk down the road from the airport and it was often necessary to have the police standing by in order to stop them going down there if for some reason they had to wait for their return flight. Once in the bar, there was no getting them out of it and so aboard the aircraft. You were stuck, and you had a problem.

One day it happened to me and I was out of luck. I had two Wessex loads coming in and the first was back sooner than expected. That meant that its load of oilies, which made up about half my passengers, had to wait. Somehow they made it through the guards. The door of the second Wessex came off in flight, whilst it was still a long way out to sea. It was winter and bitter cold. The passengers aboard it arrived at Sumburgh chilled right through and suffering. They needed to be rushed to Aberdeen in my aircraft at once, with the heat turned fully up. However we were unable to leave. Half of the contracted load, those who had come in on the first helicopter, were in the bar at the hotel and were refusing to leave it. The police were called, but it took a long time to get them away from their source of booze, then into a bus and aboard the aircraft. They had money and the bar had whiskey.

Things did not look too good. Many of them were in a pretty paralytic state and I feared that there would be trouble on the flight back. It looked as if it just might be more than the two girls could cope with. I got the gang boss, who was always known as the tool pusher, to one side out on the tarmac at the bottom of the steps. He was a vast great Texan seemingly twice as tall as me, and had no intention of being talked to in the way that I did.

It had been drummed into us that the word of the oil company that had chartered us, and their employees, was law. The tool pusher pointed out that my days in DAN-AIR were strictly numbered and that he would report me as soon as we reached Aberdeen. He added a bit more to that, rather strongly.

Apart from my job, I feared for my life, but No! I'd won. Later in the bar that night, I heard from a company office worker, who had also been a passenger on the aircraft, how the tool pusher had torn into his men and told them how 'that skipper was mad, real mad.' If any of them misbehaved during the flight, he would see that they never worked on a rig in their lives again and that they would not be paid for their last two weeks' work anyway. My beer in the Skean Dhu tasted extra good after that.

When there was no scheduled oil support work for us, the company tried to arrange extra charter flights, which meant that we were liable to be called out. We therefore had to remain on standby throughout the day, and that would obviously be an absolute bore; normally I hated it. Some occupation had to be found that would allow me to come on duty quickly if I was needed, and where contacting me would be easy.

I had kept my instructor's rating valid, so I did my standby from the cockpit of an Aberdeen Flying Club Cessna 150, usually teaching circuits and bumps. That was fine, I enjoyed myself and collected some extra beer money.

One glorious autumn afternoon, when the colours of the woodland on the hillsides were unbelievable, three taxi drivers turned up at the club and asked for an hour's joy ride round the area. I put them into the Cessna 172 and took them along Deeside. The larches were golden against the dark green of the spruce, with the high moorland purple behind. Lower down, the beeches added to it all with their wonderful colours. In the far distance, the mountain tops had their first sprinkling of snow.

They each tipped me five pounds when we landed. This was 1974; so what's the value of five pounds now? When you get tipped like that by taxi drivers, I think you might consider that you've made a success of your life.

When the oil work first started, everybody with an aircraft tried to get in on the act. The money was good, or so they thought. Some of the pilots were great characters, and George, the skipper of an Air Anglia DC 3, was a friend. He had in the past, when he had first got his licence and was trying to build up his hours, flown a Cherokee Six for a mortician in the States. It meant carrying corpses all over America. At two o'clock one morning, eleven thousand feet over the Allagheny Mountains, the corpse lying in the back, had suddenly groaned loudly and sat up. George put out a MAYDAY call as he thought that it was coming to life. But it was only the gas, which was left in the body, expanding. He was but one of the many great characters flying in the north at that time.

There was a one DC3 sized company in the portakabin next to ours. They hoped that somebody's aircraft would go sick one day and that they could get the sub-charter, thus enabling them to fly and get paid. They never did get any work, and so after a little while, they flew their aircraft back to its southern base near Ipswich and went home. The following night, a gale blew their portakabin over and for weeks afterwards it was left on its side; nobody set it up. The telephone remained connected and from time to time it could be heard ringing in the wreckage.

The old days of gold rush atmosphere and pioneering could not last. DAN-AIR set up a huge oil support operation for which the 748 was an ideal aircraft, and at one time, the company had fourteen of them based in Aberdeen. There also were all the pilots that were needed to crew them. Those of us who had done the first detachments in Scotland and opened the operation, were no longer required. The rulebook was carefully written and adhered to. We would no longer have fitted in.

My last contribution to DAN's work in the oil, was to collect one of the Argentinean 748's that the company bought, and ferry it back to Manchester. It was rotting away on a big military air base at Mendoza in the foot hills of the Andes, about six hundred miles west of Buenos Aries, and the experience of the recovery operation opened up a completely new world for me that I could never otherwise have been involved with.

I left the 748 fleet and flew BAC 1-11's, based at Gatwick. Aberdeen was just another of our numerous scheduled service destinations, and I often flew that route and night stopped in the Skean Dhu. But it was never the same, and most of the old pioneers had left for some other far corner of the world. The atmosphere that I had found there to begin with had vanished, and it was all just normal, highly organised routine airline flying.

Those five years on the 748 were good years and the happiest that I had in the airline world. There was however just one catch to it. 748 pilots were paid peanuts, so as in a year or two I would be approaching the age of fifty when there would be only ten more years to go before retirement, it was obvious to me that I needed to accumulate some money and think about a pension which would not equally be peanuts. That meant jets once more, and I decided that a conversion to the BAC 1-11 was the best way to go about it. It did mean though that I had to say goodbye to Bournemouth airport and all my friends there. Gatwick would be all hassle and straight routine with none of the fun, but I would manage.

12. The BAC 1-11 and Ten Years of Routine

I applied for a transfer onto the BAC 1-11 fleet and was accepted. I don't think that the 1-11 fleet manager quite liked the idea of having a new captain on his fleet, who had not previously been a first officer with him on the type. He was not really very welcoming when he interviewed me.

'You have not had the privilege of having being a 1-11 first officer with us,' he told me rather haughtily. He was someone on whose face, I can never remember seeing a smile.

'That's right Sir,' was all that I could think of to say as a reply, and the unnecessary 'Sir' came out automatically. It showed the state of my mind at the time. Everybody in the company, from the chief pilot down to the tea boy, was usually addressed by their first name. 'Sir' was never normally used.

It had taken me rather aback. On the Comets, there had been a sort of feeling that we were one up on the 1-11. On looking back now I know that it was rather a stupid opinion, but nevertheless one that was often there. A number of the senior and superior Comet captains had been quite open about it, but five years on the 748 had made me look at things a bit differently. I just wanted to get back on jets and the 1-11 was challenge enough. I hoped it would be a step to Boeings and I would get that promotion at sometime in the future. I had the seniority, which with ten more years to go would give me the chance of just such a step up.

First though it was back to the training centre in the big old warehouse near Horsham station. I approached it with much trepidation, and the prospect of all that the course would entail did not thrill me at all. There was however, one bright spot this time. I was moving bases so the company had to pay for my accommodation in the Gatwick area. I did not have to repeat the experience of an uncomfortable dormitory room in a grotty pub.

Much had been done to the training centre since I had last had to endure it. There was even more machinery piled into the areas between the classrooms, which was now dominated by a vast great Boeing 727 simulator. The company had never acquired a 1-11 simulator, for that we would always have to travel to Dublin and use the one belonging to Aer Lingus. I would get to know that Irish training set up very well over the next ten years, and it would always be there at the back of my mind. It formed a black cloud which hung over me, and had to be faced every six months, whenever it was time for either a competency check or an instrument rating renewal.

However, for the 1-11 ground school course, things did seem to be far better organised than they had been when I first joined the company and had been taught about the Comet by a flight engineer who had little idea of instructional techniques, but wanted to earn some extra cash. Now someone who had had ground school instructing qualifications, and had been a pilot in the RAF, was employed full time. It was he who would conduct the whole show and he did so very well. I was able to learn from him, and when it came time for us to take the ARB written exam, we were far better prepared for it. All of us passed.

After that the simulator phase was no worse than might be expected. The 1-11 was not a complicated aircraft and the systems were not difficult to understand, but that did not stop the training captains from trying to push you to your limit as the course went on. I was paired with a first officer, who had only just joined the company after four years on the ground since leaving the RAF, where he had last flown Victors. He had a really difficult time and I tried to put across all the sympathy that I could when things were going really wrong for him. I recognised all his problems and remembered my troubles when I first met civil training and the Comet.

People said that this Aer Lingus 1-11 simulator in Dublin was old and not really very good. Well, compared with the vintage Comet machine in the training set up at Horsham, it was a modern marvel. Though it was in no way up to the standard of present day simulators, it did give you a pretty good idea of the actual aircraft. Things such as the movement almost always actually worked, and the handling was vaguely similar to that of a real aeroplane. I felt that it was giving me a good start and by the time that I got to the 1-11 itself, I would have a fair idea of what to expect. This in fact did prove correct.

Once again it was Tees Side for the base training and I was lucky. The training captain who had the task of putting me through the system was really good and gave me all the help and encouragement that he could. Unlike many airline training captains, he seemed to work just as an instructor should and I could only benefit from that.

I soon began to notice a subtle, underlying difference between the Comet training and that on 1-11. Here I felt that the trainers looked for reasons to pass anybody going through the course, whilst on the Comet I had always felt that they had looked for all the reasons that might be used to fail people. Well, that really was a big benefit as far as I was concerned. More than once, I committed some sin which would have incurred the death penalty on the Comet command course, but here it was just a case of going over it again, understanding it and getting it right. A lot of hard work and concentration was needed, but I did find that I was enjoying the 1-11 conversion, and all that was entailed. Then when I actually passed, I was really right on top of the world.

'You can start the line training next week,' they told me. 'Crewing will contact you and tell you what flights you will be on.'

Oh Gosh! I thought. A jet command was really a possibility, even after five years on turboprops and an unenthusiastic welcome from the fleet manager.

I did commit one ghastly sin during the line training, which I thought would be the end of it all, and so provide me with a ticket straight back to the 748; that is if I was lucky and was not thrown right out of the company. Late one cold, dirty night in Zurich, when I was about half way through the number of training sectors that were required, I got the engine starting sequence wrong. This was stupid of me, and broke the starter motor drive shaft; so that was that until a crew of engineers could be flown in from Gatwick to fix it. Oh, this was the pit; the utter end as far as I was concerned.

The passengers had to be unloaded and found overnight hotel accommodation until the aircraft was made serviceable next morning. A lot of expense was incurred; all because of me. You are not allowed to cause an airline extra expense; it's one of the worst of all the sins, so you have to bare all the consequences.

I thought about it; I couldn't really think about anything else that night. Oh where would I go to look for a job now. Soon I was certain that they would not even allow me back on the 748 after this one. I would surely be out.

Once again I remembered Doctor Janet, 'If y'don't fly, y'won't get paid, and y'can't buy food.' Now there were the school fees as well.

Absolutely to my amazement, the training captain who I was with stood up for me, and the whole thing was overlooked. I was all right. I learnt what it meant when someone said that their relief was unbounded.

Years later, this particular training captain became 1-11 fleet manager, and dug me out of a far deeper hole which I had excavated for myself. I had been extremely rude to a passenger, who turned out to be a friend of the chairman. In fact the passenger deserved it, as he was giving the cabin staff a really bad time. But that's another story.

Line training was purely practical. No simulated emergencies were thrown at you, but you had to show that you knew exactly what was going on and were aware of all possibilities. It was just what you would have to do anyway on any normal flight as you went along, monitoring all the workings of the aircraft, thinking ahead and understanding the airways route which you would have to follow. Then there were all the let down procedures, terrain safety heights and legal weather minima at the destination and alternates, which had to be fully understood. The latest weather, not only for the destination, but for all the possible en-route alternates, was something which had to be continually updated. Add to that the very necessary team work with the co-pilot, the briefings that had to be given to him as part of flight deck management, and it can be seen that there was a lot to keep up with, and stay on top of.

Old friends and acquaintances who have never been airline pilots, but are, or have been pilots in different aspects of the profession, perhaps test pilots or just military with no civil experience, have often talked to me in a very disparaging manner about what they have seen when they have visited an airliner's flight deck. They tell me that the pilots were just sitting there doing nothing. Well, that's exactly the way that it should be. They may have looked as if they were doing nothing, but they were in fact continually monitoring everything that was going on and keeping their fingers on the pulse the whole time. That is what flight deck management is all about; if you are rushing about and in a state, then there is likely to be something wrong, or your flight deck management is very poor indeed.

When it came to my final line check, all went well. The check captain was an old colleague and friend from Hamble. We went to Perpignan, in the south of France near the Spanish border under the Pyrenees, and there was no hassle; it was a happy trip.

I had made it and on paper I was a fully qualified jet captain. I still had a lot to learn, but by then I well knew that a pilot must never stop learning. Almost every day you come up against things that are new to you, and if you don't take note of them all, it is not unlikely that you will soon get your name in the accident reports.

My ambition to get onto Boeings in due course, never materialised. The company made all narrow body jet fleets equal in pay and seniority and there was to be no promotion to different types. It saved them a vast amount of money in training fees, but it meant that I was stuck on 1-11's for the rest of my time; for all of the ten years until it was time for me to retired at the age of sixty.

After a few years as far as I was concerned, this did have a way of making the whole operation seem to be a rather monotonous day to day, routine affair. However, if you let it, that can often be the case with airline flying. I found that I began to lack ambition, simply because there did not seem to be anything really, which I might be ambitious about. All that could have been dangerous had there not been many variations in our fleet operations and the different versions of the 1-11 which we flew; so in fact, I was able to maintain quite a reasonable interest in it all throughout those ten or more years. In airline flying, letting the feeling of apparent monotony take over your way of working, can be very dangerous

We operated four versions of the aircraft, the smaller 200, 300 and 400, plus the larger 500 series, and were cleared to fly all of them. Then as far as routes were concerned, I was told that our 1-11's operated to almost two hundred different destinations over any one year. Our rosters came out every two weeks and we could find ourselves down to go to any of them at any time, by day or night.

Firstly there was the inevitable holiday work to Spain, which had not changed much over the years and was pretty well just as I had known it on the Comet. The same crowds of holiday makers were picked up from the many airports round Britain and taken to the Mediterranean, then collected a week or two later and delivered back to their homes. Once again I became familiar with such places as Palma, Alicante and Malaga, plus many more like them round the Iberian Peninsula together with Italy and Greece. Once again I became familiar with long delays whilst awaiting clearance to start up for the flight home.

However, with the 1-11, we did seem to go to a far greater variety of places than on the Comet. There were Greek islands and the Adriatic coast of Italy. I came to know Venice airport very well and often went to Rimini. Milan and Genoa were frequent destinations.

There was masses of work to Germany and on some days the company had five flights into Munich alone. Otherwise Hanover, Stuttgart and Hamburg were places that I got to know well. Nurnburg and Cologne were also on the list, as were Dusseldorf and Frankfurt.

Munich was a friendly place with helpful, well oiled air traffic control. I was always pleased to see it on my roster and soon made friends amongst the staff who looked after us there, but Frankfurt was a pain. Hamburg and Hanover were other friendly places.

Stuttgart could be difficult as there was a ridge of high ground to the west of the airfield, which was too high for a 1-11 500's legal takeoff profile, when carrying anything of a load. This made things difficult for air traffic control when take-off was in that direction. We had to ask if we might take off to the east, downwind against all the other traffic, so upsetting their procedures. However, they were always helpful and gave us a clearance just as we needed. I liked those people.

Our base in Berlin had grown considerably since my Comet days, with a number of Boeing 727's based there as well as 1-11's. The company operated a morning and evening schedule with the 1-11 between Amsterdam and Berlin. Spain inevitably ranked high on the list of holiday destinations, as did the coast of Yugoslavia. We went to Palma from Berlin, just as we did from the UK. Later we also had a daily scheduled service between Gatwick and Berlin.

There were the same three destinations in Norway, Kristiansand, Stavanger and Bergen, that I had become so familiar with on the 748, but now we had charters to two more. Gardermoen near Oslo, came up occasionally, as did Trondheim, much further on to the north and near to the Arctic Circle. The latter carried holiday makers going in completely the opposite direction to the majority, north rather than south, and was a more common destination.

The Comet had no takeoff weight problems, and with its four Avon engines, had masses of power reserve. It easily carried sufficient fuel to give it ample range for all these routes; but not so the 1-11. All takeoffs, especially from those hot destinations in the summer, entailed getting out large reference books. These gave exact details of length, altitude and obstruction heights for all the runways which we used. Graphs, which brought wind and temperature into the equation then told us what safe, legal weight was allowed for departure. The passenger load and the fuel requirement had to fit into that figure.

The passenger load was revenue for the company whilst the fuel was cost, and so came a bad second in their view of priorities. When you had been told your passenger load, you could work out what fuel you were able to carry, and you just hoped that it would be enough to cover all the requirements for your flight home. If you couldn't carry enough, it meant that you had to make a refuelling stop somewhere along the way; and that obviously caused a late arrival back home.

Athens was always a trick. We operated there at night with the larger 500 Series aircraft. Load wise, these were the most critical of the 1-11's and it was always a toss-up as to whether we could get home or not. You would uplift every last litre that your weight limit allowed, and the aircraft would then be at its absolute maximum; takeoff being timed for about two o'clock in the morning, when it was at its coolest.

The ensuing takeoff always amazed me. When you were lined up to go, you would run up to full power, holding the aircraft on the brakes until you felt it trying to push forward, but when you released them, there was suddenly no urge after all. The beast seemed to sit there like a vast bull making up its mind to charge, but not doing so. Then gently, without any of the mighty shove in the back, which I had associated with many types that I had flown, it would begin to ooze forward, accelerating very slowly.

Then began a period, which seemed to last interminably. The two magnificent Spey engines, mounted either side on the tail, would have to work at their absolute rated power setting for such a seemingly long period that I could never imagine how they could possibly keep it up. Something would be bound to blow up; how could they possibly have been designed for this, I felt. But they were designed for it and they always did manage. I never had the least trouble from them. They were magnificent engines and with the 500 series 1-11, they had to push out their absolute maximum effort.

As we rolled down those long hot summer, Mediterranean runways, gradually accelerating to takeoff speed, I always wondered what would happen if one engine did fail above V1, the speed above which we had to continue with the takeoff and get airborne. It always worked on the simulator, so I always hoped it would work on the aircraft, but I never had to face the problem in actuality. Contrary to some aircraft, it was said that the 1-11 would always do everything that the book said it would. Over ten years, I found that to be the case in actual fact, but I often wondered how.

Once in the air and through the knife edge noise abatement procedure, when you climbed to three thousand feet without reducing power, and at an airspeed that was uncomfortably close to the stall, the aircraft handled beautifully.

So when returning from somewhere such as Athens, you had what for the 1-11 was a long stretch back to the UK. You inevitably found that the winds, which you encountered at altitude, were against you, and also that you were held down to an uneconomic flight level. Initially this would be because of your own weight, but later as you burnt off fuel and became lighter and so able to climb, other aircraft occupying the levels above you, which you needed, would prevent any chance of that climb. Air Traffic Control did understand our problems however, and did their best for us if they were able, but you had to play all the tricks in the book, plus more that you could dig out from your own experience. Without a technical stop on the way, it was never easy to make the flight back to Gatwick with the fuel load that we had been able to squeeze on. But we usually did manage somehow.

If you did land on the way, as this was a night flight you had to face some airport at about four in the morning where the duty staff were fast asleep, the refuelling crew had vanished and nobody wanted to help you anyway. Refuelling stops were always a pain in the neck. The only one which I found to be really efficient at that time was Romagna, situated in the country a little way inland from Rimini. However, there was still some distance to go from there, and committing yourself to a stop at that early stage, was certainly over cautious, so I only used them when I knew definitely, right at the start that I would not have enough fuel for the full flight home. Circumstances always threw difficulties at you but then, that was what it was all about.

However, the economics of the 1-11 were easy to see. The Comet 4 carried 108 passengers in charter configuration, whilst the stretched 4B and 4C each carried 119. To do this they were powered by four fuel guzzling Avon engines, brilliant engines in themselves and then still in widespread military use, but uneconomic in the civil world. The 1-11 500 in charter configuration also carried 119 passengers, but only used two Speys, which were much more modern and far more efficient engines, though even then, they were becoming outdated in the civil world for various reasons, mainly because of the noise that they made. Fuel consumption was becoming more and more important, and on this front the Comet was left far behind.

Flights on our network of scheduled services round the UK and Ireland were quite the opposite to our four hour charter flights to such places as Athens, few being over an hour in duration, chock to chock. Operating such flights was an entirely different business and Jersey was as good an example as any.

I did not go to Jersey as often as I had done from Bournemouth on the 748, when the Islands were one of our two main operations, but on the 1-11, early morning and late evening commuter services every day from Gatwick, plus regular weekend shuttles, meant that it was quite often on my roster.

Just as we did for Zurich where we had a similar schedule, we would operate the evening Jersey on a split duty basis and after a short night in a hotel, depart for Gatwick at seven the next morning. If you weren't used to it, it was all a total rush and on the sector back from the Island, there was a great deal of work to do on the flight deck, in a very short time indeed and of course for the girls as well, who were rushed off their feet in the cabin. Always just about when you were crossing the Isle of White and starting the let down into the Gatwick approach procedure, one of those hostess's who always looked after us really brilliantly, would bring in trays with a huge great hot breakfast on them, and dump then on our laps. Gobbling the meal, following air traffic instructions, flying the aircraft and carrying out the drills, all smoothly and correctly, not in a completely rushed muddle, took a lot of team work, practice and experience on routes like that.

Those ten years on the 1-11 might have been ten years of routine, but there were so many variations in it, that it would really have been very hard to get badly bored, unless I had been stupid and let it get that way.

One thing that I did like about the UK schedules was the way that they enabled me to keep up the old friendships amongst the ground staff that I had made round all the airports whilst on the 748. These 1-11 schedules covered Newcastle and Aberdeen, where there were all the people who helped make everything work so smoothly on the Link and the Oil and I could never thank them enough for the way that they worked now. Inverness was another happy place for me.

Then there were the handlers at Jersey, where British Midland were our agents. They continued to be superb members of the team, just as they always had before. On one ghastly afternoon when everything fell apart for me after we had set out for an easy, straight forward Gatwick, Jersey, Cork, Jersey, Gatwick duty, they saved the day for me. Some passengers from a 748 that had gone sick, were stranded at Cork. Their destination was Bristol, and we were diverted there by our operations set up at Gatwick, in order to drop them off on our way back to Jersey. However the operations staff at Gatwick made things particularly difficult for me and having given me the alteration to our schedule, did nothing to alert staff at Bristol, or help. Due to an early closure because of striking firemen at Jersey, we only had fifteen minutes to uplift fuel and turn round there on the return. The duty handlers at Jersey pulled out all the stops and we made it work in the most fantastic way, so avoiding a night stop with a load of passengers for whom there was no accommodation. I owe them eternal thanks for that one. If we had not been friends of long standing, I would never have received the help that I did that day.

Friendship could have the opposite effect sometimes and that happened to me on one occasion at about midnight in Munich. Things had been very difficult for a month or two and I was absolutely tired out after numerous roster changes, call outs and general problems that had just built up or had jumped out at me, one after the other. Tiredness was something that you got used to in the job, but I had had enough of it for a bit.

That particular night I was on the way to Rimini, when over southern Germany, the controller came up and announced that Padua radar in Italy had broken down. It was off the air. Padua radar was part of the controlling authority for all northern Italy, so the Italians had closed their airspace. No aircraft might enter it from other countries, nor were takeoffs from Italian airfields allowed.

That meant that we had a choice and a quick decision was necessary. In a case like that, you could either divert straight away and sit it out on the ground, or hold in flight at some en-route point, hoping that everything would soon be put right and you would be cleared on. The latter course used up fuel and you had to monitor it very carefully. There would suddenly be a time when you no longer had enough to reach your destination safely and so had to divert quickly, before you were caught out and in trouble. Other aircraft in the same situation as yourself always seemed to need to divert at the same moment. So with minimum fuel, you would all be shouting for diversions and that could obviously mean difficulties. Diverting too soon could also be the wrong decision, as the problem which was holding you up might soon be put right. Having landed, you would need to uplift fuel anyway which cost a lot, and there would also be the extra airport charges. Difficulties always had a habit of mounting up!

In this case, being familiar with Italian radar problems and the usual length of time that it could take to fix them, I called for a diversion into Munich straight away, before the rush started. I had had enough. I would sort it out from there and anyway Munich had a strict night ban on all jet movements. They would not let me take off until the next day, so I would go off duty. Then having gone off duty, we would not be able to carry on again until after a minimum rest period. Ha! I would get some sleep tucked away in a hotel, so blow it.

We landed, taxied up to the ramp and stopped the engines. There I was greeted in very friendly manner by the duty officer, who came on board as soon as the steps were down. He was someone who I knew well and was always friendly and helpful.

'I know that jet takeoffs are band here at night, so we will all go off duty. I want accommodation for one hundred and seven passengers, plus the crew.'

He gave me a big grin, 'It is good now Mike. Padua say that they will be working again in about ten minutes and will clear you into their air space. You can get airborne as soon as you are refuelled. You are a friend, so we will call this an emergency and ignore the night ban'

So much for making friends with everyone. We flew on to Rimini, and then back to Gatwick.

I think that the engineers were the people for whom I had most respect amongst all those who formed the team that kept the airline flying and operating as smoothly as was possible. After a while as a 748 skipper, I had realised that being able to count some of them as friends, was in fact something of a privilege. Now on the 1-11, I got to know many more of them, and became even more convinced that the artificial aircrew/ground crew, officer/other rank barrier that I had known in the RAF, was not at all a happy state of affairs. Both sides of the operation missed a great deal in the way of friendship, and also comradeship, without ever realising or understanding it.

The people who really had power over us and just about ruled our complete existence almost all the time were first rostering, then crewing. Both departments had the ability to make any aircrew member's life an utter misery if they so chose. In fact I'm quite sure that they were totally fair in the way that they treated all of us, but nevertheless I did my best to make friends and co-operate with both. They both had tremendous difficulties in doing their jobs successfully, and I felt in fact that they deserved a lot of respect.

First the sales team went to the charter market, and sold the company's aircraft capacity to the travel agents; the details of the resulting flight requirements being then passed to the planners. The planners drew up a list of all the flights that were thus needed in order to cover those sales, plus the scheduled services that the company operated. These in their turn were passed to the person responsible for crew rosters in each aircraft fleet. He was known as the rostering officer and had to nominate crew members for each of those flights.

Obviously every one of those flights had to be covered, and how rostering managed it was quite beyond my imagination. There were masses of things that came into the equation; legal duty times and numbers of sectors to be flown, travel to the various airports where the flights had to operated from, accommodation away from base, then rest periods and time off, to name but a few of them. Then there were pilots' base checks, instrument ratings, medicals and leave to fit into it all. How they managed it without going crazy, I have no idea.

Regularly every two weeks we received a roster which covered a two week period, and started two weeks ahead. Thus when you got your new roster, you knew exactly what you would be doing for the next four weeks. This really was very good and much better than many other airlines, where sometimes it had been almost a day to day business.

Obviously some flights were easy, some were a pain in the neck and often you had days such as family birthdays, when you really wanted to be at home. As much as possible, I made quite sure that I was on very good terms with rostering. Because of that, if I gave the person who devised our day by day destiny plenty of warning, he was usually able to give me time off when I needed it for such things as those all important family reasons. I kept very quiet about all that, but I knew some pilots who were definitely on bad terms with rostering and often seemed to ring them up in order to grumble and complain about the flights that they had been given. It seemed to me obvious that their problems were probably their own fault.

Then there was crewing, who were the people that you had to check in with as soon as you came to work. It was they who covered the hour by hour, daily situations for every flight that went out and to my mind it was a really terrible job. They had to fill in for people who called at the last moment to say that they were sick and would not be able to come in that day. Also there were those crew members who really made it difficult for them by often being late as a matter of course and sometimes just not turning up anyway. Then there were last minute changes made by the charterers and sometimes extra flights might suddenly be needed, whilst aircraft might suddenly go sick. All of these hiccups had to be covered somehow or other.

Having staggered in from the car park, often at some ghastly hour when nobody should be having to go to work, and then reached the floor, high up in the operations building where it all happened, you stood at the crewing counter and greeted the person behind it. He would usually be staring intensely at a huge sheet of paper on which were listed all the flights for the day and the crews allocated for each of them. He was obviously lost in a world of his own as he tried to sort out the impossible situation that was building up. At the end of the period, whatever it might be, that sheet of paper could be a total mess of scratchings out and alterations. There would be quite a few already, however early in the day it might be.

'Morning then, Mike Holmes for the 0725 to Geneva,' or wherever it might be, I would say, cheerfully I hope, to this person with the lugubrious expression.

'Ah yes Captain. There have to be some changes. We want you to operate the 0745 to Faro.'

'Oh...,' you think. That's a lot longer, but then the crewing bloke behind the counter says, 'Your aircraft will be Whiskey Alpha, however it's running an hour or so late, and won't be in until 0730. We will get you a new slot time as soon as we see how things go on, but it's very busy today and there are delays building up already.'

That is just one of the ways that they had of altering all the careful arrangements that you might have made for your time off after you had managed to get back home later in the day.

Then there were your standby days or nights. Different companies have different requirements, but we had to live within two hours drive of our base. Gatwick just fitted into that pattern for me and I always gave myself plenty of time for the journey. However, when it was a call out from standby, it meant that I had to drive as fast as I safely and sensibly could. Once again, it was necessary to be friends with the people in crewing, so that they would make allowances for those of us who had a long distance to travel.

It was no good ringing me up at about 1600 and saying, 'Captain there has been a problem. We want you to operate a Palma, departure 1640. Come in right away, the first officer has done all the planning and we are just about to board the passengers.'

That sort of thing happened to those who lived locally. I was glad that I lived a long way off.

They got to know this and generally gave me plenty of warning for roster changes or call outs. Some people though, just did not seem to be able to co-operate with crewing and they certainly paid for it.

We all generally thought of Gatwick as a pretty ghastly place. On the ground there it was all hassle, agro and dozens of problems to overcome before you could get away on your flight. The problems sat there waiting to assault you as soon as you had parked your car and walked into the airport. All of them had to be disposed of in order to get away on time with all your passengers and everything organised as it should be.

Our regulations stated that we had to report to crewing one hour before departure time. This was nothing like enough for me, even if things did by chance happen to be running smoothly, in exactly the way that the book said they should. In order to have plenty of time to defeat the problems, most of us checked in at least half and hour early, but as far as I was concerned, even that could sometimes mean rushing it a bit.

Having been given your slot time by crewing, which was the time when you had to be at the holding point and ready to roll, and having been informed of all the changes to your original programme, you were also told what your expected passenger load might be. From that you could work out how much fuel you would be able to carry and so phone your requirement through to engineering. They would then organise the bowser from the fuel company.

It was then quite a good idea to go next door to the ops room and try to learn from them just what the general situation might be air traffic wise, all down your route. The French might be about to strike, the Spanish might also be having trouble in some way, or an area radar in Germany might have gone off the air. Then there might be a strike by baggage handlers at your destination, which obviously could course a lot of bother.

A vast board on the wall of the ops room, showed all the current company flights for that day, worldwide. It could give you an indication of how long aircraft were having to wait at their destinations before getting clearance for their return flight. Inevitably there were delays, except perhaps in the middle of the night. However, as Gatwick had a night ban anyway, aircraft returning after 2300 had to wait on the ground at their departure point as a matter of routine. They could then time their takeoff in order to arrive back after 0600 in the morning.

So far so good; if crewing had not told you that as yet you had no aircraft allocated or that the one that had been allocated to you needed some rectification; or again perhaps, that it was not due in for an hour or two. If none of these upsets had occurred, you could consider that things had a chance of getting off to a reasonable start.

Of course, all these people had stacks of other possible problems for you that they could pull out of the bag. There was a never ending list of difficulties that that you might be presented with.

They would also tell you who your first officer for the flight would be, and that could certainly present you with a major difficulty if you were unlucky, and it was someone who you did not get on with particularly well. Naturally there were some that you did not like, but that was part of life, and had to be accepted as it might be in any circumstances between two people working together.

Team work on a flight deck could not be affected by personal likes and dislikes; they just had to be ignored and the standard procedures maintained. However, there were some first officers who were extremely difficult to get on with for some reason or other; usually those recently out of the Services, with no previous civil experience. They often thought that they knew best, and because of their background, had no real basic idea of the team work and flight deck management that was required in airline flying. Inevitably at times, perhaps because of their erstwhile military rank, such people thought that they should be captain and had a very low opinion of the ancient civilian, who sat in the left hand seat.

If you found that you had one of these allocated as your first officer, you could expect that the period ahead of you was going to be really dreary. Naturally first officers had the same sort of thoughts about the captains that they had to fly with. You just had to work together and carefully follow all the laid down company procedures. If you did not do so exactly, the problems could be immense and the operation would be dangerous.

The two of you would probably meet in flight planning, where you collected all the data that you would need, such as weather and Notams. Over the eighteen years that I worked for the one company, the actual planning of the flight had been continually simplified, streamlined and made easy. Initially, when I was a new first officer on Comets, I had had to work the whole thing out from basics each time. All that would be provided was the approved route. For my last few years, everything was completely computerised. All that you had to do was to key in your flight number, and out would come a complete flight plan with the fuel requirements. Even the wind component was worked out for you

You no longer visited a met office and talked to a met man, who would brief you from a beautifully prepared chart. You just picked up pieces of paper which had also come out of a computer. They showed the overall weather situation, the winds, the forecasts and actual weather, not only at your destination, but also at all the en-route airports which you might need as alternates in an emergency. I always missed being able to talk to a friendly met man, but learnt to accept the modern system. The world was becoming computerised and I had to catch up with it. Anyway the computer was much better and quicker at flight planning than ever I had been. It saved me, and all the other pilots like me, a lot of trouble

Crewing had been told where your aircraft was parked, and ten to one this would be somewhere in a distant corner of Gatwick's vast ramp system, not conveniently close on one of the fingers of the terminal. That meant that you had to go out to it by bus. The crew bus was always busy and you waited for it just outside the building, whilst the number of other crews who were also waiting for it, would steadily build up. It had probably had to go to another far distant corner of the ramp, and would be sometime getting back. Then after it had got back and you had all boarded it, it would make many stops, in order to let off other crews at their own particular aircraft, whilst on its long and roundabout way to yours.

At this stage of the game, the need to be all ready and waiting to go at your slot time was beginning to be uppermost in your mind. It was absolutely essential that you were ready to roll down the runway, right at that particular moment. Being a little late was just not allowed and if you did miss it, the next available slot might not be for another two hours at least. That would inevitably cause masses of hassle down the back. The passengers could see their holiday slipping away and would be absolutely fed up, having every right to be so. That in its turn would mean that the girls would get off to a bad start, and that boded ill for the rest of the trip.

At least two, sometimes more people were waiting to grab you as soon as you got off the bus. They were busy people and had masses of other urgent things that had to be done, probably an hour ago. They had been waiting some time for you, and were naturally getting fed up with the whole situation.

There was the duty traffic officer whose job it was to organise the passengers, get all of them out to the ramp in a coach and safely settled aboard the aircraft. It could often be a difficult job. The passengers considered that they were on holiday and many intended to start it as soon as they reached Gatwick, if not during the journey there. Also on some airports where the handling company did not employ specified load controllers, the load sheet would be this person's responsibility. Then if the cleaners had not turned up, or the number one hostess had told him that something, which was desperately needed, had not arrived, it was his business to get on the phone and chivvy things along. Traffic officers often wore very strained expressions on their faces. I did my best to be helpful towards them, and over the years that bore dividends.

Then there was the engineer who had been given the job of seeing you off, probably together with a number of other aircraft. If everything went on time without problems, he would have no difficulties, but everything seldom did go on time without a problem or two of some kind or another. To begin with the girls would almost always have found something wrong in the cabin, which required fixing, and that could take up some of his time.

He would almost always be an old friend, so a cheerful, but hopefully short chat was the order of the day. He would tell you about all the things that were wrong with the aircraft. These were allowable deficiencies, as listed in the Ops. Manual, but having to work with any deficiency could always make things a little difficult. Individual aircraft often had their own particular and generally well known problems, so when told about it, you would not be too surprised. It was often something that you expected anyway.

The engineer also needed the tech. log sheet after you had signed it, but the fuel uplift, together with details of all the maintenance and repair work had to be listed before you could do so and give him his copy. He might have to put up with quite a bit of hanging around. However that could please him sometimes as it kept him out of the way of his boss, back in the office, who might otherwise grab him for some other particularly unpleasant job.

You were then able to go aboard and the first thing to do was to put your head into the cabin and say hullo to the Number One. Again I always tried to be on friendly terms with all these people down the back. It was important. When I had been a first officer, I had seen captains who were bossy, overbearing, sexist and unhelpful towards the cabin crew. That I thought, was not at all necessary and I soon noticed how the girls reacted to friendly skippers. You all needed to work together in order to produce a good operation, and it was far more successful when you could do so as a friendly team. Then you would all have had a happy, cheerful flight

Inevitably the Number One would tell you of some dire state of affairs. The caterers had not brought this, that had not turned up, the loos were dirty, and would you get on the company radio at once and tell them to organise something or other else for her.

So it was then time to do the walk around, outside check of the aircraft. After that, you could go back to the flight deck, sit down and start all those pre-flight checks. There was a whole string of them, and a lot to do before you would be ready to start up and meet your slot time. The first officer would be there first going through all the checks that he had to do. He would also have got out the relevant navigation manuals and charts, plus checking in with ground control and with any luck getting the air traffic clearance, which would give us our departure routing. The navigation instruments then had to be set up accordingly. This was long before the days of modern computerised flight decks, so everything had to be done manually. We would hand-fly the aircraft through all the departure procedure and also most of the let down, approach and landing at the other end. Our aircraft had no auto-land system. Well, letting some black box fly the aircraft right down the final approach, and then land it automatically in zero visibility, whilst I just sat there monitoring everything, would certainly have been something, which would have scared me stiff.

Just at the moment, when we were in the middle of trying to sort out some tricky point, the hostess who had been allocated the job of looking after the flight deck, would come up and ask us whether we wanted coffee, tea or fruit juice to drink during the flight. With any luck we would be given a cup of tea there and then, but it depended on how busy she was. There were plenty of other things that she had to be look after.

At about this time the first bus load of passengers would arrive. With them would come the traffic officer, who would tell us that the second bus was also on the way, but three of our passengers had been lost between check in and the departure gate. Calls had been put out over the loud speaker system, but so far there was no sign of them. This was often the case with charter passengers going on holiday. As far as they were concerned, slot times meant nothing and the aircraft could wait for them. They were on holiday. There was all the duty free shopping area to explore, and the duty free bar where just at that moment, they were probably well stuck in and making the most of it.

This often became critical. You could not go without them as their hold baggage would have been loaded along with everybody else's after they had first checked in. Should any passenger not actually board the aircraft after having checked in, all the baggage had to be unloaded, laid out by the aircraft, and identified by the owners who were present. Then the unaccompanied cases could be found and removed by security people. That of course took ages, but was important because there just might be a bomb in one of them.

The terrorist threat had then just begun to descend upon aviation, and one of the early ways that terrorists had of trying to get bombs onto aircraft, was to put them into baggage, which was checked in normally. The bombers then just walked off and left it to be loaded, so blowing the aircraft up when it had got airborne. You did not fly with unaccompanied baggage.

Ninety nine times out of a hundred, the traffic staff did find the missing passengers and get then aboard. You hoped that they would not be drunk, as if they were it meant the time consuming business of getting the police out and having them thrown off, as the law allowed.

Another thing that had to arrive on time was the tug, which was needed to push you back off your stand. Usually there was no problem with it, but at busy periods when a lot of aircraft were departing, there might be a cliff hanging few moments whilst you waited for it, staring all round the taxiways, looking for one that seemed as if it might be heading your way.

All the time, whilst all these last minute problems were working themselves out, you would be sitting there beside of the first officer, playing the *I'm absolutely calm and not worried at all* game. This was an act that by the very nature of aviation, had to come up every now and again for many reasons, both on the ground and in the air. You both knew it and had learned to be quite expert at it. In this case though, the only danger would be that you might miss your slot time, and so have to have to sit there for another two hours perhaps, before a new one was available. But finally the tug almost always did arrive in time and would hitch up. The operator would plug into your intercom system and you would be ready to go.

Your checks were complete and there were no more problems to sort out; wonderful. It was time to move, you could call the tower, requesting clearance to push back off your stand and start your engines. At that point, inevitably, there would be a tremendous sense of uplift and freedom on the flight deck. It was all your business now, no more interference from the people on the ground.

With any luck there would not be too great a congestion of aircraft trying to get to the holding point at just the same time as you, and you would be cleared straight onto the runway. As you taxied out, you completed all your final checks and the Number One would tell you 'cabin secure.' You called the tower, 'Ready for departure,' but if necessary, you had to wait your turn to enter the runway. Then the tower would give you 'clear for takeoff'; you opened the throttles, checked the engine instruments, released the brakes, and rolled.

The take off roll was always tense, but in a way that I found incredibly exhilarating as we accelerated towards flying speed; all the time closely monitoring all the engine instruments and warning lights. But only once in a 1-11, over the ten year period that I flew the type, did I ever have trouble at that point; and then only a minor problem.

When we reached the required speeds, the non-handling pilot called 'V1' and 'Rotate'; then we were airborne, checking the aircraft's attitude, airspeed and height, calling for the gear to be raised and climbing away, first through the noise abatement procedure, then whilst following the standard departure route.

The long climb to cruising level was a time of settling down, changing frequency to London Radar, synchronising the engines into their climb power settings, checking that the nav aids and radios were all in order and that everything was working just as it should be.

The cabin door would fly open and in would come mugs of tea or coffee in the hands of the hostess who was looking after us' just what we had asked for. The *No Smoking* sign could go off and later if their was no sign of turbulence ahead, so could the *Seat Belt* sign; that was unless the cabin staff needed to keep everyone strapped in for some reason.

There ahead of you if you were not in poor weather, the Channel would show up, all shining and glittering in the sunshine. After that it would soon be the French coast. If you were heading away to Switzerland with your destination there or beyond, you would soon be able to see the great bulk of the Alps, possibly sticking up above a layer of lower cloud. If you were bound for Spain, it would be a hazy view into the distant centre of France. If you were on the way to Portugal, Malaga, Morocco or the Canaries, you would soon see Cherbourg and then the Channel Islands.

All the stress and problems inherent with getting out of Gatwick would be left behind. It was totally you and your crew now. The only other people to have any say over you were the various air traffic controllers in the ATC Centres that covered your route, and I never really found them a problem, though some unfortunately did have a poor reputation.

Cruising Level; and you could really settle into the flight, into the routine business of fuel checks, weather checks, system monitoring and all the other dozens of things that the operation of an airliner entailed. But it was also a moment of tremendous satisfaction. It was all yours and it was all a wonderful experience, something that you could never get bored with, however many times you did it.

I vividly remember just that moment on one occasion when our destination happened to be Malaga, but it could have been any one of many other places. The first officer was a friend; we got on well together and made a good team on the flight deck. We had levelled off at the top of our climb and had completed all the cruise checks. The Channel Islands had slipped below and we were approaching the coast of Brittany with the distantly flashing, silver glint of the Bay of Biscay beyond.

We happened to turn and look at one another, exactly at the same time. We both grinned and knew what the other was thinking. This was a marvellous job, there was no other like it in the whole world, and who could ever possibly want to do anything else anyway. There was a great day of flying ahead of us and we were both absolutely on top of the world. Though part of the day would be loaded with inevitable difficulties at our destination, we would deal with them, and would generally enjoy every minute of it

13.   On Finals

No Never! I had done all my flying. I was over sixty and I had retired. That was it. I had plenty to do. I managed a large acreage of woodland and was involved with a number of wildlife conservation and survey projects both here and overseas. This included research into bats as an English Nature Bat Warden. I did a lot of bird watching and also did voluntary work such as bird counts. With all that going on, I had no more time for flying; it was all a thing of the past, and how had I ever had time to work anyway.

I had in fact thought seriously about it as I approached sixty, the age when the airline that I worked for retired its pilots, and the CAA reduced the status of pilots' licences. To stop flying, or any work for that matter, just because I had reached that age was to my mind ridiculous. Flying of one kind or another had been my life for over forty years; it was imbedded in me, and I could continue with a job on commuter aircraft. The thought of cruising backwards and forwards to the Channel Islands again, though now in some smaller aircraft, did entice me, especially if the load in the back was just fruit or flowers, not passengers.

Then there was the possibility of part time instructing at a flying club. Goodwood was the obvious one for me to try. It was closest to home, so I went there to have a look at it. First I would need to resurrect my instructor's rating, which I had let slip years before, but a trip with the club CFI there turned me against that idea straight away. I found that all the necessary patter was long forgotten and a lot of expensive practice would be necessary in order to bring it back to life. I fumbled with it and just stuttered, when in the past it had flowed out naturally, just as it should. Besides, I took an instant dislike to the instructor with whom I flew. He obviously did not like me either and was not at all friendly. He played back a tape of my patter which he had made during the flight, and it was obviously a load of rubbish. I threw out that whole idea at once.

Another thing had become apparent over the last couple of years, which helped to put me off the idea of going on flying. This was the stress of the job, which had built up a great deal as time went on. The airline was having financial trouble, so causing extra stress throughout the company, and things seemed to be getting difficult. I decided that it was time to forget the sky and to get reacquainted with the country. No more flying, and that was the way it was to be for a few years.

I had made up my mind but inevitably, more and more often, the thought would suddenly take shape in front of me, 'Oh it would be good to get up there into the sky amongst all those puffy little clouds again, just to remind myself what it was like and to feel the controls of an aircraft, alive in my hands.' It took quite a few years though, to actually do anything about it.

When I drove along under the South Downs, I often used to see the aircraft from the local gliding club, which operated from a small airstrip near Storrington. I would sometimes see one being towed up behind a Pawnee, and when the wind was in the north, they would be cruising along the line of the hills, staying airborne in the updraft that was produced by the air currents which rose in a wave over the ridge.

I knew nothing about gliding, I had never done any. With that total lack of knowledge that I had about it, I used to say rather pompously that I would never want to fly without an engine. What a ridiculous thing to think of doing anyway. But that was a very stupid way to look at it.

One day when the itch to get into the sky again was making it obvious to me that I must do something about it, I suddenly realised that gliding might be just the answer. No licence was required, neither was a medical needed at that time, so I might as well go and see what went on. I turned in through the gates of the little airfield at Parham and drove up to the clubhouse. It was a Tuesday, there was no flying going on, but a few members were doing maintenance work round the place. There I saw an old friend who had been another skipper on 1-11's at the same time as I had. Also there was an engineer, who I recognised from somewhere in the airline world. I was amongst friends.

I was made welcome at once. It was wonderful, I was back in the world of aviation, albeit amateur, and a very small, insignificant part of that vast world, but I realised at once that I felt at home again.

They said, 'Come and have a cup of tea. We fly on Wednesdays and at the weekends. Tomorrow's Wednesday, so get here good and early. We'll show you how to get your name on the flying list. You can join the club and start right away.'

I did just that, and it was marvellous. I flew with a very good instructor in a K13 glider, which was the type that the club used for basic instruction. Formed out of a canvass covered metal framework with a very basic cockpit, it did at first glance look a little ancient when compared with all the shining, high performance sailplanes alongside it at the launch point. That did not worry me in the least and when we hitched up to the Pawnee tug, I was both as thrilled and nervous as any ab initio young pilot might be on his first ever flight. I had a sudden vivid memory of the back seat of the Tiger Moth at White Waltham over forty five years before.

Then people were waving their arms, shouting and making hand signals, which as yet I knew nothing about. The Pawnee's engine opened up and we were moving forward behind it. It was my first takeoff since my final airline flight in a 1-11 over five years before. That had been at Toulouse on a normal, routine schedule, returning to Gatwick. Now I was back in a cramped little cockpit on a grass field, learning about what was to me an entirely new form of flying, and I knew what being 'thrilled to bits' really meant.

The instructor's patter came over, telling me what was going on and all about it, but the first thing which amazed me, was being able to talk quite naturally. Except for the airflow over the aircraft, there was utter silence when we released from the tug. Well without any engine I thought, of course there should be no noise. It still surprised me, though I naturally came to love it; another of the wonderful things about gliding, which I was to discover as I went along.

First there were all the old, standard flying training exercises, which had to be covered; effects of controls and straight and level to begin with, though of course it was not actually level in a glider. Unless you were in rising air, you naturally had to be in a descent. Then there was turning, stalling and even spins, plus how to recover from them. I had not done a spin since instructing at Hamble years before, but it all came back and it was marvellous.

One afternoon when I had managed to impress an instructor sufficiently into making him think that I might not immediately crash, I was sent solo. That was an incredible moment. To fly solo again and be in control of an aircraft, all by myself, was wonderful. I'm not sure that I wasn't more thrilled about it than I had been many years before at White Waltham, when at last Bill Hampton had sent me off on my one and only, first ever, real first solo.

From then on it was a case of progressing steadily to more advance gliders as I gained experience, and learned more about soaring flight. Wednesday was my day for the gliding club and it was sacred as far as I was concerned.

First, in the morning it would be a case of getting there early enough to have my name near the top of the flying list. There were strict first come, first served, and take your turn rules over the use of club gliders. The club owned only three single-seaters, so if it looked like being a good flying day with plenty of thermals, those who had not got their name near the top of the list, might not be able to get a flight at all. People made their flights last for at least an hour, moving from one thermal to another under the cumulous clouds. If your name was at the bottom of the list, you might have to wait all day, until most of those thermals had died away. Getting to the club early was therefore a very necessary part of the day's programme.

Learning all about finding and using lift in all its forms was just as important as learning how to handle the aircraft. Until then during my flying life, the weather, when it took any notable part in the proceedings, had usually been something that hindered aircraft operation. I had spent years getting on terms with it, and learning how to cope with it in all its worst forms. Now it was entirely different; now the weather was the thing that had the power to keep me in the air and discovering just how that worked, fascinated me.

After a time I came to realise that gliding was the most exciting and most satisfying form of flying that I had ever done. There was so much to learn, which I had never dreamt of during the previous fifty years. I soon found that I was looking at the sky in an entirely different way, and thinking, 'Oh yes, those clouds would be the ones; there could be a super thermal under that particular one and then that ridge of hills seems to be at just the right angle to the wind for the air to rise as it crosses it, and so provide all the lift I might need to stay cruising along it.'

It took me a long time to learn these things with any degree of accuracy and I was never near to being anything like an expert during the few years that I spent chasing parcels of rising air round the sky. But I always regretted not having concentrated on it as a hobby, and taken it up fifty years before when I had first started my flying career.

Many flights, especially those in my early gliding days, just consisted of releasing from the tug and then because I did not understand where to look, being unable to find any thermals or other form of rising air. It would then be a case of doing no more than drifting overhead the airfield and setting up in the circuit to come back in and land straight away. Every landing of course was with without power, so comparable to a forced landing in a powered aircraft after an engine failure. A go around was quite impossible; you had to get it right first time, but no one in the gliding world thought twice about that, it was the natural way of going about things. I learnt a lot, which was the way that it should be for a pilot.

The first trick that had to be mastered was to learn just how far from the airfield I could go, and having made an unsuccessful search for a thermal, still have sufficient height to glide back to the overhead. Stretch it too far and you were in trouble and had to quickly pick a field and land out, which to my mind, showed a terrible failure. Luckily I only once ever had to do so.

But then, when I began to learn just where those parcels of rising air might be found and what caused them, I steadily gained confidence and began to have some really happy flights, enjoying myself immensely.

When the wind was in the north, there was lift over the whale back hump of the Downs, or in gliding language, 'the ridge was working.' We could easily reach it from our release point after a winch launch, and then cruise along, perhaps only two or three hundred feet above the ground.

Small print in the Air Navigation Order states that a glider when ridge soaring, is exempt from the low flying laws, which normally make it an offence for an aircraft to fly closer than five hundred feet to any obstruction on the ground. So, when flying a glider as opposed to a powered aircraft, you are given lots of scope for whizzing along low with your wing tip only a few feet from the hillside. Otherwise, if you like, you can just fly sedately backwards and forwards along the ridge, for as long as there is an updraft to keep you flying. You had to think again though, when you reached the gaps in hills where either the rivers Arun or Ader, ran through their valley in the Downs on their journey from the Weald to the sea.

Crossing those gaps always presented a challenge as obviously there was also a gap in the rising wave of wind, which usually made me very hesitant to attempt the jump. The experts in their high performance sailplanes, would cruise the ridge happily all the way between Lewis and Harting, with the Arun and Adur gaps presenting them with only a modicum of challenge. Not so me. I would drift easily along the hillside, and then suddenly, there in front of me, would be this yawing chasm with the far side seemingly an impossible distance away. I would search for a thermal, which might give me more height, but usually with no luck. And then my nose pointing way out over the flat river valley, I would look at my rate of descent and the distance that I still had to go. Usually to my mind, it seemed obvious that I hadn't a chance of making it; those far hills on the other side just did not get any closer, so in desperation I would chicken out and turn one eighty degrees, making a dash back to the safety of the ridge that I had just left. I had to accept second best; I was just an inexperienced beginner.

By simply releasing from the tug at two thousand feet and drifting back down to land on the airfield once more, a flight of about twenty minutes could be achieved. To add any more flying time, you had to find thermals that would give you lift, and allow you to soar. In the various steps towards becoming an efficient glider pilot, one of the first things to achieve was a flight lasting for an hour, and my first hour amazed me. I had found one thermal after another. By then I had learned a little about how to interpret clouds, and how the rising air below them moved across the sky, but the main thing was to learn how to follow and remain circling round in that rising air. Having spent a lifetime being kept aloft by the lift created by my engines dragging me through the air, and so causing airflow over my wings, I was now learning how to use the movement of air itself and so stay aloft that way. I felt another tremendous elation and excitement.

After that first hour, it was easy to repeat it on other occasions and extend it for as long as the right weather held. But we had an unwritten rule between us when flying club aircraft; an hour was the limit. You must be fair to all your mates so that they could also have a go.

It would be a happy hour over beautiful countryside. There were the Downs stretching east and west as far as the eye could see, with beyond them the glint of the sunlight on the sea. Through them ran the Arun, after it had wound its way amongst the water meadows and the Wildbrooks south of Pulborough. Yes, it was always a very happy hour.

When you were not actually flying, there was all the work to do round the launch site in order to keep the whole thing going. Gliders had to be pushed into place and hitched up to the tow rope, then recovered from the far side of the field after they had landed. Work never ceased, and it was all very different from a trip to a flying club for a pre-booked hour's flight at a set time. You went to the gliding club for a days work, and everyone had to chip in.

Something which might have been a resurgence of my old spirit of adventure took over and I went off to find other clubs and places where I could go gliding. That search led me to the Long Mynd in Shropshire, which I had first seen distantly from the cockpit of a Chipmunk years before, when I had been stationed at Cosford and part of my duty had been to give RAF Boy Entrants air experience. There, somewhat beyond the range, which could be achieved in the half hour that each BE was allotted, was what looked from far away, like a long, whale backed hill near the Welsh Border. On top of it was an airfield where I could just see the glinting sunlight reflecting off the wings of parked gliders.

Gliding was then something, which I knew nothing of, but I determined that one day I would learn about it and fly from that hill top. It was exactly my kind of place, but I left Shropshire and it became just a vague memory, pigeon holed away to acquire dust in a forgotten recess at the back of my mind, whilst I followed a career in entirely different forms of aviation.

Now all that vague memory crystallised and found its way out of the recess. I felt that I just had to do something about it and the thought was really exciting. One day I had to give a lecture about how bats used trees, to a group of County Tree Officers at Iron Bridge. My way home led past the long hump of the Mynd, which rose out of the broken Shropshire countryside. It was raining heavily and visibility was down to just a few yards higher up, where everything was covered in thick cloud, but I found a narrow little road which climbed up steeply though gullies onto the moorland above. There near the top was a fork with a little notice pointing the way to the gliding station. A couple of miles further on, after splashing through ruts and stopping for ragged sheep which could never make up their mind as to which side of the road they would rather be on, I came to a single barred, iron gate and a cattle grid. Beyond that was the airfield, and distantly through the mist and rain I could see a windsock, a small hanger and a clubhouse with a row of glider trailers parked outside.

In those circumstances it hardly looked inviting, but I found the office and in it were John the chief instructor and Janet his wife, who was the secretary.

I was made welcome at once and told, 'Yes they ran week long courses for non-members. You did not have to stay the whole week, but could book for just a few days if that suited you best. There was accommodation there in the club house, where meals were served.'

That was it, I booked up at once and hoped that the weather would remain clear and the cloud would not sit on the deck whilst I was staying there.

There on the Long Mynd during many visits, I spent wonderful days gliding under John's supervision and his excellent instruction. The scenario and culture was totally different from anything which governed my home club. Nobody was shouted at. If you committed a sin, you were gently taken aside and told what you should have done, sensibly and reasonably. There was no scrabbling rush to get your name on a flying list. John had his own plan and you would be told when to fly. He was a professional, not an amateur club member who held the Chief Flying Instructor position temporarily. He knew exactly what he was doing and I appreciated that. It was a very happy, well organised place with a good way of going about things. Above all, the flying was absolutely marvellous.

On my home club's small airfield we seldom winch launched. To do so, we needed a pretty strong wind as the field was rather small. Even then, with the available distance over which the wire could stretch out being so short, we could barely reach one thousand feet. We normally clambered into the air behind a tug, either a Pawnee or a Super Cub, and unless we opted to climb further, released from it at two thousand feet. The higher you went, the more it cost, so two thousand was the standard release height unless you needed more to get to some obvious lift. At that time, I had never winch launched at my home club.

On the Mynd it was different, there all the launches were by means of a winch, and with the huge distance available across the moor, you had to be pretty inept, as I was to begin with, not to reach two thousand feet before having to unhitch from the wire.

For my first visit I was taken in hand by John's deputy at that time, a superb instructor named Rowan, and it was his job to introduce me to my first winch launch. Well, this was totally unlike any way that I had ever got airborne before. We sat at the launch point and went through all the relevant drills and checks, then with Rowan demonstrating and explaining everything, it was suddenly and unavoidably time to go.

By then, I had developed considerable trepidation towards the whole procedure; perhaps this was not after all my thing; I must be mad at my age. There were the usual shouts and exchanges of hand signals and suddenly we were snatched forward and dragged into the sky at an initial climb angle that I had never before dreamt might be possible; or anyhow it seemed that way. I felt as if I was on the end of a powerful slingshot, which in a way of course, I was.

Involuntarily and loudly, I shouted at myself, 'You stupid old man, what on earth do you think you are doing.'

However Rowan, who was not at all an old man, had obviously heard my shout and it took a lot of talking on my part to persuade him, and make him realise that I was not actually addressing my shouted remarks to him. We became friends.

It's not the way that I usually behave, and the shout was entirely for my own benefit. At that I age I did not really consider myself old, but this was something that I had absolutely no experience of, or been involved with in any way during all the years that I had been flying. I could only contrast the whole procedure to the way that I had previously got airborne. Then it had often been in a heavily loaded 500 Series 1-11, lumbering along as it tried to accelerate down a long hot runway at the peak of a Mediterranean Summer. It was utterly different!

When I found time to settle down and think about it; out of the blue it came to me that this was the most exiting way of taking off that I had ever known. After that I could never get enough of it.

K21's were used for dual at the Midland Gliding Club on the Long Mynd and they were far superior to The K13's that I had known at home. With their composite construction and clean lines, they were also much more modern. They were very strong aircraft and needed to be so because of the rocks and rough surface of the moorland on which they had to land and manoeuvre, then be heaved around behind the busted old Landrover ground tug. Solo was on their single-seater version, the K23. Though far more sedate and gentlemanly an aircraft than some I had flown, this soon became my favourite glider and I have wonderful memories of the flights which I made over Shropshire in the two that the club owned.

There was also an ancient K8, which was the single seat version of the K13. I had happily flown one at home, and it was my first single seat glider. But this one on the Mynd was totally basic with no electric audio variometer to let the pilot know whether he was climbing or descending. Everything had to be done by visual means and feel; completely by the seat of your pants. I really enjoyed that old glider, finding it a great test of skill.

More experienced glider pilots have told me that there are far better gliding stations than the Long Mynd, and I have no doubt that from their points of view they are quite right. Some are within reach of the great wave systems that can carry a glider many thousands of feet up over the Scottish Highlands. Another which lies not far from the Mynd, under the Black Mountains, has a number of ridges within easy reach, which means pilots don't have to wait for just one particular wind direction before they can go ridge soaring.

All that may be quite true, but I loved the Mynd. I loved the view across the Borders, and into the distant Welsh mountains to the west. I never ceased to be amazed by the way that the panorama just expanded tremendously whenever I pulled off the winch cable at two thousand feet and started to soar away; that is if I was lucky and could find that elusive parcel of rising air. Anyway, if as often happened to me, there was no lift to be found in time and I just had come round in a wide circuit back to land, there were still the fascinating views into all the gullies, which ran up the steep hillsides from the rolling Shropshire countryside bellow. To the east were the Clee Hills, and away to the north, vanishing into the haze, lay the wide Cheshire plain.

Then there was my other great interest. I loved watching the buzzards soaring in the rising air currents, far more expertly than I ever could. I always hoped that I might manage to join one in a thermal and formate on him, but it never happened.

Outside the great wide bow window of the clubhouse, which looked west into Wales, the first thing that I would often see in the morning when I came in to breakfast, was up to half a dozen ravens putting on one of their amazing aerobatic shows, no more than a hundred yards away at the point where the land dropped steeply away to the next valley. What a great start to the day.

Best of all was to try to join the ravens soaring high in a thermal, as I also attempted to do with the buzzards. Though I never managed to circle with them, I did manage to climb up with four ravens one day, and then to chase them round the base of a cumulus cloud. But, whatever tricks I tried to play, I was totally inept and they easily out flew me.

Then one day my son-in-law, who was very much involved in the microlight aircraft world said, 'Why don't you take up microlight flying.'

'No,' I replied, 'I would have to have a license and pass a medical.'

The doctor, who used to do my six monthly ATPL examination, had just laughed when I once suggested to him that I try to pass a medical again. He certainly would not sign me up after a ten year gap. To begin with, in his eyes I was as deaf as a post.

'Ah,' said my son-in-law, 'You only have to get your own doctor to sign up your medical for you on microlights, not a CAA examiner.'

I did just that without any difficulty. But now, as my ATPL was long out of date, I would have to work for a new licence, a microlight PPL which would allow me to fly these little aircraft.

A week later, I went to Popham, a little grass airfield near Basingstoke, well known in the sport flying world. I had driven past it many times, and it was one which I had often thought might be fun to fly from. The idea this time was just to visit and look around, as I had heard that there were microlights there. I thought that I would go and explore a bit; just to see what things were like. Then I could go back home and think about it a bit more.

I drove up and parked by the row of unpainted, and what at first appeared to be rather dilapidated wooden buildings. It all had a very country appearance, and one that I liked immediately, very different from most of the more modern and up to date flying clubs that I had happened to visit in the past. I liked it all straight away, and felt at home there.

There were masses of aircraft parked about the place, a number of the usual Pipers and Cessnas, but amongst them were some fascinating older types, which I had not seen for years. Then again, there was a row of the most extraordinarily shaped stick and string, canvas covered affairs, with their little two-stroke Rotax engines seemingly attached precariously as an afterthought, out in front of the high wing above the windscreen. They looked very odd to me.

At the end of the row of wooden buildings, I found a little café with a desk in the corner. Behind the desk was someone who looked out of wide bow windows and appeared to be operating something of an air traffic control system. This was the airfield operations centre. I asked him where I might find anybody who could tell me about microlight flying on the airfield.

'Next door along; Airbourne, ask them,' he said. Then, 'There, just out there, that's Phil, the man with the cloth cap on. Ask him, he'll put you right.'

I did ask Phil, and got grunted at. 'Have you made a booking with Paula,' he said. 'You're not on the list.'

'No,' I said, 'But I came on the off chance. I would like a flight if possible please.'

There were more grunts and I was cross examined a little. It seemed that all flights had to booked through Paula, who was at home on the end of a telephone. This it seemed, was some way off at Verwood in the next county, but I was lucky.

More grunts, 'All right, I can fit you in now. You can have a trial lesson,' said Phil.

I did not want a trial lesson. Flying was something that I considered I knew a bit about and I was current on gliders. I wanted the first lesson in a series that would check me out, get me a licence and enable me to fly microlights. It would really be a refresher course as far as I was concerned.

Phil looked doubtful, and his doubtful expression continued to remain with him for the first couple of flights that we made together, but by then he had got the measure of me and we had become friends. Initially, I realised that he was a bit bothered about flying with someone who was vastly more experienced than he. As a retired airline captain, I was in his estimation, bound to be over bearing and awkward when given any instruction by someone such as he. So, I made a point of being as friendly and responsive to his instruction as I could. Before long all was working out well and we enjoyed our flying together.

But now, on this first occasion, Phil led me to one of the extraordinarily shaped objects, which he told me was an AX3. He showed me how to unlash it from its moorings, refuel it and get it ready for flight.

'You'll only get shown once,' he said. 'In the future, it will be your job to do all this. I'll watch, and then walk out to the aircraft when I see that you have everything ready.'

He made it plain exactly who was boss, and the captain of the aircraft. I had a quiet chuckle and we got on well together.

This was MAC, the Microlight Aviation Club. The holding company was Airbourne, and it was all run by a wonderful couple, Mac and Paula Smith. They both made me really welcome when I got to know them, and I found that the little club that they had built from scratch over the years was great. It had a really happy atmosphere and a good operation, which was well respected throughout the whole microlight world. I soon felt at home.

Very unhappily, Paula had a long lasting illness and has now passed on. I expect she runs a super flying club somewhere up there where all aviators go when they die. Mac, with his daughter Shelly, has since streamlined the whole affair with modern aircraft and an expanded operation. I don't fly any more, but when I visit it, I can see that it's holding its place amongst the best.

The AX3 might have looked very odd, but it taught me many things and brought back others long forgotten; things that I had first learnt on Tiger Moths many years before, filing them away somewhere in some forgotten corner of my mind. It soon came to me that like the Tiger, it was another trainer that if handled properly would give you a very good grounding, and prepare you for anything that you might fly in the future. Though on the ground, it appeared ugly and unlike any aircraft that I knew, once up in the air it came alive, and could be made to fly really well. So all over again, it taught me how to fly light aircraft.

The Popham runway had once been part of a wood, so there was still woodland on either side, with the odd gap between the trees. Any wind can find such gaps and twist itself into knots, so turning in all directions. Never believe the windsock as such twists cause the oddest of sudden crosswinds and wind-shear, just as you are about to touch down. They come from a direction that you never expected, and can catch any unwary pilot totally by surprise. The combination of the AX3, together with those winds from the trees, taught me things that I had long forgotten during a lifetime of operating from big wide airfields, and flying much heavier aircraft.

Apart from the flying, Popham was a happy place where the staff were all friendly and welcoming. Dick, the airfield manager, also ex-RAF, was an out and out aviation enthusiast, which he combined with a love of motor bikes. He was just perfect for the job, and it was obvious to me that I had picked the right airfield on which to base myself. It was all exactly what I was looking for, and just right for me.

After the AX3, the club began re-equipping with Thruster T600's. They were super, and soon became my favourite microlight. I never felt the need to have something faster, something which could take me over the horizon to far away places.

The Thruster, originally designed in Australia and used in the Outback as a farm implement to muster sheep, though now based in Lincolnshire under the able control of Malcolm

Howland, was when I got to know it, built in this country in part of a farmyard close to Harwell. The owner of the set up, Gordon Pill, and his people all became firm friends, as I often visited the place when ferrying Mac's aircraft to and fro,' for the various maintenance work that was necessary at times. The farm was the Pill family home, and was worked by his brothers. The Thruster was perfectly at home there

The little farm airstrip there was another of the places where you had to dodge trees and sideslip round them in order to touch down near the threshold, so giving yourself a reasonable length of runway in which to stop.

It all provided me with a lot of fun, but mainly I was just happy to get up in the air from Popham, sometimes landing down the road at Chilbolton, or pottering off down into Wiltshire to land at Old Sarum. At other times I would fly further on into Dorset for some lunch at Compton Abbas, that beautiful little airfield near Shaftsbury.

That, I think, was my favourite destination. Perched high on a chalk hill, the view from there across the rolling country-side was magnificent and I loved it. There were many other places to land, but none so beautiful as that. Many were much closer to Popham, and I searched out all the farm strips in the area where I would be welcome and which were not on some private estate, to be used only by the owner with his personal Cessna. You could usually see the aircraft's nose poking out of a small hanger, off to the side of the field. Apart from him, it would surely be reserved for just his guests and wandering microlights would not be welcome. I also visited White Waltham, where it had all begun for me over fifty years before, but that was now very upmarket and I could no longer visualise Joan Hughes, Bill Hampton or one-eyed Mac.

The type hunting, which I had always worked at in the RAF, came to the fore again. Whilst gliding I had flown about fifteen different species and now it was the turn of the various breeds of microlight. I made a nuisance of myself at the Popham trade fairs and badgered anybody I met in order to get trips in the aircraft they were trying to sell. I evaluated a number of types and wrote reports about them for Mac, as he

Also by Mike Holmes and published by Woodfield....

Apprentice to the Red Ensign

Memories of the British Merchant Navy in the late 1940s
ISBN 1-903953-85-5 | 248 pages | softback | 140 x 205 mm | £9.95

This book is a first hand account of life in the Merchant Navy as it was in the latter part of the 1940s, just after the end of World War Two. It tells of the ships that made up the huge British merchant fleet and of the men who served in them.

The author grew up in the Berkshire countryside, far from the sea, but was educated at what was then **Pangbourne Nautical College**, where he learnt the rudiments of seamanship and 'how to do things smartly, at the double' – also developing a strong feeling about being of service to the Empire.

He left Pangbourne aged just seventeen and went straight to sea, joining the **Ellerman & Bucknell Steamship Company** as a cadet, always known aboard ship as an 'apprentice'. He served in three of the Company's ships and one Royal Fleet Auxiliary store ship, which the Company manned; these being the *City of Carlisle*, the *City of Rochester*, the *City of London* and the RFA *Fort Constantine*, in all making six voyages and visiting ports in many parts of the World.

In those days the Merchant Navy was the vital link, connecting the various parts of the vast British Empire, providing the means by which the lifeblood of trade could flow, and the Empire's people travel.

Among those who manned the ships a strict pecking order existed, which held discipline together. A junior apprentice started as the very lowest of the low, slowly progressing to become a trusted member of the ship's company.

The British Merchant Navy as it was in those times has long since disappeared. The Red Ensign is no longer flown by a great percentage of ships at sea, 'flags of convenience' are the order of the day and very few crews are British. Because it describes a way of life which has now vanished into history, this book is sure to be of interest to all those who remember life as it used to be under the 'Red Duster'.